Everyone's Guide
to
Buying Art

By Peggy and Harold Samuels

Illustrated Biographical Encyclopedia of Artists of the American West
The Collected Writings of Frederic Remington
Frederic Remington: Selected Writings
Contemporary Western Artists
Frederic Remington: A Biography

Everyone's Guide
to
Buying Art

Peggy and Harold Samuels

Prentice Hall, Inc.   *Englewood Cliffs, New Jersey*

Prentice-Hall International, Inc., *London*
Prentice-Hall of Australia, Pty. Ltd., *Sydney*
Prentice-Hall Canada, Inc., *Toronto*
Prentice-Hall of India Private Ltd., *New Delhi*
Prentice-Hall of Japan, Inc., *Tokyo*
Prentice-Hall of Southeast Asia Pte. Ltd., *Singapore*
Whitehall Books, Ltd., *Wellington, New Zealand*
Editora Prentice-Hall do Brasil Ltda., *Rio de Janeiro*

© 1984 *by*
Peggy and Harold Samuels

*The paintings reproduced in the text are from the
authors' private collection, and were photographed by
Robert Reck.*

Library of Congress Cataloging in Publication Data

Samuels, Peggy.
  Everyone's guide to buying art.

  Bibliography: p.
  Includes index.
  1. Art as an investment. I. Samuels, Harold.
II. Title.
N8600.S25   1984   332.63   84—2076

ISBN 0-13-293382-9
ISBN 0-13-293374-8 {PBK}

Printed in the United States of America

Introduction

Because a lot of people are afraid of art, one purpose of this book is to get everyone to feel comfortable with paintings, prints, and sculpture. To this end, we will strip away the mysteries of the business to help you lose any fear you might have of buying art.

What will be left for you is all of the beauty and none of the ballyhoo, all of the pleasure and none of the pain.

Whatever the level of involvement in art that you then choose, whether that of casual appreciator or lover, infrequent buyer or insider, you will fall into one of the four major classes of buyer. The most demanding category you can achieve is that of the insider. Next is the serious collector, followed by the casual buyer. The lowest level is the patsy, the uninformed acquirer who "knows what he likes and that's what he buys," regardless of the authenticity, suitability, or price of the object he purchases.

After reading this book, you can become any kind of art buyer that pleases you, casual or serious or expert, but you will never be a patsy.

Contents

Contents

Everyone's Guide
to
Buying Art

CHAPTER 1

The Flowering of Fine Art

To start with, talking about the way insiders buy art is a bit of a contradiction. Insiders are usually dealers, and if they can avoid it, dealers generally don't buy art for their galleries. They take art on consignment for resale.

Also, dealers normally don't talk about what they do. The way they select the art they buy is a trade secret, occupational information to be sold as a service and not given away. If dealers ever did decide to talk about what they do, however, what follows in this book is what they would say.

Those dealers who do buy art for inventory in their galleries face a range of problems common to most merchandisers. They have to keep buying during all sorts of business conditions in order to have stock for sale. When the country is prosperous, they buy art at relatively high prices from a restricted pool of offerings, yet they must be confident that their practices will protect them against losses in a downturn.

When the country is economically depressed, dealers must still buy art, but at lower prices on the average and from a wider availability of art works. Every day, regardless of the economy, their buying procedures must allow them to acquire good pieces, safely, that will generate gains.

That is what watching the insiders will do for you. You will learn how to buy when the market is strong, to purchase art works for your pleasure, pride, and profit, both while the market continues bullish and after the market starts to weaken, if it does. You also will learn how to buy when the art market is soft, how to take advantage of price breaks and wider options, and how to sell.

Let Your Left Arm Dangle

As the first tip on acquiring art, you should know that every prudent insider has a personal painting size, a go-and-no-go gauge to set the dimensional limit on what he or she buys. Before you are ready to begin buying art like an insider, you too must know your painting size, a fixed measurement like your hat size or your shoe size.

This measurement is something you can take yourself, at home. You simply hold a yardstick in your right hand, if you are right handed, and let your left arm dangle at your side. With the yardstick, you then mark the distance in inches from a loose fit under your left armpit to the first joint on the middle finger of your left hand. The result is your personal painting size. A man of medium build would be a comfortable 24. A woman of medium build would be about a 21.

You apply this personal painting size the way the insider does. That is, you use it to determine whether any particular painting you want to buy will fit under your arm. The reason for this is that, if you make a mistake in what you buy, or if economic conditions worsen drastically, under your arm is where the painting will be while you carry it from place to place, trying to resell it at a price close to what you paid. The limitation on size prevents you from buying art that is too big for you to lug around. There is an equivalent limitation you can employ for bronzes, this one based on weight rather than size.

The admonition is an old one. In 1915, the American painter Arthur B. Davies (1862–1928) advised his students to follow a variation on the same theme. Students should not paint pictures bigger than would go under their arms, he said, because that is where their pictures would be most of the time while they were starting out. In the days before transparencies, going from gallery to gallery was easier when the young painter was transporting smaller pictures.

Even though this caution is given softly in the form of an anecdote, a size and weight limitation on what you should buy may still be a downer for your hopes when you are just beginning to think of acquiring art. Nevertheless, the careful strategist always looks to his defenses before he takes a position.

As you will see, buying art is quite safe as a form of investment for the initiated. Art prices soar when other investments rise, and on the whole they are steady when other investments collapse. The average return can be high when profit is the goal. However, assembling any art collection involves a series of transactions, and one transaction out of many could involve a loss. You must be sure, then, to stick to the rules in order to minimize the chance of an unprofitable purchase.

Your first acquisition is likely to be the riskiest. You will be acting with the least knowledge you will ever have. Painting size and sculpture weight are thus symbols of prudence, and the little anecdote about size is an exercise to fix caution in your mind. When you see a piece of art and it seems to suit you, think for a moment before you buy: Is this work really my size?

Anyone Can Buy Art

To understand the art market, you ought to be aware that quite apart from questions of prudence, historically there has been a psychological impediment to buying art in America. For hundreds of years, some ordinary people have believed that owning art was morally wrong, because the Puritan ethic made no provision for expenditures for decorations or frivolities. There has been a prejudice against displaying art and an instilled reluctance to acquire art objects that perform no function.

Today, this Puritan ethic is becoming passé and the idea of owning art has found a more accepting climate. Few feel guilty about watching the value of a picture appreciate at the same time they appreciate the picture. In fact, there are now millions of people in the United States who buy art. Twenty percent of all American homes contain at least one piece of original art, a high level compared to even a decade ago. Sales of many art objects are increasing in price and in volume, and the circle of buyers continues to widen. Fine art is no longer a luxury for the rich.

Here, as in parts of Europe where art is woven into the fabric of life, the usual motivation for buying the first piece of art is aesthetic pleasure. You purchase a limited edition print or an inexpensive painting casually, for personal enjoyment, simply because you like it. Sometimes, after the picture is hung, visitors praise your taste. This can evoke a second reason for art acquisition, pride of possession, along with the enhanced social status that results from the admiration of your picture by others.

A third reason to buy art can surface when you compare the original purchase price with the larger amount that may well be the current valuation. In good times and bad, the price of well-chosen works can be booming in categories like old-time Western paintings, contemporary sculpture, American Impressionist paintings, or wildlife prints. The result is that the buyer for pleasure may enjoy an unexpected potential gain in addition to the social enhancement.

Len Green is a Denver dentist. At an auction five years ago, he saw a John William Casilear (1811–1893) oil painting of a Colorado mountain landscape he liked. After buying this nineteenth century painting for $5,000, he hung it in his office. Some patients admired the picture, and

1. *John W. Casilear. "In the Rockies," 1876. Oil on canvas, 20 by 16 inches.*

said so. One patient was aware of the rising prices of art of the Hudson River School and kept the dentist informed of the jumps in auction prices of other Casilear paintings. In five years, the value has tripled.

To Dr. Green, who had never before owned original art, this difference between purchase price and current value sounded overwhelming, especially at a time when it is chic among the more successful young professionals to say that money is worth little. In a deflationary economy, good art will generally hold its value, while in an inflationary period, tangibles including art are the preferred assets. What better tangible than an attention-getting painting, particularly if that painting makes money for its owner while it is just hanging on the wall? A buyer for beauty like Dr. Green has been made aware that art can be an investment for profit.

The aesthetic reverse may also occur, with investors in art gradually coming to recognize the beauty of the works they own. According to the head of a London auction house, "the combination of inflation and money devaluations plus growing distrust of traditional methods of investment have made art into a marvelous long-term investment. Most of these nouveau riche slobs become something else when they buy fine art." The mundane investor in art may thus become the new frog prince, made over into an appreciator of beauty. Pleasure, prestige, and profit go hand in hand, regardless of which end of the "P's" the art buyer starts from.

Not everyone, however, agrees with using art to make money. There are museum curators and European-oriented critics, the elitist portion of the art crowd, who debunk the investment aspects of art ownership. "One should collect art only for sensual and intellectual enjoyment," they say. "Spiritual enrichment should be the true goal. Art is for beauty and maybe nostalgia but never for status or profit."

Spiritual or not, a large number of people are now investing in art. As an example, a veterinarian in Hartford who is not wealthy says he knows nothing about art. A Connecticut museum curator referred him to a New York City gallery where, ingenuously expecting to turn a profit in the near term, he paid $15,000 for two oil paintings of Italian landscapes by a minor living artist. Since an investor is just a collector who buys with resale in mind, the veterinarian has automatically become an investor, without any real idea of what he has bought or when if ever the pictures may be worth what he anticipates.

Another example is a doctor in Memphis who has set up a private pension fund for his ten-person staff, using nineteenth-century English watercolors as the fund's assets. He flies to England at the fund's expense in order to make his selections on the advice of a dealer there. With his employees' money, the doctor is holding himself out as an expert to bring back pictures he personally enjoys.

Investors like the veterinarian and the doctor and collectors like Len Green assume they can count on an ethical art gallery not to take advantage of them, if they can define what "take advantage" means. Reputable galleries should set asking prices based on their appraisal of the retail market, as we will see.

Still, most of these investors and collectors would prefer to assume a more meaningful role in the decision-making process, if they only knew how. Fortunately, that is accomplished easily, by following an educated path and by purchasing under protected terms. Anyone can succeed in buying art pleasurably, safely, and profitably by following the rules. Collecting or investing in art is not restricted to the elite any more than buying stock is, and automatic buy/sell plans are now being adapted to fit the ownership of art for those who want such structured programs.

You can trust reputable experts, but you should first learn the ground rules in this book. Every seller of products or services can have a built-in conflict of interest.

Some Businesses Buy Art

Historically, even the businessman who buys art for himself has ignored original art either as decoration or as an investment. A publisher like Harper & Brothers that worked with commercial art every day saw no value in Frederic Remington's (1861–1909) original illustrations in the 1890s, and happily returned them to the artist. The more important of Remington's early works have since brought $500,000 to $1,000,000. When Harpers could not meet its financial obligations at the turn of the century, assets like Remington illustrations might have helped them.

In the 1960s, the publisher Street and Smith, on the advice of a leading art dealer, gave away as valueless hundreds of paintings that had been used as illustrations in its pulp magazines. Some of those paintings, the ones by N. C. Wyeth (1882–1945) and Nick Eggenhofer (born 1897), are now worth $50,000.

Most businesses leave the purchase of their wall hangings to the interior decorators who buy mass-produced art of the size, subject, and color that suits. Decorative art like this is allied to the desks, the chairs, and the carpeting, possessing no resale value other than as used furnishings.

It is strange, but common, for example, to enter the offices of a law firm decorated in the style of the 1920s and come upon furniture upholstered in genuine leather and, on the walls, prints that are not originals and have no value apart from the frames. In today's informal atmosphere, however, a service establishment like a law office is no longer required to seek a Dickensian anonymity in its decor. One good investment-grade painting can be featured on an entry wall to express individuality and to assure the client that he will be seeing a sympathetic human advocate.

Although the number of businesses buying paintings, original prints, and sculpture is still too small to be competition for the collector, that number is increasing. Because these art acquisitions are outside the normal operation of these businesses, experts have been retained to counsel on buying and selling.

A big New York City bank, for example, has made an alliance with a leading auction house to guide the bank's major depositors on art investments. A Washington law firm has spent $250,000 to acquire 85 pieces of contemporary American art. The firm is buying from galleries, bidding at auction, selling, and trading—on the advice of dealers. A Wall Street brokerage house buys contemporary American paintings, employs its own curator, and sponsors a living artist. In the Southwest, it has become common for financial institutions and public utilities to collect local art.

The executives of these businesses are consciously fostering public service images by supporting the arts. In addition to enlivening their office walls, businesses invite tour groups to view their collections and make up traveling exhibitions that promote the business name. Because of the variety of benefits that result, there are art-minded business managers who have called paintings and sculpture their companies' best investments.

In addition to those businesses that acquire art for their collections, there are now funds that buy art for investment, either for diversification or as the primary holding of a fund formed for the sole purpose of profiting from the buying and selling of art. General funds are minor factors in the market, reluctant to buy any great quantity of art for their portfolios because of the delays inherent in selling art.

In an art fund, the usual organizational plan is to employ the founder as the operating manager and to retain a dealer as the expert consultant. The function of the fund is to combine small shareholdings to make possible the purchase of expensive works. After art is acquired, the fund tries to place the pieces on loan with a museum for exhibition and storage. If no museum will undertake custody, the pieces are stored in a rented vault where they remain unseen.

Individuals who buy into these art funds do not participate in the choice of the works to be acquired or sold. Instead, selections are made by the fund's management. Art has on the average been a profitable investment, so art funds have on the average shown a profit, and it will take a prolonged recession in the art market to determine long range viability.

Even in good times, though, the shareholder in the fund has a basic disadvantage—he does not get the art to display for himself. He might just as well be participating in a commodity or a stock fund, as far as handling the merchandise is concerned. Art bought to be hidden from view is a contradiction.

Art funds are too new and too few to allow conclusions to be drawn about how they will develop. As they grow, though, and as the art holdings of commercial institutions increase, the time will come when art valued at hundreds of millions of dollars will be owned for investment. The effect will be to make the forecasting of art prices more complex, to enlarge the demand for investment grade art, and thereby to make galleries and auction houses prime beneficiaries of the increased volume of trading in art.

Art Competes for Dollars

It's clear that you can make money buying and selling art, if profit is your goal, but the exact amount of money you can expect to make, based on an analysis of what has been made, is hard to pin down. Should you be looking for a five-times gain, or for 50 percent growth? Art competes for your dollars with the other collectibles, tangibles, certificates, and equities, but there is no reliable gauge to measure the exact rise in the value of art relative to other assets.

One way to compare is to listen to the advocates of investment in an alternate area, because most of them make claims for their specialties that sound minuscule in relation to art. When buying businesses, for example, professional investors say they are satisfied if two out of three ventures are profitable and if their average return is ten percent after adjustment for inflation.

In contrast, you are entitled to expect that every piece of art you buy will be profitable, at worst in the long term, and if you are an experienced buyer, you should look for a gain of at least 25 percent a year. Veteran art dealers will tell you that there are very few times when they lose money on art, and they do not buy art at all unless they can see selling it for double the cost, as a minimum.

When you talk about buying "art," though, you mean a single transaction, not an average for a series of transactions. Averages of art prices are mostly meaningless, because different pieces have widely different values. There are countless kinds of paintings and sculpture, and innumerable individual works within each kind, especially when compared to a more uniform commodity like gold.

For what it is worth, there was one reputable analysis of European Old Master painting prices as a group that indicated an increase of 13.4 percent per year over ten years and of 15.2 percent per year over the last five years. Old Masters have been notoriously slow movers, however, compared to almost any other kind of art. While these results do seem modestly productive, averaging about two times the gains from bonds and five times the gains from stocks in the period ended in 1979, they were not quite equal to opportunities like gold at its peak price or even to other kinds of art.

American paintings offer a better standard of comparison to other kinds of investments. This category has enjoyed a much greater boost in average prices, amounting to a cumulative rise of 225 percent over five years, a figure almost double that for Old Masters. Antique paintings of the American West have experienced an even stronger surge, as a reflection of the nostalgia for simpler social relationships. Works by the two top names, Frederic Remington and Charles Marion Russell (1864–1926), have increased almost 50 percent each year in 1980, 1981, and 1982.

Specific examples are more revealing than averages. The gouaches (opaque watercolors) and oils of Henry Farny (1847–1916), painter of the American Indian, have regularly sold at premium prices just below those for Remington or Russell. Five years ago, a fine small Farny gouache of Indians in an action scene brought a high of $28,000 at auction. Four years ago, a comparable gouache was $35,000 at auction and a medium-size oil sold for $195,000, a breakthrough in Farny prices. Three years ago, a small gouache brought $52,000. Two years ago, the price was increased to $60,000 at auction, and one year ago to $115,000, more than four times the first auction level. To cap this, a large Farny oil sold for $460,000 at auction last year.

Prices for the works of contemporary Western artists are also available for comparison. One source is the autumn Cowboy Artists of America exhibitions held at the Phoenix Art Museum. Ten of these Cowboy Artists were reported on by *Artists of the Rockies* in five recent years.

- James Boren (born 1921), for one, priced his watercolors at $2,250 in 1977, $3,000 in 1978, $4,000 in 1979, $6,500 in 1980, and $8,000 in 1981, with an oil at $15,000.

- John Clymer (born 1907) priced his painting at $20,000 in 1977. The price for a comparable work was $40,000 in 1979, $80,000 in 1980, and $150,000 in 1981.
- The work of John Hampton (born 1918), a sculptor, was priced at $6,000 in 1977, $7,500 in 1979, $12,000 in 1980, and $18,000 in 1981.
- The work of Harvey Johnson (born 1921) was $5,800 in 1978, $8,000 in 1979, $13,500 in 1980, and $24,000 in 1981.
- Bob Lougheed (1910–1982) was $7,000 in 1978, $13,000 in 1980, and $17,500 in 1981.
- Tom Lovell (born 1909) was $15,000 in 1977, $80,000 in 1980, and $110,000 in 1981.
- Frank McCarthy (born 1924) was $14,000 in 1977, $26,000 in 1980, and $40,000 in 1981.
- Bill Owen (born 1942) was $6,300 in 1978, $15,000 in 1980, and $21,000 in 1981.
- Jim Reynolds (born 1926) was $14,000 in 1978, $22,000 in 1980, and $30,000 in 1981.
- Gordon Snidow (born 1936) was $8,700 in 1977, $18,500 in 1978, $20,000 in 1979, $40,000 in 1980, and $40,000 again in 1981.

In 1982, the theme of the CAA show was small paintings and bronzes for the little collector. Most prices were not comparable to the major works offered in previous years, but a James Boren watercolor was $12,500. A John Hampton bronze was $22,500. Bill Owen brought $26,500 and Gordon Snidow $48,000. The trend was still up, in a market where collectibles other than art were down.

These men do not make up some artificial grouping contrived to prove a point. They are the Cowboy Artists of America, the original cowboy artist organization. In this instance, averages help tell the story, too. In 1977, the average price for the work of the members named for the year was $11,125. In 1979, the average was $15,900; 1980 was $30,800, and 1981 was $45,850—an increase of about 40 percent from 1977 to 1979. Prices doubled in 1980 and added another 50 percent in 1981. In what other field that is reasonably honest could such increases have occurred?

One answer is that of original prints—a similar success story, particularly for the new collector with less money to spend. *Prints* magazine publishes regular reports on the secondary market for limited editions; that is, the resale values of editions of prints that have been sold out. There are hundreds of artists involved as printmakers, but if you take just the artists who were listed as investment grade in *Contemporary Western Artists* (Southwest Art Publishers, 1982), you can get an idea of some of the price increases that have occurred.

- A Pati Bannister (born 1929) signed and numbered offset lithograph published in 1980 in an edition of 200 for $200 had a value of $600 in 1982.
- The George Boutwell (born 1943) "Roadrunner" published at $2.50 in 1970 was $60 in 1982.
- Guy Coheleach's (born 1933) "Bald Eagle" published at $75 in 1968 brings $1,050.
- Jerry Crandall's (born 1935) lithograph issued at $60 in 1979 is worth $400.
- T. Phillip Crowe's (born 1947) 1980 issue at $50 became $100.
- Chuck DeHaan's (born 1933) $75 in 1979 became $450.
- Ray Padre Johnson's (born 1934) 1981 $50 was $100 by 1982.
- Jacob Pfeiffer (born 1936) went from $150 in 1978 to $300.
- Gordon Phillips (born 1927) from $100 in 1979 to $300.
- Roger Preuss' (born 1922) "American Goldeneyes" issued at $15 in 1949 was quoted at $2,600 in 1982.
- Terry Redlin (born 1937) went from $40 in 1979 to $750.
- Olaf Wieghorst's (born 1899) $125 issue in 1979 was $1,000.
- David Wright's (born 1942) litho issued at $25 in 1974 was $400.
- Bob Wygant's (born 1927) 1979 issue at $50 was valued at $75 in 1982.

As you can see, some portions of the art market have shown phenomenal increases in value in recent years, and even the relatively cheaper art categories fared reasonably well. When art does compete for your dollars, it puts up a pretty good show against other possible investment areas.

Art Beats Stocks

The stock market has been the most popular of all investment opportunities, and now that investing in art is coming of age, comparisons can be made between stocks and arts.

Although the business magazine *Forbes* has reported that art "Sure Beats the Hell Out of Stocks," stocks still hold the advantage over art in many procedural ways. There are daily published stock prices, for instance, arrived at openly. Brokerage commissions can be less than one percent. Trading in stock is governmentally regulated, protecting the investor. There are hundreds of pseudoscientific formulas and charts to help the investor decide whether to buy or hold or sell. When you decide to sell, your investment is liquid, getting you out of the market in one day, again at a published price. The possibilities are so varied, you can even sell stock you don't own.

Moreover, stock is a more convenient instrument than art. A painting or a bronze obviously requires maintenance and should be insured. There is no current income from art to compare to dividends or interest. Paintings and sculpture can take four months or more to sell at a price close to retail. Art bought at retail usually has to be sold at wholesale, like an automobile, and the commission for buying art at auction averages about ten percent while the cost of selling is generally higher.

On the other hand, stocks are by definition a gamble, guided a little by formulated gibberish and a lot by mass psychology explained after the fact. It is only the following morning that you are told by pundits why the stock market acted the way it did. The art market is more logical than this, and some of the functional buy/hold/sell theories that have developed in stock transactions over the past 80 years are being converted to art to soothe tentative art buyers. The art market is becoming a more professional business all the time.

Art has a superior potential for gain and is an investment producing few losers among the experienced. When the stock market surges 50 percent, the President of the United States takes the stump to claim national significance, while knowledgeable art buyers look on doubling as routine. The absence of governmental controls over art offers wider entrepreneurial leeway for the knowledgeable, permitting piratical practices that would be criminal in securities.

Art is not as sensitive to economic downturns as it rides the trends of price and spans the short-term waves and ripples that can capsize stocks. In bad times, decreases in the prices of prime paintings may lag a year behind falling stock quotations. Prices of art may even rise in a depression.

Also, the constant advantage for the investor in art is that he has the work to display, as opposed to paper transactions in equities or most other commodities. Stockholders seldom frame and display their certificates. A stock certificate is a neuter, while a work of art has an apparent personality. Art provides a profusion of aesthetic and social rewards as well as economic.

Art has more mystique than alternate investments, too. At economic conferences attended by proponents of investment in art, real estate, oil, gold, diamonds, colored gem stones, stamps, coins, stocks, commodities, rare metals, and so on, most of the different guest lecturers also attend the art sessions. Paintings and sculpture intrigue them.

In contrast, art dealers seldom attend other lectures. Most of them put their own investment dollars back into art, just what they advocate you do. It is the rare gallery owner who deals in art for a living and then invests his profits in real estate or gold. The stated reason of such a maverick may be to circumvent the eccentric tax structure that applies to an art dealer, but the truth is that he does not really believe in the uniqueness of his own merchandise.

Clearly, art is flowering as a collectible and as an investment. You get more for your money.

CHAPTER 2

Once Over, Lightly

It used to be that running an art gallery was a stable and quietly growing occupation engaged in by a relatively few expert dealers. They were the insiders, the ones who spent their days examining, buying, selling, trading, authenticating, appraising, and exhibiting art, counselling on art, and reading about art. Art was their only business.

Something New Is Going On

In recent years, there has been a tremendous increase both in the number of dealers and in the quantity and the value of the art they handle. Auction houses have grown similarly. And, keeping pace with these increases, there is a dark side to the business that is also growing larger.

Something new is going on, particularly with respect to art done before 1950. A greater percentage of works offered requires careful scrutiny. The problem is sometimes price, because cost is always a factor, but more likely it is other considerations that make a work questionable. The work may be by the wrong artist, or it may be the wrong subject, or the condition of the art may be poor or suspect, from an investment standpoint.

The 1920s painting by Hayley Lever (1876–1958), for example, that was offered for sale and rejected in Scottsdale because the signature had recently been repainted, came back again, within months, at a higher price. Someone believed in the painting, and bought it for resale, despite the flawed signature.

A sketch signed George Bellows (1882–1925), turned down in Chicago because the quality was not fine enough for a Bellows, reappeared in the hands of another dealer at a lower price. The first rejection had panicked the original owner.

A painting of trench warfare in World War I, refused at any price in New York City because wounded soldiers were an unpopular subject, was offered again at auction, although the market is limited. The picture may be more suited to gun dealers than to art dealers.

In the same vein, an auction catalog illustrates a turn-of-the-century painting that is signed, its authenticity guaranteed. It is a painting that was discovered ten years ago, however, when it was not signed.

Another auction catalog illustrates a Remington wash drawing of horses, but either the catalog illustration has been cut down or the drawing has. When the artist had the drawing in the 1890s, there was more to the work at the top and on the left.

A third auction catalog reproduces a painting signed lower right. The original signature was lower left.

Again, a dealer in Oregon wants $18,000 for a J. E. Stuart (1852–1941) Indian painting when a more detailed and larger Stuart painting recently sold at a New York City auction for $3,200.

These are extreme examples of a variety of flawed works, and they occur regularly. As in any trade that is expanding, there are many sellers who are pushing pictures, promoting the concept of art as a safe buy. Most of these sellers have training in art or experience as dealers. Some do not. High prices inevitably lead to the introduction of questionable merchandise, and there are works of art being bought that should not have been offered.

How to Buy Winners in Art

Telling you how to buy winners in art is relatively easy. The rules are the same ones the insiders follow in their personal profit-producing procedures. Any veteran dealer who owns his inventory has bought thousands of pieces of art, putting out his dollars when he buys. Until the pictures in his inventory are sold, they are his investment portfolio, his money-makers. Thus a dealer's internal routines are not just theory propounded by a writer; they are an insider's practices.

To this point, people who have written about how to buy art have generally been outsiders, repeating what the insiders have told them and relating surface principles that sound good but don't give the game away. In the rare instances where insiders have written, they have confined what they have said to self-serving recommendations. Dealers prove that dealers are the only reliable sellers, and auctioneers advocate auctions.

Unfortunately, there is no mystical formula for purchasing any one picture. If art could be weighed and measured and then graded like peanuts, perhaps cut-and-dried advice might do for everyone. Buy nineteenth century Hudson River School landscapes this week, dealers could say, as a stockbroker might tout a certain issue because of its book value and its prospects for earnings. Unfortunately, though, telling all investors to buy a given style or school of art fails to recognize the diversity that exists even among the slender Hudson River School of paintings, without regard to the individual investment needs of different buyers. No generalized recommendation to buy can be made to apply to everyone.

So, in addition to telling you what and how an insider buys, we must explore the patterns that will be suited to you as an individual and provide you with the cautions to go with them. To give you an idea of where this will take you, the balance of this chapter is an outline of the rest of the book, once over, lightly.

Touch Is the First Key

The initial focus is on the buyer himself. Some buyers just want to know enough about art to make casual purchases safely, or to diversify their investment portfolios. This can be accomplished quickly through the guidelines we provide for choosing experts as counsellors.

Others who want to become collectors or insiders are asked to concentrate on art, to apply themselves the way a professional does. They should begin by reading a few art history books and by familiarizing themselves with art reference materials. The books are named, and so are sources for obtaining them.

Next, collectors should start looking at art to apply what they have read. Although the usual advice would be to go wherever there are quantities of works to see, such as museums, galleries, and auctions, a better place to begin is in the lower grade shops that allow handling of the art.

Reading the books and handling the art develops the collector's "touch," the knack of being able to pick the right picture for himself in a room full of pictures. Touch is the first key to buying art.

Those who want to go on to become insiders will need much more exposure to art works than can be gained casually. This means treasure hunting, the easiest exercise to find out about art quickly, and the right way to generate start-up funds, if you need them. The hunt is not for everyone. It calls for a dedication far beyond what the collector can usually give, but it is guaranteed to make you an insider.

Treasure hunting provides exposure to every form of art, antique and modern, paintings and sculpture, originals and prints. All that is required is proximity to the shops, transportation, reference lists, and calling cards.

The common problems that arise are telling a painting from a print, a bronze from plated white metal, and an original print from a mass reproduction. You will need to find and read scrawled signatures, verify the signatures in reference books, and evaluate the asking prices when there are neither pre-sale estimates as in an auction nor researched price tags as in a gallery. When you have mastered the treasure hunt, you will know as much about art as many dealers do.

Instant Expertise

The second key is the specialization that results from confining yourself to a single category of art. Whether you want to be a casual buyer or an insider, you must pick the specialty you need by immersing yourself in art objects until you find the kind that you are most comfortable with, or that reflects your life's experience, or that the authorities you trust recommend for you.

The number of available specialties is infinite. Tens of possibilities are suggested, along with methods to help you choose any other category that might appeal to you. The narrower your area of specialization is, the better, as long as there are enough possibilities in it to give you room to buy.

The advantages of specialization include "instant" expertise, minimized efforts for maximized results, and an investment area defined specifically for you. The risk of picking an inappropriate classification is slight. Antique Western bronzes and paintings by artists like Jean Baptiste Camille Corot (1796–1875), George Inness (1825–1894), and Ralph Blakelock (1847–1919) who are frequently forged are to be avoided by casual buyers. So are American paintings done before 1850 and primitive paintings that are difficult to authenticate, along with fads and other passing fancies. The Southwestern phenomenon of current cowboy art is considered in detail and compared to art of the American West done before 1950.

The third key is to know yourself in relation to collecting art by exploring your own physical, emotional, and budgetary limitations. As a group, today's collectors are more likely to be female, younger, less well off financially, and more numerous than they were a decade ago. The average budget for buying art is relatively smaller but oriented toward self-satisfying acquisitions rather than the conventional. Old financial maxims like limiting money for buying art to ten percent of net worth, or buying art only from capital accumulations and not from income, are dead. Experienced collectors may plunge on art purchases, and young professionals may find budgets hamstringing and buy from income.

The warning is to keep an eye on the milk money. Establish a budget for art, and make realistic "worst case" analyses before exceeding your budget. Even when art prices are strong for good pieces, you must still remember that the art market has not historically lent itself to short-term investment. The conclusion is a paradox: Buy when you see your best piece, but pause to think of resale before you leap.

The fourth key is understanding that a crucial part of the purchase of art is to know who signed the work. Who the artist was controls the value of the art. To be investment grade, the work should be by an artist listed in the reference or source books, a question that is resolved by good library practice. Listings are based on honorary memberships, gallery representations, published reviews, education, awards, public collections, and so on. If an artist is not listed in reference or source books but has equivalent credibility, he still can be regarded as investment grade, although marked for careful monitoring.

These factors that lead to listings are the earmarks of professionalism, and the point is that the artist must have been a professional to be worth buying. If artists who worked before 1950 are not listed, they are not likely to have been professionals because they did not conduct their careers in a manner that would be normal for a professional artist. There were few closet artists of quality.

If contemporary artists are not listed, it may only be that they are too new, and you will have to satisfy yourself as to the quality of their backgrounds. What you are looking for are indices of professionalism, not necessarily of excellence. The art market is expanding so rapidly, it is running out of works by the most famous artists. Today, second- and third-tier listed artists are also sought after.

Buy the Best

"I don't know anything about art but I know what I like and that's what I buy" is a know-nothing excuse for the purchase of the wrong piece of art. Instead, the rule for everyone should be "buy only the best."

For some, the best is the highest priced. You get what you pay for. For others, the best buy is the cheapest. There are also your individual best, the best at the time, the best by objective test, the best for the purpose, the best provenance, the professional best, the one that is the singular best, the scarcest best, the expert best, and so on. That makes for a lot of "bests," but what "buy only the best" comes down to is buying your personal best, the one that most appropriately fits your own collecting pattern. All of the other bests are just modifiers to help you make up your mind.

The next key takes you into the subterranean world of the physical condition of art, particularly of old paintings. In the reality of the art business, price is meaningless without a statement of physical condition. Some auction houses will verbally reveal what they believe the condition of a work of art to be, but no guaranty of condition is made. Other houses require the buyer to bid at his own risk. Some dealers will guarantee condition, if requested, while others will not even admit to a knowledge of conservation practices.

The casual buyer may never learn to see condition because his untrained eye will go only to the beauty of the surface, and the auction house and the dealer will not educate him. In the absence of disclosure of condition, the art buyer who gets no warranty is no better off than the buyer of a used car. He is reduced to the equivalent of kicking tires and slamming doors.

For the protection of the buyer, a painting's physical condition should be described in every offering. Five categories are suggested, from fine to very good to good to fair to poor. The basis for the distinctions would be the extent of the deviation from the original condition when the painting left the artist. Good is average condition, and an ethical seller would be required to disclose any lesser state.

In a seller's market, art in poor condition may be sold to less knowledgeable buyers, but physical condition will inevitably become a factor when buyers get pickier. A conservator should be consulted about any questionable circumstance.

Appraisal Is Theory

You also need to know about appraisals and how to ascertain that the appraiser has expertise in your specialty so as to be able to authenticate your work and determine its condition as well as its value. Appraisals are subjective and should be on a level that reflects the purpose of the appraisal. There would be different appraisals for insurance, for a retail sale, and for wholesale.

Appraisal is supposition, compared to price paid, which is reality. Appraisals may be closer to value than prices because flukes in sales are excluded in appraisal practice. A dealer's asking price is an appraisal that starts with his actual cost, and moves through reality factors adjusted by gut feeling. An auction house may influence prices by jockeying its pre-sale estimate, by nurturing supply, and by intensifying demand.

For the collector, price within reason is of lesser importance than whether a work of art is his "best." He may properly pay as much as 50 percent above appraisal to get his best work.

An Auction Is a Contest

For many years, auctions were regarded as shady proceedings, but auction houses have long since improved their images. Essentially, an auction is a contest between the auctioneer who strives to increase the price for himself and his seller, and the buyers who seek to dampen the action. Before selling at auction, collectors must have some idea of value. One way to find out what a piece is worth is to contact several auction houses and judge from their responses.

Buyers should realize that auctions dispose of sellers' mistakes as well as art of importance. The rule is buyer beware, although protection for the buyer is getting better at some auction houses. Authorship, for example, may be guaranteed to a limited extent. Consignments with minimum prices called reserves and consignments owned by the auction house may be disclosed, and condition reports may be available on request.

Nevertheless, an auction is not a safe place for the casual purchaser. As long as auction houses get important art, however, collectors and insiders have to participate in the bidding.

The Dealer Is an Expert

Like the auction house, the dealer is usually a middleman. He sells at a negotiated price. There are many kinds of dealers, and the collector should seek the kind and the individual that suits him. The ideal dealer should be a moral and mature expert who has been in the art business long enough to be able to serve as preselector, pathfinder, and professor.

The fringe benefits of buying from a gallery include the privileges of asking the dealer to hold a picture for a short period while you make up your mind, to let you test the suitability of the art in your own home, to grant interest-free installment payments, to accept a trade, and to allow return of a purchase for a refund.

To recapture the initiative from auction houses, galleries should adopt a uniform bill of sale that would describe the piece of art, provide for guaranties of authenticity, signature, and physical condition, and specify the price, terms, and any right of return. When the casual buyer gets a full bill of sale from an established gallery, he is as protected as he is likely to be.

A Program for Selling

Once you have begun buying as a collector or insider, you should also have a program for selling, in terms of whether, when, how, and where to sell, and at what price. Don't wait for an emergency. Sell your unwanted art when you believe that your piece is close to its high price relative to other investments available to you, or, when the automatic buy/hold/sell plan that you follow calls for selling.

The most appropriate way to sell is sequentially, if you have the time and the stomach. Try to sell privately, then to dealers, then on consignment with a dealer, and when all that fails, go to auction.

Selling privately saves a commission, as long as you can set and obtain a fair retail price. Selling to a dealer is possible only when you know the value of what you have. Selling on consignment through a gallery calls for a careful statement of the terms of the consignment, just as selling at auction also requires that you cover all of the procedural bases in advance.

The Ten Keys

Those are the ten keys to collecting or investing in art: Touch, specialization, personal limits, the professionalism of the artist, your best, physical condition, appraisal and price, auction, dealers, and selling.

In addition, the conclusion will cover management, maintenance, insurance, framing and crating, hanging and storage, and finally, how you move from being a casual buyer to a collector and then to an insider, if you want to and if becoming an insider is worth the effort in your circumstance.

CHAPTER *3*

Touch as
a Sensual Connection

The question of how to buy art is like a layer cake. How deeply you bite into it is determined by what you want out of it. Casual buyers and diversified investors, for example, may be seeking only simple rules for purchasing safe pieces, while reserving the bulk of their attention for other markets. Investment portfolios have historically been diversified, and art has not been the primary holding. For these occasional buyers, a few hours of reading a week will suffice to learn the basics.

If you want more concentration on art, to have paintings and sculpture as a major concern, your preparations will require more dedication. Before you contemplate any purchase, you must start to make yourself into an informed buyer. Acquiring real expertise may take six months or even longer, but the more consideration you give the process, the more competent you will be as an art buyer and the better equipped you will be to cope with the unexpected.

There are three parts to this initial exploration, all centering on you as the collector. The first is the matter of your knowledge, experience, and touch, what they are and how to get them. The second will be to decide on the focus of your personal involvement in art, and the third will be setting your budgetary limits.

Knowledge Comes from Books

The starting prerequisite is knowledge, and that comes from books, although there is relatively little reading required to introduce you to the general art history background you need. The step after knowledge will be exposure to the art itself so that you can learn to relate what you have read to what you see. That is experience. Touch is something else, a flair that can be either innate or a way of viewing to be developed from multiple exposures that provide a basis for confidence. It is what is meant by saying a person has an "eye" for a particular subject. In art, touch is the ability to make a sure-handed selection of one picture from a group of pictures.

Touch is different things to different people. To some, it is almost a sensual connection, a real emotional high extending to a particular work of art, a velvet and sinuous tie that is the foundation for an instinctive feeling of dash and bravado and risk taking. For other calmer souls, it is a developed extension of background and experience producing assurance.

Whichever way touch comes to you, it has to be supported by knowledge and practice. There are some whose confidence comes in advance of knowledge and lets them make fools of themselves by acting precipitously. A few years ago, a middle-aged woman who knew all about stamps skipped around the art gallery to choose her booty in a trade and stopped before the least valuable painting in the place, absolutely certain she had picked the winner. Whatever touch she had in stamps, she did not have in art. Her flair did not carry over.

In contrast, there are those rare sensitives who have the innate capacity to choose the best among good pieces, though knowing nothing. There are children, for example, who intuitively respond to an unsigned watercolor by Georgia O'Keeffe (born 1887). That is innate touch and is rare.

For the collector, knowledge is just work, and experience is just time, but touch, that's the edge to distinguish the eventual insider from the routinely successful buyer. Fortunately, innate or developed touch is a truly democratic knack. Some degree of the necessary flair will be found and cultivated in all of us.

Collecting art can be for anyone who is sighted, and even the marginally sighted can function perfectly well if they have close-up vision. Three-dimensional works are available for the blind.

Age is no barrier, either. Indeed, the life experience of older persons generally provides an advantage. Some people only begin to buy art at an advanced age, after they have retired from unrelated jobs. Collecting art is not like starting school where the institution has to grab you young to make you stay in. Rather, if you are caught up in the desire to become involved in art, you will generate an emotion independent of years, to last for the rest of your life.

A physical handicap is not an impediment to collecting art; art *is* a driving force, and an old art dealer who walks with a cane will still leap toward a sculpture by Constantin Brancusi (1876-1957) if he sees the piece at the head of a staircase.

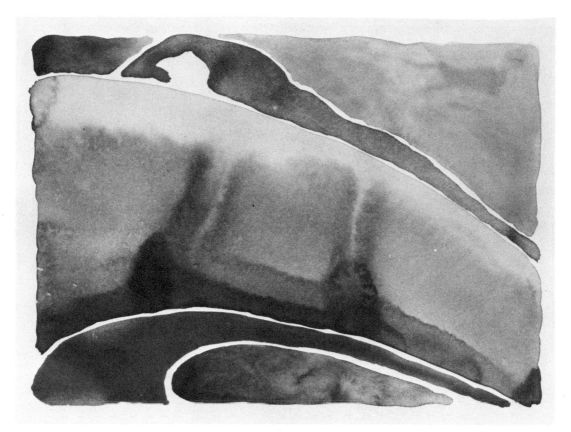

2. Georgia O'Keeffe. "Pink and Green Mountains."
Watercolor on paper, 9 by 12 inches.

Pairs and Couples

Pairs and couples are usually an advantage in the art business, if only for the prosaic reason that when traveling is required, two travel more easily than one. Couples have the edge in buying, too, as demonstrated by the number of dealers who function as marital partnerships today. They buy only what they both agree on, and they make offers and set prices by averaging their independently arrived-at estimates.

The recommended way for couples to begin collecting is to leaf through a book of art reproductions. If they choose paintings as their field, they can try publications like a print house catalog of pictures available at a framer's, our *Contemporary Western Artists* (in print at $50), or our

Biographical Encyclopedia of Artists of the American West (in print at $30). Art magazines are good, too. Each person chooses his favorite pictures and his hates independently of the other, listing the choices in writing, and then the two compare and discuss the lists. The types of paintings both like represent the consensus group to be considered, and the hates of either are excluded.

The usual stereotype is that one of the pair is adventurous and bold while the other is the balance, slowing down the buying process and emphasizing the negatives. The combination works well. The confidence couples have feeds off each other. In investment, couples may not make the quickest million dollars but their progress will be more even, happier, and surer. Couples are less likely to lose their investment stake before they reach their goal.

Begin with American Art

In acquiring the knowledge to serve as the foundation for collecting art, you should begin with American art history because in this country it is the insider's field. American art is just attaining its national significance. Collecting American art lets you take advantage of the gap that still exists between current price and ultimate worth.

European art is closer to having reached full value relative to other investments, and so would be a poorer choice for most collectors. It is an international market, not available to all American buyers, whereas American art is a national industry, our own country's record. A substantial proportion of all American art is sold in the United States; in comparison, only a fifth of quality French art is sold in France.

Within ten years, American art will be international, too, broadening the market and rewarding earlier collectors. In addition, the tremendous growth of American art both in sales volume and in price is leading to the availability of simple statistics that will permit technical evaluation for automatic investment plans.

Besides, the same principles you will find applicable to American art will carry over to collecting in any other field of art. What you learn in the one can be practiced in the other. Usually, rules governing American paintings also govern American sculpture, drawings, European art, and even prints, to a lesser extent.

There is no one perfect text for American art history, but the best background source has continued to be Oliver Larkin's *Art and Life in America* published by Macmillan in New York City in 1949. Also recommended are Samuel Isham's *The History of American Painting* published by Macmillan (the 1927 edition with the Royal Cortissoz supplement), Virgil Barker's *American Painting* published by Macmillan in 1950, Rilla Jackman's *American Arts* published by Rand McNally in 1928, Barbara Rose's *American Art Since 1900* published by Praeger in 1967, and Milton Brown's *American Painting from the Armory Show to the Depression* published by Princeton in 1955.

Art and Books

Your horizon is expanding now as you prepare to look for these two things, art and books. Where you can, take the books out of the library before you buy them, to see which fit you. If you can't buy the books, because of economics or availability, make photocopies of the indices. Names of the famous artists who are discussed in the art history books should be on your person, at the ready.

When you start with limited funds to buy art, you are likely to be a long time finding an affordable work by one of the ranking artists listed in these history books, but if you are ever in such a position, you will know what to grab.

In addition to the background books, there are reference texts which are longer lists of substantially all of the professional artists who exhibited and sold, minus the descriptions in the history books of the schools of art and the personalities involved. These reference books are not to read, but you should become familiar with them so you can use them in the field to check names.

The books of lists start with the two volumes of Mallett's *Index of Artists* published by Bowker in 1948 (in print at about $40), Fielding's *Dictionary of American Painters, Sculptors and Engravers*, published by Carr in 1965 (in print at about $20), or one of the later editions of Fielding.

There are also Groce and Wallace's *Dictionary of Artists in America 1564–1860* published by Yale in 1957 (in print at $52.50), the *American Art Annuals* that included *Who's Who in American Art* published by the American Federation of Art and others beginning in 1898 (some *Annuals* do not have the *Who's Who* section and are of little value), MacDonald's *A Dictionary of Canadian Artists* published by Canadian Paperbacks starting in 1967, and Benezit's *Dictionnaire des Peintres* published in ten volumes by Librairie Grund in Paris in 1976 (in print at about $500). Earlier and cheaper editions of Benezit are equally good for the older artists. The *Dictionnaire* is in French, but locating names is the same in any language.

The general art magazines also provide background. Old copies of the defunct *American Art Review* are worth having. *Art & Antiques*, *ARTnews*, and *Antiques* are helpful. Try the *Maine Antique Digest* published in Waldoboro for frank reporting.

Get catalogs from auction houses. Names and addresses of major houses are available from your library. If you subscribe, avoid the auction houses that make you buy catalogs for all kinds of art in order to get the one kind you want. Instead, take the subscriptions that let you concentrate on, for example, American painting and sculpture of the nineteenth century. Being swamped with information on Old Masters and European Post-Impressionists and Latin Americans is confusing and divisive.

Take a course in art appreciation, if you can find one on American art that is worthwhile. Join a couple of museums that collect American art to get their mailings telling what the museum owns, buys, and exhibits.

As you will discover, some of the recommended books and magazines are out of print and must be obtained from dealers in used art books. Your local book store may have them. Otherwise, try Olana Gallery, Drawer 9, Brewster, New York 10509; R.W. Smith—Bookseller, 51 Trumbull Street, New Haven, Connecticut 06510; or Kenneth Starosciak, 117 Wilmot Street, San Francisco, California 94115. Editions Publisol, P.O. Box 339, Gracie Station, New York, N.Y. 10028; The Reference Rack in Orefield, Pennsylvania 18069, or Timothy Trace in Peekskill, New York 10655 have the in-print books.

When you need to dig deeper, get the weekly trade magazine *AB Bookman's Weekly* (P.O. Box AB, Clifton, New Jersey 07015). In *AB*, you can look under "books for sale" to find what you want, if you are patient, or you can excerpt the names of dealers in used art books and write to them. You can also advertise in *AB*.

Book scouts are another option, but they are expensive, they insulate you from the fun of your own quest, and the books named here are not all that difficult to find, except for some early out-of-print *American Art Annuals*.

Getting on the mailing lists of dealers in used art books is the usual procedure. Start by requesting the lists of book dealers who do not charge for mailing, or who at least offer you a credit against purchases coupled with a nominal charge. You may be surprised at the high cost of these used art books, but they generally cost less than new books and they are worth the money.

Start Looking at Art

After you've begun the process of obtaining history and reference books or copying lists, it is time to start looking at art. Go wherever there are original works in some quantity. The usual sources are galleries, museums, auctions, historical societies, schools, collections, shops, and businesses, anywhere there is art for show or for sale.

The best places to look are the shops that will let you handle the art, pick up the sculpture and look at the bottom, take the pictures off the wall to examine the backs, bounce reflected light off the paint, hold the signature close to your eye in direct sunlight, and see how the paint was applied. These are experiences that will become more meaningful to you as you proceed.

The approach of touching the art limits where you can go. Art that is valuable is properly restricted, and you may have to extend your visits to "junk" shops, that is, charity outlets, used furniture shops, used book stores, less expensive antique shops, country auctions, flea markets, and anywhere else there might be art you can physically explore. Look in the Yellow Pages under both "Furniture—Used" and "Antiques—Dealers." The antique dealers you want to start with are not the elite but rather the ones that are only a cut above the used furniture stores.

Junk shops serve a real educational function for collectors, particularly when the collectors recognize that they really should buy art to get their feet wet, yet, conversely, they should not buy art at all until they have some experience to guide them. The answer to this riddle is to begin by buying inexpensive art in junk shops, but only according to the rules.

Wherever you are, however, ask permission before you take anything off the wall. Be careful with what you handle. Glass breaks. Paper and fabric tear. Don't put your finger on the front of a picture. Don't lick the signature to be able to read it better. Remember, old frames can come apart while you hold them, and pictures can fall out of frames. Don't scratch a casting to see if it is bronze.

Part of the routine for the development of "touch" is the engendering of respect for all art objects, regardless of their condition or what you think the value is.

CHAPTER 4

Specialization
Is a Key

With the knowledge and experience you have gained and the touch you are beginning to test, you are now ready to choose a specific arena for your art collecting. The question is, will you act as a generalist in your collecting, purchasing art in random categories, or as a specialist, buying only within a small homogeneous group personal to you? That is, will you consider buying art of any kind where there may be a bargain or a gem, or will you confine your explorations to a predetermined class of art you can study more intensively?

Deciding whether or not to choose a specialty is one of the most important steps in learning about art.

Whether to Specialize

An example of what specialization means comes from the career of a bill collector who liked art. To learn more about paintings and sculpture, he drove a dealer to galleries and stayed in the background while the dealer bought and sold. His next step was to become associated with a major Madison Avenue dealer in New York City. When that operation was suspended, he was thrust on his own about 1976. He opened a small gallery in New York with his wife, handling profitably whatever came to them from contacts he had made. The Western pictures he found, he offered to a dealer in Western art, taking in trade good paintings that were not Western.

On one visit to the Western dealer, he saw a group of paintings by an American abstract artist of the 1930s that the Western dealer had bought to encourage a "picker," although the style did not fit his market. The New Yorker, who was an aggressive and personable man, ascertained that the artist was still alive, contacted him, and became his agent for the scores of 1930s paintings the artist had retained.

Success in this representation led him to seek out more of the American abstract artists of the 1930s who had long since slipped from the current art scene. Some of these artists were still alive and the work of others remained in their estates in the absence of a market. He took on consignment all of the early American abstract paintings he could get and was soon running one of the most profitable galleries in New York City, entirely because he was able to recreate and meet the substantial demand for this specialization he had revived. When he exhausted the 1930s abstract artists, he added the 1940s.

Another example is an illustrator who had as a hobby collected a large number of original illustrations drawn by the great commercial artists of earlier days. The illustrations had cost him comparatively little. He wrote the first comprehensive picture book on these illustrators, starting with the turn of the century artists, and, to sell the original illustrations he set up a little shop in the attic of the publishing house where he worked about 1972.

Over the years, he maintained his shop as a sideline, promoting illustrative drawings and paintings as a salable art form. Partially because of his efforts, original American illustrations representative of the period from 1900 to 1950 make up an important new area in the art world, and he now has his own gallery, carrying on as his vocation what he began as a specialized personal collection.

By sticking to a small turf, the former bill collector and the former illustrator reaped great rewards relatively quickly. If you focus on a selected group of paintings, as they did, the same kind of opportunity will be yours for collecting and investing in art.

You have much to gain. One advantage will be the acceptance of you by those you would like to have as your peers. When you specialize, you will be surprised to discover that in one month, you will acquire enough of a veneer of experience to talk the language of the experts in your specialty. You will impress the general dealers, and you will find they prefer to work with knowledgeable and decisive buyers, the kind you will be. This is one benefit of specialization, "instant" expertise. The longer you stay with your specialty, the deeper your expertise will become.

Narrowing Your Scope

Specialization in art is thus a primary key to profitable collecting. Narrowing your scope means minimizing effort for maximized results. When you are starting out, you cannot expect to be an authority on all aspects of art, so you must confine yourself to just one type of artist, one subject or style, or one time period, and fit yourself to that one aspect.

The reason for this is that the art market is not the big undivided enterprise it may appear to be, but a composite of separate and specific markets, each with its own patterns and participants. There are separate dealers and separate auction departments, separate museums, separate painting and modeling characteristics, and separate trends. There is even a separate literature. You will gain from recognizing that the art market is made up of this combination of specialties. Concentrating on just one will let you move ahead much faster.

Another advantage of specialization is that works of art well chosen in a popular category will be exhibitable and will lend themselves to mention in books and articles. Art shows and art literature are proliferating. Curators, editors, and writers are glad to know about private collections pertaining to their fields.

For example, one collection touring museums and featured in periodicals has as its focus the singular characteristic that the artists included were "undiscovered" minor Western illustrators who worked for the popular magazines and pulps before 1950. The point of the collection is that there were professional illustrators such as Edmund F. Ward (born 1892) and Walter Baumhofer (born 1904) who were fine talents even if they were not quite Norman Rockwell (1894–1978) or Remington.

Lesser artists like these will become more marketable when they are placed in a homogeneous grouping and publicized. They become better known and their work commands a premium. The museums that exhibit the collection may even buy a piece. As a result, individual paintings and bronzes which once might have been bought for a modest amount have been upgraded many times in resale value. This is investment properly made, through the selection of a specialization that succeeded.

Confining your attention to a specific area is a further advantage because you will be dealing with relatively few people. There may be only 500 persons in the country who are selling, buying, and exhibiting art in any one really narrow category. You can more easily get to know the decision makers and the style setters, to share views on events and trends. Contacts like these will bring you to an understanding of the inside factors in both buying and selling, an insight you might never otherwise achieve.

As a specialist, you may be able to deal person-to-person with other collectors and investors rather than through middlemen like dealers and auction houses. You will save commissions. You will be better able to protect yourself against fakes, too, and where there are no recorded selling prices for a given artist, you may have private sources of data you can tap.

Being part of a small group might tip you off to a market trend early enough to get in on it, or out of it.

You might even get to set your own trends. If you were to buy 50 Joseph Imhof (1871–1956) drawings of Taos Indians, say, and you promoted Imhof as a specialty, you would see the somnolent Imhof prices awaken with a bang as the consequence of your action.

You might find there is no one recognized expert in the field you have chosen. This would be a real opportunity for you. Collect the literature and original memorabilia, do the research, publish articles, and you will find you have become the expert. Instant expertise may sound like pie in the sky, but scores of authorities were established just that way, by art students as well as art hobbyists.

Specialization Is Preferred

In art collecting, specialization is thus the preferred practice, fostering all three of the usual reasons to buy art: pleasure, prestige, and profit. As in other good things, however, a few nay sayers claim there is an inherent danger in specializing. The investor, they say, who sticks to one type of art may be seen as not having the hedge against misjudgment that a generalist has who buys any work of art in any subject promising gain.

Admittedly, picking the wrong specialization is possible and could indeed be a blow, but this will not happen. In the nature of things, it is inevitable that one category will peak before another does, and one specialist will thereby gain his reward earlier, but even the specialist who suffers a delay is likely to be better off than the generalist. The specialist will obviously be more informed about his subject and will tend to make wiser decisions, as by avoiding fads.

Actually, the suggestion that the art collector should diversify as a generalist is not even an art concept. It comes from some of the veteran stock brokerage houses where diversification is practiced because the stock market is innately such a gamble. The brokers recommend a combination of stocks, bonds, and cash for balance, and a truly spread portfolio also would include tangibles, perhaps even art. In the contemporary stock market, however, there are experts like Adam Smith who espouse concentration in stock ownership rather than diversification, for much the same reasons as in art. You cannot be the master of everything.

There is a substantial difference, though, between buying more and more identical shares of one issue of stock, and, buying more and more different works of art, even if in the same category. Advice to diversify does not really apply to art at all. Every work of art is inherently different from every other work of art, so the second piece you buy must be distinct from the first. The only reason for true diversification in art would be to cover up bad judgment through averaging of errors, a situation you will not have to face.

Keep in mind that in the beginning the definition of your specialty should be a little broader than your ultimate scope will be. The category you select at the start has to be sufficiently wide so you can readily find enough of your kind of art to keep those first searches exciting for you. Later on, the more you narrow the classification, the better.

Western art created before 1950, for example, is a broad subject, allowing you plenty of opportunity to buy. You can later refine the subject to bronzes of buffalos or early paintings of the Taos School or of the Utah localists or whatever else West of the Mississippi your intuition and experience lead you to. If your original purchases do not fit your final portfolio, you will still be able to dispose of the discards profitably.

It will always be difficult, however, for some people to make the initial purchase of any work of art. It will be easier if a person tailors the collecting pattern to his individual interests establishing his personal compatibility as the primary consideration—and also if he assures himself that the specialty he selects has good possibilities for gain, is insulated against loss, and is not too difficult to enter. If the casual buyer who is reluctant can just be coaxed into such a suitably cozy category, profits are built in for important pieces of art today and losses will be very few.

Go Back to the Pictures

The appropriate way for the individual to make the choice of a specialization is for him to go back to the pictures in the art history books and the magazines once again, not for general knowledge this time but solely as an aid in selecting his specialization. He should submerge himself in a large number of preselected "good" pieces of art, wherever he can find them. In addition to the usual sources, look at albums of commercial prints like the catalogs of The New York Graphic Society that show hundreds of paintings of all types.

Very briefly stated, you will find that the American paintings you will see begin with eighteenth century Colonial portraits done typically by Gilbert Stuart (1755–1828) and John Singleton Copley (1737–1815), followed by early primitive painters like Edward Hicks (1780–1849). In the mid-nineteenth century, there were the realist painters of genre like George Caleb Bingham (1811–1879) and William Sidney Mount (1807–1869), along with the Hudson River School of Thomas Cole (1801–1849) and Asher B. Durand (1796–1886).

The nineteenth century still-life painters were men like William M. Harnett (1851–1892) and John F. Peto (1854–1907). The marine painters included Fitzhugh Lane (1804–1865) and James E. Buttersworth (1817–1894). The painters of the Old West were led by Frederic Remington and Charles Marion Russell, while the American Impressionists included The Ten with Childe Hassam (1859–1935) and John Twachtman (1853–1902). The Ash Can School was made up of The Eight including Robert Henri (1865–1929) and John Sloan (1871–1951). The Regionalists were represented by Thomas Hart Benton (1889–1975), and so on. These artists' names are just to identify the schools for you, not to suggest that their art is readily available within the limits of your pocketbook.

Pick Your Specialization

After you have considered the schools of art, it is time to proceed to pick your personal specialization. One way is to be introspective. Think of what you are really like in your heart, in your aspirations and dreams, and extend this feeling to reach out to the type of art that is most consonant with you.

Relax with a book full of pictures. Which appeal to you? Where do your affinities lie? The book you are looking at should be thought of as a department store that stocks all kinds of professional art, waiting for you to wander through at your leisure before you pick a gift for yourself, the specialization that suits you.

To oversimplify the way emotions affect choice, if you see yourself as action-oriented and a decision-maker, you might respond to the movement and mass in pictures of military action. If you are quiet and reflective, you might prefer traditional landscape watercolors. If you are committed to the issue of women's rights, you might feel comfortable with paintings by or of women in an appropriate context.

The fundamental goal is to make a sincere and intuitive choice. However you decide, the specialization should reflect you. Someone who knows you and looks at your art should see the connection and be able to say, "Isn't that just like you!"

A second approach is for you to pick your specialty based on your individual experiences apart from art. What is your personal opinion of what the next social focus will be? Will the trend of the 1980s reflect a return to the 1950s in art as it has in clothes and furniture and politics?

Or, if you are knowledgeable in a related field like antique furniture, can you sense the drift there and carry your beliefs over to art? If there are style changes you expect in these other areas you know, the category of art you will consider could reflect those changes and thereby offer a way to use your own background to get ahead of the art market. If you collect Mission furniture, for example, you could select paintings such as Barbizon landscapes that are compatible with Mission and put them in Mission frames.

A third approach is to seek advice from curators, dealers, auctioneers, or advanced collectors. Some of us will choose a specialty only if the choice dictated by our feelings and judgment is confirmed by an expert. We often do not trust our own decisions and may need reinforcement. This sort of indecisiveness exists even in great institutions and so is nothing rare. The problem, however, is sorting out the good advice from the bad.

The early collections of many of our leading American museums, for example, were arrived at by consultation with European-minded dealers, resulting in the absence of American art in these museums in favor of specialization in European Old Masters and the academics who were the products of the Ecole des Beaux-Arts in Paris.

More recently, a small museum on Long Island in New York which had been distinguished by its major collection of old Western art discarded the Western pieces and replaced them with a pedestrian holding of twentieth century moderns, on the advice of a new curator who had been trained in contemporary European art. Giving up an important specialization like this was a national loss.

What You Know in Your Bones

Experts are usually art historians, and analyzing the past is a lot easier for them than forecasting. Be sure to pick a sympathetic and aware advisor for yourself. You cannot, though, just depend on experts. You should not abandon your own intuition and experiences. If you take outside counsel without regard to whether it makes sense to you, you will have no confidence in your collecting and you may drop out at the first hint of a reversal.

Instead, pay attention to what you know in your bones. Let the visions, memories, and recommendations all flow through your head until they fall into place. Then determine your specialization by yourself and it will bring you substantial personal rewards. Even if your only reason for collecting art is investment, you will do better with works that appeal to you.

You need to trust your own feelings, but within sensible limits. Some collectors have a tendency to go too far in their independence when they are starting out. As an example, a new collector marvelled at his acquisition of a George Inness (1825–1894) landscape at a country auction. The cost was low for an Inness, $2,000, and any established dealer could have told him that many such Innesses are likely to have been forged. This collector did not ask for advice, although buying an Inness without provenance is a classic con in the painting business, almost like buying the Brooklyn Bridge in real estate.

Other new collectors solicit recommendations, and then do not use the advice they asked for when it is contrary to their feelings. Buyers like these have been known to ask a dealer which of two pictures in his shop is the better investment, and then buy the other, simply because they think the dealer would knock what he would prefer to keep. These collectors represent the contrarians in art.

Once you have decided to specialize, as you should, what is called for in picking your category is balance. Use all of the aids available to you.

CHAPTER 5

Your Personal Specialization

Whether your choice of a specialization is dictated by your emotions, your background, or the experts, there is literally no end to the possibilities for personalized specialization patterns.

As Varied as You Wish

In American art, the categories can be as varied as you wish, reflecting almost any point of view you might want to express. The options are wide, classifying first by school, as nineteenth century Academic, Barbizon, Pre-Raphaelite, Realist, Abstract, Impressionist, and so on. Or the approach can be by way of the subject, such as events, portraits, animals, landscapes, marine scenes, people doing things in everyday life, or still-lifes.

If you pick landscapes, you might start with the Regionalists, or with localities like San Francisco or Boston, or particular sites like the Statue of Liberty, the Hudson River, or an Indian pueblo, or frontiers such as the Arctic or space. Events could include the Gold Rush or Custer's Last Stand.

Narrowing the subject further could provide works on domestic animals or sporting themes or wildlife. There are also railroads, airplanes, the cavalry, the Civil War, art by or of American Indians or blacks, and so on. See which of these suits you. If you are a bird watcher who lives in Massachusetts, what could a better specialization be than art by Louis Agassiz Fuertes (1874–1927) or Allan Brooks (1869–1946) that shows New England birds?

From the standpoint of time, you might feel you are a person who would have been more comfortable if you had lived in the past, say 1900. You could then pick art showing what people were doing then, how they lived, and what their homes were like. You would discover that people look different today than they did in 1900, so the works you would want are the ones done then. Artists working now are not likely to reproduce accurately the nuances in what they never saw.

Alternately, you might prefer to specialize in the works of one painter, like Frederic Remington, the Western artist. There is a supply of Remington paintings regularly available from the 2,000 or so that he made, at prices from $100,000 to $1,000,000. If this is too strong for your budget, there are complex Remington drawings from $5,000 to $50,000. Even cheaper are simpler Remington sketches like the marginal notations from *Hiawatha* or from his sketchbook.

If this still does not bring Remington within your means, you may wish to search out a less expensive Western artist whose work pleases you. Will Crawford (1869–1944) whose drawing technique was the model for Charles Marion Russell might be such an example. Good Crawford drawings of cowboys in action can be found for less than $1,000. As a forester, as one of America's great pen and ink men, as a friend of writers, actors, and artists, as a radical, and as a hunchback, Crawford was eulogized as a "most unforgettable character." He merits the biographical study that would increase the prices of his drawings by bringing back into the limelight a highly professional but forgotten commercial artist.

As you can see, your personal pattern can follow any one of a tremendous number of specializations. You can even limit yourself to one painting medium, such as oil, gouache, watercolor, wash drawing, or ink, pencil, or charcoal drawing, or to murals on canvas or lunettes rather than to conventional sizes and shapes.

Different styles of painting and subjects and times all overlap, too, allowing even further narrowing of a category for you. If you enjoy paintings of domestic animals like horses, dogs, cats, cows, or sheep, you can choose one animal, opt for the late 1880s as the time, and pick Barbizon as a suitable style. Pigs as a subject might be too hard to find at the start, but horses were always popular. So were chickens. You will discover that there is a typical price differentiation among animals, with sheep generally priced below cows, and cows below horses, and horses below cats, and so on.

Another specialization is to concentrate on artists under 30, if you are sure you can pick the ones who will eventually be recognized in the contemporary art scene. The reverse of selecting the promising young artists is to buy the works of older living artists, in anticipation of a price rise when they stop working.

Beware, though, the longevity of the artist. Mary Theresa Hart (1829–1921), wife of the Hudson River School painter James M. Hart (1828–1901), lived so long that some of her paintings were mistakenly attributed to her daughter, Letitia (1867–c. 1936).

Your Last Literary Excursion

After you have chosen your specialty, you should consider acquiring a new set of appropriate books on a last literary excursion. You will need background materials to place you in the scene you picked, and you will need descriptions of the art plus biographies of the artists.

If for example you selected pictures of the old-time West, you should have fun reading about the period in the books of the time. You can also try current magazines like *Southwest Art, American West, Art West,* or *Artists of the Rockies.* It will be helpful to you to know what the cast of characters looked like, what they wore, what gear they used, the terrain that was their backdrop, and the nature of the painters' "light" they saw.

Remington himself recommended early Western books by George Catlin, Josiah Gregg, Washington Irving, and Francis Parkman, along with Andy Adams, Mayne Reid, and Theodore Roosevelt. Remington thought of Andy Adams as the reality of the West and Owen Wister as the stereotype, but they are both pertinent, as are Remington's own stories in our *Collected Writings.* For biographies of Western artists, look at our *Biographical Encyclopedia.*

You will find this reading essential to specialization in Western art because American art history books minimize the space given to genre painters of the American West. Larkin in his *Art and Life in America*, for example, did not even mention Charles Russell or Henry Farny or the Taos school, simply because they were not innovative painters in the sense that Remington was.

If you think of the Hudson River as your subject, you might check the turn-of-the-century "view books" of the river shores and also the picture book on the Hudson River school of painters by John Howat. For background on American illustrators, try Walt Reed's *The Illustrator in America* or Henry Pitz's *200 Years of American Illustration.* For paintings by American Indians, there are books by Jeanne O. Snodgrass and Clara Lee Tanner. For still-life, there are books by William H. Gerdts and Alfred Frankenstein. And so on. See your bookseller and library.

There are also books on artists of the various states, and *The American Guide* by the Federal Writers' Project gives names of regional painters.

Landmark catalogs include Domit on *American Impressionist Painting*, Bermingham on *American Art in the Barbizon Mood*, Hoopes on *American Narrative Painting*, and Fink and Taylor on *The Academic Tradition in American Art*. The library will recommend additional books and articles, in your specialty.

Pictures by the Localists

Before you decide to act on a particular specialization, however, there are cautions on how to proceed. Some are apparent, some not. For example, pictures by the localists, the artists of specific places, are becoming increasingly attractive to the residents of those places. In San Francisco, New Orleans, San Antonio, Washington, Philadelphia, Detroit, Boston, and other cities, local artists who had been neglected for 50 or 100 years have suddenly surfaced as highly collectible in the cities where they painted. Prices for local scenes have increased as much as 15 times in five years.

The caution is that the prices of the works by some of these localists may have risen too much in their home areas to warrant puchase at those prices. Perhaps you cannot profitably buy W.A. Walker (1838–1921) in New Orleans, Robert Onderdonk (1853–1917) in San Antonio, Lucien Powell (1846–1930) in Washington, or Carl Weber (1850–1921) in Philadelphia. These are painters of national rank, though, and well worth considering if you have access to markets at a distance from their locales. Lucien Powell's landscapes of Virginia may still be available at a reasonable price in Los Angeles, if not in Washington.

There are also some strictly local painters who are highly collectible where they worked, but who are not known a hundred miles away. They have no national standing and are not listed in standard reference books. Carl Von Hassler (1887–1969) was a superior Albuquerque artist who brings high prices in central New Mexico but nowhere else. A routine Von Hassler was appraised at $17,000 for donation to a local museum, although his value for investment is questionable on a national level.

Buying the work of a listed artist in his home town may be expensive, as we have seen, but buying the work of a locally celebrated artist who is not nationally recognized may be disastrous.

Old Western Bronzes

A few other common kinds of American art are not recommended because collecting them may be too difficult or too risky. For instance,

Western bronze statuettes modeled before 1950 are a problem for the collector, unless he is irrevocably drawn to their considerable charm and is willing both to do the additional preparatory investigation and to face the extra danger of loss.

One reason for the note of caution is that the price of these bronzes is depressed in comparison with paintings of the same period because of the huge number of relatively undetectable forgeries and recasts.

The most typical example is Remington, who was the primary sculptor of the Old West. He died at the end of 1909, but his wife authorized new castings up to 1918, a date when forgeries had already begun to appear on the market. No chemical dating test for authenticity could be wholly meaningful when the forgeries antedate authorized but posthumous castings.

There were less than 400 authorized bronzes cast of Remington's "Bronco Buster," and yet there are more than 4,000 castings in existence. Moreover, forgeries were authenticated even by experts. Ten of the 27 Remington bronzes in a famous museum collection may not be originals. This would be typical of many museum collections where the castings did not come directly from the artist.

On some antique bronzes, foundrymen themselves have difficulty identifying originals, although they talk in a learned manner about changes in the style of gating, the formula used for the bronze itself, and the traces left of the plaster core. There are even different levels of recast bronzes, distinguishing those where the subject has been resculpted from those that were recast over an original. These recasts may be given the mark of the original foundry, or the mark of a new foundry, or no mark.

There is thus a very gray area in validating old bronzes. In one instance just a few years ago, a panel of five experts met to decide whether a 1905 bronze was authentic or not, and the panel split three to two in favor of authenticity. If you had purchased such a statuette with seemingly good provenance and its authenticity was later questioned by a recognized expert, you might never be able to resolve the validity of your bronze and you might not then be able to recoup your purchase price.

You can see that antique bronzes would be a dangerous specialization, although contemporary bronzes do qualify for collection and investment, provided you can resolve the professionalism of the sculptor.

Other Subjects to Avoid

Other subjects to avoid are more personal. In forming collections of paintings by one artist, insiders would stay away from Ralph Blakelock

(1847–1919). A mystical painter of Western Indian subjects, he was forged even immediately after his death when his daughter was painting the same subjects in the same style. Much of what is offered as his work is now questionable. There have been several so-called indisputable authenticators of Blakelock over the years who soon proved to be quite disputable.

You should also be chary of American paintings before 1850. There are relatively few of them, and knowledge is hard to come by. Most of the pictures are what are called ancestor portraits which might not suit collecting today. Ancestor portraits were in vogue a decade ago, to provide instant antecedents, but a group of such portraits might be monotonous as a collection unless they were sub-specialized into portraits of sea captains, for example, or children with cats.

There is a continuing interest in old primitive paintings, but many experts exclude these from safe specialization, too. There never was just one artist named "Peter Primitive" whose style you could study. Instead, there seem to be an unlimited number of unnamed artists, some of them working today. There are few objective standards you can record, and "in" experts control the market for all of the countless examples of primitives. There is just too little that is defined that the amateur may learn or rely on.

As in old bronzes, you might have difficulty maintaining an authentication of a primitive. Forgeries and questionable authentications are plentiful, and even museum curators have problems analyzing old primitives. A recent incident involved a wooden weathervane carved in 1976 to replace an antique that was stolen. Dated "76" because there was no room for the "19," it was accepted and advertised as an antique by the highest level of experts in primitives, until the carver happened to learn of the mistake.

Another Caution Is Fads

Another caution is to avoid fads, where the price of a work of art is temporarily inflated because the subject or the artist is in momentary vogue. Immediately after an artist sets a newsworthy record at auction, for instance, his poorer works are elevated in price for a short time, until interest in that artist flags.

Auction records show that booms are sometimes launched by mistake. At an auction in 1973, one Yasuo Kuniyoshi (1893–1953) painting was sold for $160,000 and another for $220,000, amounts that were astonishing records for the artist then. An explanation rumored after the sale was that two agents of the same Japanese principal were unknowingly bidding against each other. Kuniyoshi prices soon receded, and buyers who had taken the record prices as real indicators were fooled.

Fads are an unnecessary hazard. It seems frivolous to invest in a subject where you have to worry about the precise moment to get out, while you try to hold a position until just before the walls fall in. That would be stock market mentality. Few of us could count on such prescience.

Buying art at the height of a fad is like buying from a seller who tells a romantic story about the background of a piece in order to provide a promotional aura. Experienced buyers pay only what the piece would be worth if the story evaporated, because that is exactly what it is likely to do by the time you get the piece home.

A work of art bought during a fad has extra value only during the life of the fad, and the duration of the fad is not predictable.

Western Paintings Done Before 1950 and After _____

Because picking your specialization is such an important affirmative step in buying, it is worth taking time to contrast two similar but different categories, art of the Old West done before 1950 and contemporary Western art. The reason for breaking off at 1950 is that the artists painting the West before then saw different scenes. Also, the earlier arrivals have claimed that they were the ones pulled to the scene by the subject, whereas some of the latecomers were in just for the money.

The total of all of those earlier artists working before 1950 is still a manageable number, and they did see a sort of raw life on the range, even if the buffalo, the unfenced land, the wild Indian, and the cavalry were beginning to fade from the stage between 1880 and 1890. Remington went to Montana and Wyoming in 1880 when a million buffalo grazed the open land. Russell was already there, working as a cowboy.

Antique Western pictures enjoy a national market, as strong in New York City and Los Angeles as it is in Phoenix or Chicago. The subject matter is attractive to most men and the subdued side has feminine appeal, a picturesque slice of uniquely American history, painted by artists who saw some of the events happen. Old Western paintings are an innocent art form for a cynical post-Watergate society, and in the last ten years, investment in Old Western pictures has been most profitable. There is no sign that prices are softening for prime pieces.

Old Westerns benefit from the margarine maxim. The wider you spread one pat, the thinner it gets. There cannot be any more Western pictures painted before 1950. All of them taken together constitute "one pat," and topnotch examples have been swallowed by institutions and collections. Major Remingtons and Russells are more and more difficult to find. With supply diminishing and demand rising, the price is escalating. This makes for the textbook definition of a sound place for investment.

In 1965, the Cowboy Artists of America was formed to improve the supply side, "to perpetuate the memory and culture of the Old West as typified by Remington and Russell." The first CAA exhibition in 1966 drew 100 buyers who paid $50,000 for the Western art they purchased. In a dozen years, there were 1,400 buyers paying $850,000. By 1981, there were 2,000 buyers, and the sales were $1,762,000.

The success of the CAA has launched the careers of hundreds of other artists who are followers of the Cowboy Artists, just as the Cowboy Artists followed Remington and Russell. This contemporary cowboy art has been primarily a Southwestern phenomenon, where paintings of the Old West done currently have been sold for as much as $300,000 to $400,000.

The top cowboy artists have had scores of customers available for each major painting. They cannot always keep up with the demand, and the scarcity controls the prices. The practice at exhibitions has been to post the price for each picture shown and then place a box alongside so that prospective buyers can register on "intent to purchase" slips. As many as 300 slips have been entered for one picture, requiring a lottery to select the winning buyer.

An Auction at Burt's Place

The highest prices for current cowboy art are generally realized at auctions. An example of such a private auction, fictionalized from actual happenings, might have been held at Burt's place. Burt could be some Hollywood film star with his own collection of current Western art.

The 1,100 invited guests who paid $100 a head to attend are treated to patio dining with plenty of booze. Gents are in Texedos, which are tuxedos with black tie, ten gallon hats, and lizard skin cowboy boots. The ladies wear Dior gowns with three-diamond studs in each ear.

It is de rigueur for the artists to attend. As much on exhibition as their art, the artists stand around, hanging on to one glass of whiskey and water while leaning away from the clutches of their liquored patrons. This kind of contemporary Western market is aided by the capacity of the artists to resemble Westerners rather than the Eastern daubers some of them might once have been.

After dinner, the party moves to poolside. The auctioneer is on the balcony and his spotters are on the deck of the pool. A celebrity who looks like John Connally, the former Texas governor, makes the opening remarks, giving the crowd his three rules for buying art. "Quality, quality, quality," he advises the crowd. "Buy the best, 'cuz a good horse eats no more than a sorry one."

The auctioneer starts the bidding in the same high-pitched chant that has sold thousands of "heifers and hosses." When the bidding reaches $50,000 on the first lot, the auctioneer breaks from his song to admonish the buyers. "Folks," he says, "You're making so much noise, I don't believe you know what the bid is." He wants the guests to reassure him that the bids he hears are really true. As each lot is sold, the name of the winning bidder lights up in eight-foot-high letters on the scoreboard borrowed for the evening from the Dallas Cowboys' Texas Stadium. Gross sales for the auction amount to $1,500,000.

Pictures of the Good Old Days

This kind of auction is a social happening, staged for a new type of culture consumer. These are Southwesterners who had been depressed by the Puritan work ethic and by the agricultural economy but who are now transformed by money, leisure, and the new educational emphasis. Their old life was gray, but this vivid contemporary art portrays the cowboys as true American heroes and it rewrites the buyers' own biographies. "I am an old country boy," an energy-rich Texan says, "and I like pictures of the old country, the way it was in the good old days."

Patrons of the current artists who paint old scenes are generous to the extreme with money spent for art. This binds the cowboy artists to them and gets the attention of the Eastern elite. To earn big pay-offs, the artists must paint "quality, quality, quality," which in this case means a nonviolent ranch or Indian or mountain man scene in realistic detail, rendered with a slick illustrator's finish on a 24 by 48 inch or bigger canvas.

Despite the "quality" sales talk, however, some of today's cowboy art following Remington and Russell is designed to have its greatest appeal for buyers who know the least about quality in art. Nothing innovative would be tolerated by these patrons who say they have a "madman's rage" or a "gluttony" for their kind of art. Galleries who sell to them state that they are "really the avant-garde. The Eastern art establishments think they're avant-garde, but they're still going for dots and dashes that no one can understand or enjoy. But while the Eastern critics keep writing bad reviews," they say, contemporary Western paintings command prices that are among the highest in all of current American art.

Hindsight and Foresight

Purchasing Old Western paintings of the Remington school done before 1950 is an investment based on economic hindsight. There have been decades of published sales prices to use as a guide.

The long-term values of some of today's Western art, however, are not yet protected by hindsight. The work is too new to have had public sales over a long period. What is required, then, is foresight in choosing among the hundreds of current practitioners of Western art. Buying the work of current Western artists must be selective.

You need to be sure that the artists are professionals, listed in the specialized reference books like our *Contemporary Western Artists* or possessing other indicia of recognition such as dealerships, memberships, articles, honors, exhibitions, and sales. Otherwise, buying contemporary art of the Old West may not be an investment at all, but rather participation in a fad.

Use these standards to help you to distinguish between the professional Western artists whose work will be of permanent value and the unlisted Western artists who are along for the sweet ride but who will be quickly unseated if the extraordinary Western interest comes to an end. After all, when prices being paid for current Western art can be the same as for a small Cezanne or equal to ten times the prices being realized at conventional national auctions for equivalent old-time Western artists, some discretion is called for.

The collectors who are buying Western art indiscriminately must suspect they are paying more than some of the art will be worth when the business all shakes down, but they feel wonderful so far and they are hooked. Good advice for them when they buy art that is unprofessional, though, would be the same as for the men holding the bear: Don't be the last one to let go!

Of course, the field of current Western art is constantly broadening, as shown in *Contemporary Western Artists*. It now goes beyond the wave of Eastern illustrators who migrated westward beginning about 1950, the ones who then took center stage despite being criticized as ignorant of authentic Western practices and gear.

Instead, many of the best of today's Western artists are not cowboy artists at all. They would resent being called that, and they even resist being classified as Western artists. Not Old West oriented, most of them are regionalists, painting or sculpting the West they know only because that is where they live.

They went to school at the Art Center in Los Angeles, not the Art Students League in New York City, and their influences are not Remington or Russell but rather Andrew Wyeth (born 1917) and Nicolai Fechin (1881–1955). They live mainly in small towns in the Southwest, the Mountain States, and the Far West, although some do inhabit art colonies like Santa Fe and Sedona.

These living Western regionalists are as good as any other group of contemporary American artists, Eastern or Southern or Midwestern. Within the decade, they will be recognized with the highest honors in art, including memberships in the National Academy of Design.

They do represent a sound basis for current investment.

CHAPTER 6

Budgeting for Art

The measurement of your personal painting size that was taken at the outset, along with the development of your touch and the determination of your specialization, relate to you personally as buyer or collector rather than to the art. In addition to this physical size of yours, there are also your emotional and monetary "sizes" to be explored in order to fill out the individual pattern that will control your buying and selling.

Thinking Small

From the standpoint of size, there is economic sense to thinking small. Little works of art, for example, serve special functions related to money. If an appraisal of a painting could be calculated by the inch, the smaller physical sizes would be figured at a substantial premium, if only because any work by a professional artist has a minimum value that attaches to the name.

Also, in times of runaway inflation like the one in Europe after World War I, little objects of value were the most marketable. In West Germany where the memory of that inflation lingers, small paintings are still especially desirable because they are the easiest to move. Moreover, as tangibles they could not be defaulted on the way paper obligations were. Small paintings are unique works of art whose prices cannot easily be artificially rigged as small collectibles like diamonds, for example, have been.

In addition, Americans who had cash a few years ago and wanted to export the money without paying taxes on it were acquiring good small paintings with international appeal, like the Dutch "Little Masters." They shipped the small paintings overseas clandestinely and sold them there, taking payment in a currency and place of their choice rather than in U.S. dollars in the United States. Advertisements for overseas shipment, sale, and deposit still run occasionally, and the advantage is to the little works of art, the ones that fit under the arm on the way abroad.

Size-wise, new buyers should play it safe when they begin. They should stay well within their physical and monetary sizes, to be emotionally comfortable with their program for buying art.

Your Worth and Your Income

If you are a serious collector, figuring your monetary size also means analyzing your financial condition to ascertain your net worth, a step you should undertake at the end of every year for comparison with previous years and to plan ahead. Your bank will furnish you with a form for this purpose.

All that is involved is adding your assets—your cash, accounts and notes receivable, stocks and bonds, real estate, mortgages owned, value of life insurance, automobile, and other real and personal property. From this you subtract your liabilities—the total of your accounts and notes payable, income tax payable, mortgage and loans payable, installment contracts, and other obligations. The excess of your assets over your liabilities is your net worth.

You should also figure your annual net income, that is, the total of your salary, interest, dividends, rentals, and other income, less your property and income taxes due, mortgage payments, insurance premiums, living expenses, and other expenses. The determination of your net worth and your net income will help to set your budget for buying art.

Regardless of your circumstances, however, the practical minimum for any investment budget should be $1,000. For this amount, you can purchase a small investment grade painting by a lesser artist, one who is on the verge of coming into popularity so you can expect to double your money in four years or so. If the investor has to start with less than $1,000, he can still buy a drawing, a secondary market compared to paintings but another good medium for specialization. Drawings can be used as a way into paintings.

How much you have to spend will determine where you go to spend it. Art at auction is available for any budget, if you are patient and willing to seek out special sales. When you go to dealers, however, you will find that they all operate differently. Some dealers open their doors only to collectors who can spend $100,000 or more a year. Other dealers will not handle a painting worth less than $10,000. Obviously, the small collector will not be welcome in these galleries. There are, though, plenty of dealers who handle drawings as well as paintings at various prices, and there are superb yet relatively inexpensive drawings to please any collector.

Seed Money and Milk Money

The first financial resource that is required for a collector or investor to buy art is seed money, the budgeted stake for getting started. Historically, seed money has come from capital, the accumulated assets that are your net worth, not your current income. Consequently, one traditional rule to ease the worries of new collectors has been, never invest current income in art. If you do, the funds may not be there when you need milk money for the children.

Also, the art market has not lent itself to short term investment, that is, for periods of less than a year. This means that if you buy art expecting to sell in less than a year, it may be you will get stuck with something you cannot quickly move at a profit. Short term dispositions of art cannot be counted on. Even an established dealer who purchases his inventory of art instead of taking pieces on consignment must plan on holding a less salable piece as long as two or three years if he wants his full return.

As you can imagine, selling is substantially more difficult for the collector than it is for the dealer. The individual has far fewer sales outlets than the dealer, and he generally has to sell at a discount. The collector may be shocked when he purchases a painting at a major gallery and then discovers that its immediate resale value to another gallery may be half or less of what he paid. Selling is a separate technique from buying, and the skill takes time to develop.

To protect themselves from such illiquidity, conservative collectors keep fluid assets like cash in reserve, apart from the art budget. How much cash is held depends on the individual. If he has no regular income, he might want to hold aside enough cash for six months, his short-term needs. Of course, "holding cash in reserve" these days does not mean under the mattress or even in a regular savings account, but rather in an appropriate money fund or deposit arrangement.

How Long the Long Term?

How long the long term is differs with the state of the market. The classic advice on investing in art used to be, plan to invest for the long term because you cannot expect to make a big profit in less than ten years. More recently, five years was accepted as the average minimum time for realizing on an investment in art.

Conditions now, however, are more volatile. Enhancement in value can be rapid. A painting bought at 100 percent of retail and worth only 50 percent of retail for immediate resale to a dealer may show a 30 to 50 percent increase in value in a single year, so a profit can be realized after two to three years.

Paintings sold at auction in the recent past and then resold at auction demonstrate this upward movement. An April 23, 1981 Sotheby's *American Paintings* catalog provides examples of seven lots previously sold at auction. Lot number 15 was a small oil painting by the early nineteenth century landscapist George Henry Durrie (1820–1863) which had sold three years previously for $8,500. It resold for $16,000.

Lot number 69 in the same sale was a small oil on paper by John Frederick Kensett (1816–1872) of the Hudson River School which had sold a year and a half earlier for $3,250. It resold for $9,000. Lot number 73 was a small oil by Sanford Gifford (1824–1880) also of the Hudson River School which had sold three and a half years earlier for $3,250. It resold for $10,500.

Lot numbers 88 and 107 were letters written and illustrated by Charles Marion Russell which had sold eight and a half years earlier for $4,000 and $9,000. They resold for $10,500 and $20,000. Lot numbers 111 and 119 were Russell watercolors which had sold eight and a half years earlier for $23,000 and $14,500. They resold for $125,000 and $45,000.

The poorest return among the seven lots was ten percent per year. For superior works of art, the long term gets shorter and shorter, although this was one auction buyer compared to another auction buyer, not gallery buyer to gallery buyer. Buying at auction presupposes expertise. Buying at a gallery may be better or worse, depending on the dealer's discounting.

When large gains like some of these do become quickly available, values have to be monitored regularly. While average prices in the art market gain steadily, there may be pockets of advances that are phenomenal. There are few losses in value, so today's aggressive investor regularly considers selling the profit-producing works of art he owns, especially when he believes there are other pieces available for purchase that are candidates for even greater profits.

What this means is that when there has been a fast run up in the value of a piece you own, you have to analyze how the rise came about in order to decide whether to sell. Is the increase the result of the inherent worth of the investment or the result of extraneous causes? You may simply have bought a bargain below the true value of the work, and you may wish to resell at the current market price, taking your profit in order to be able to look for another opportunity.

Or, your purchase may have anticipated a fad that is running its course, and you may want to resell to take the profit while you can.

Conversely, if you have bought into a rise caused by new awareness of a native school of art like American Impressionism, you may believe that prices will continue to increase for the foreseeable future. Then, you may want to hold on.

The Contemporary Profile

As a new collector or investor, you must determine how high to set your own art budget. In addition to the analysis of your net worth and your net income, this also involves who you are, in relation to collectors in general.

In the last ten years, great changes have occurred in the composition of collectors as a group. First, the number of buyers of art has increased substantially. More than half are now women buying in their own names, presumably as single persons. This by itself is a remarkable difference.

Second, the average age of collectors has dropped to 35 years, an equally startling statistic compared to the average age of 50 for collectors a decade earlier.

Third, buyers are still mainly white collar workers, but they now include many more people with lower earnings. As a result, the average earnings level of buyers as a group has actually decreased.

This contemporary profile demonstrates that collecting and investing in art are no longer just for the rich. The value of the average art holding has declined, though, as large numbers of these younger, less well-to-do, better educated, and to a greater extent female, new buyers come into the art market, looking to acquire lower priced painting and sculpture within their means.

The Human Factor

In addition to computing how much capital and income you have available and determining where you stand in the group, you will also have to consider such individual factors as your age and the ages of your dependents, your health and the health of your family, the constancy and expected duration of your income, your insurance and pension coverages, and whether you own your own home. These factors are then examined both for anticipated future expenditures and for the impact of extraordinary expenses that might arise from illness, accident, and acts of God.

Those are the relatively measurable items. The process of budgeting also should include human elements like your temperament, your willingness to assume risk, your ability to manage money, your dependence on income from your investments, and the time you have to devote to learning about collecting art.

All of these factors taken together—capital, income, and tangible and human elements—will determine what kind of an investor you will be, financially, emotionally, and intellectually.

You may be a conservative investor, one who seeks primarily to preserve capital, or an active investor who buys and sells more frequently to meet a goal of a 25 percent annual gain on available capital, or a speculative investor who wants the largest possible gain in the shortest possible time, even though risk is involved. If an investor analyzes his position every year, as he should, he may take different stances in different years.

A new investor with a younger profile, for example, might tend to establish a budget that allots a larger proportion of his wealth to art investment. Younger people may not yet have full family responsibilities calling for more conservative fiscal planning. If they can stand the risk of loss, the objective might be more for growth of capital than for security. These active young investors are suited to investment fields like art that, historically, have been thought to be more adventuresome despite art's strong track record for stability.

On the other hand, you may be what used to be the stereotype of the conversative investor, an older person with family responsibilities and a need for a secure, fluid, and conventional investment portfolio. You should be concerned then about the shorter life span available to you to recover from a major error in investment. If so, you may wish to spend the dollars cautiously, devoting a reduced proportion of your budget to art in relation to your wealth and concentrating in defensive art categories. Protecting assets would be one of your goals.

An example of a middle-ground investor would be a New Jersey policeman a decade ago. He went to a dealer he trusted whenever he had accumulated a thousand dollars in savings. That was the amount of capital that he saw as a satisfactory stake. Over the years, he assembled a superior collection of nineteenth century Hudson River School landscapes. He did his homework in the period, and paid in advance for what he took.

A little more complicated example is a university professor who had gone through unsettling times in Europe before coming here. He was comfortable only when spending relatively small sums. Treasure hunting worked for him—the modest amounts he paid for his finds kept his total art budget small.

He then located an old painter who was willing to try art restoration, and so the professor was able to buy from dealers the damaged works that needed too much repainting to be salable at full prices. His caution was overcome by his energy and inventiveness and proved to be no bar to his success, although as you will see, using an artist as an untrained restorer was an eminently unethical practice.

Traditional Rules Are Dead

As a result of the huge recent gains for investors in art, however, old monetary maxims are breaking down. The standard advice to conservative investors used to be, put no more than ten percent of your capital assets into art. Another way of stating practically the same thing was, put into art no more than 20 percent of your net worth exclusive of real estate. Art, it was said, should complement, not replace your traditional investments, and you should never sell a conventional investment like stock in order to buy art.

Today, those long-standing investment rules are dying. Traditional investments like silver and gold are not working out for many people, while art purchased as an investment is offering superior rewards. Instead of applying the same old rules to everyone, the personalized patterns that have been developing are presenting a different way of looking at investment in art.

While the new investor should certainly begin cautiously, many who have gained confidence in their judgment in the specialization they have adopted are putting virtually all their net worth into art and are doing very well.

As a case in point, a federal bureaucrat decided to specialize in the work of a single artist. After a few years of buying the artist's work in a small way, he grew to be very sure of himself. When a major painting became available, he did not hesitate to mortgage his home to obtain the money that was needed to make the purchase, risking the real estate asset thought of as the family untouchable in order to buy one picture. This picture became the cornerstone of his holdings. He was able to pay off the mortgage quickly, and he went on to be recognized as the leading specialist in his artist's paintings, as well as the definitive biographer and authenticator.

Another investor in art was a cab driver enamoured of American academic painters of the nineteenth century. He would pawn his wife's wedding ring whenever a desirable purchase became available. This was his practice for five years, until his accumulation was profitable enough to keep the ring securely on his wife's finger.

The bureaucrat and the cab driver were full-speed-ahead and damn-the-consequences investors. They sound like gamblers, but they were not. They had paid their dues by learning their specialties. Even if the economy took a down turn, the quality paintings they had bought were protected in value.

Despite what would conventionally be regarded both as great risk and as undermining the usual family standards of marriage and homestead, the solid purchases each made eventually started a substantial investment package. They might have been improvident as farmers. They reversed the standard wisdom by putting all their investment eggs in one basket of paintings, but their confidence paid off handsomely, although they never made a formal budget for art investment and the milk money went down the drain as a part of the initial expenditures that launched their success.

This course of action is definitely not for everyone, but these two unusual art buyers succeeded handsomely. The point is that budgeting, like developing your touch and your specialization, has become a personal venture. There are standard ways of budgeting, based on a proportion of net worth, and these ways offer an easy access to controlled buying of art. In contrast, many collectors, especially experienced ones, no longer pay any attention to traditional restraints in budgeting. These collectors can be influenced by a steady rise in art prices to become quite aggressive in their buying practices, although they still do limit themselves to buying art solely from accumulated capital.

Art from Current Earnings

On the other hand, many young purchasers of today, the doctors, dentists, lawyers, accountants, and other professionals, literally do not believe in the value of currency. They cannot visualize a decrease in the present high level of their earnings, and so they pay no attention to the traditional prohibition against investing current income in art.

They retain planners to husband their capital, design tax shelters, and find tax deductions for money spent lavishly on condominium housing, vacations in exotic places that are taken in combination with conventions, food and drink in haute cuisine restaurants, and entertainment at shows and concerts. After all their indulgences, however, they still have leftover earnings they are reluctant to entrust to banks or to conventional investments.

Buying art with these excess funds suits them, not only for the investment features but also for the prestige of being able to display beautiful objects in their homes and offices. Young professionals generally have good taste, and they lean toward art that has been reproduced or that has other promotable aspects they can tell their associates about.

There is also the middle-aged medico syndrome, the fiftyish doctors who are bored with treating sick people and who are looking to expand their horizons into an engrossing field like art. Their conventional investments are also made from a capital account handled for them by tax advisors. Art they buy on their own, not for profit but as an emotional release in return for the extra earnings that fall to them.

Purchasing art with spare income means that these buyers become borrowers, paying the galleries on the installment plan. They cannot obtain a conventional bank loan using the art as collateral, unless they are preferred customers of an art-minded bank. So, depending on how well the dealer knows the buyer, how profitable the sale is, and whether there is anyone else who might want the work, the dealer extends his credit and may hold on to the piece until he is paid.

Buying from current income rather than capital is a practice that suits some professionals, even though it is contrary to conventional budgetary preachings. Again, the approach would not fit everyone, but it does help to get the adventurous into art.

Budgets that Hamstring

One trouble with budgets for investment in art, however, is that they can hamstring you. You may become reluctant to buy because there is only so much money in the pot for the budgetary period and you fear the pot may be drained before the period is up.

When you can't buy, you worry about what you are missing. If you do buy, you worry about what might come up later that will be better than what you have.

Mistakes can be made in not buying as well as in buying, if only because new collectors do not know as much about what they are looking at as they will later. They may not recognize a major work of art because it is priced too low, or because it's dirty, damaged, or badly framed. They may not yet be able to read a famous signature. Consequently, the rule for new collectors is, never look back at a piece you should have bought but didn't. Failures of omission like that can happen to everyone. Mistakes are to learn from, not to moan about.

On balance, it is better to have missed out on a painting about which there is doubt than it is to have bought one that is questionable. An investor who specializes in Taos scenes did not recognize this rule. He could not make up his mind whether to buy a large painting of an Indian from a major dealer. The painting was priced relatively low for a work attributed to an important artist, but it was not signed or guaranteed. After the painting was acquired by a museum and catalogued as by the named painter, the investor declared sorrowfully that the museum acquisition and authentication proved he had made a serious mistake in not buying the picture.

He failed to understand, however, the the dealer was the real expert. If the dealer had thought the painting was authentic, he would have priced it as though it had been signed.

Also, if the investor had actually bought the unsigned painting, the museum's authentication even if correct might not have been available to him. He would today be complaining about his error in taking a chance on an unsigned painting he could not get authenticated and so could not sell profitably. His budgeted amount would have been spent for the period, with no money left for better buys.

Think ahead. The best is yet to come, and new opportunities arise all the time. Your next chance should be a better one. An experienced dealer would not be able to think of six pictures he should have bought over the years and failed to buy. Sometimes when you buy a few great paintings from a source with a hundred paintings in stock, you do so well on what you bought that you think you must hurry back to pick up what you missed. For the experienced buyer, there seldom is a single thing.

Buying right is important. All of these budgetary suggestions are intended to give you confidence so you can snap into your first purchase and keep going as an active and successful collector of art.

Buy at Once, but Pause

There will inevitably remain, however, those few casual buyers who will still be wary of taking that first step, unable to decide which of these alien tangibles called art is the one they should select. They have the specialization and the budget worked out, but they doubt their touch.

To such people, the advice seems conflicting. Buy at once when you see the perfect work of art, but pause to think of resale before you leap.

These same late starters in art may be regular investors in stocks and aggressive in collecting other tangibles, while art puts them off as fragile-looking and mysterious. They are waiting unrealistically for that one paragon of a purchase, a steal of international proportions that is as safe as a government bond.

   The solution for these potential investors is to examine and handle a lot of art work so familiarity will ease their way into the initial transaction. To a collector, art must be physically manageable, compatible with his or her personality, and economically comfortable, fitting into a personalized budget.

   If art is still alien after all this, it just may be that other investment opportunities are in order rather than art. If you do not ever get a special feeling for a superb work of art, then art may not be for you.

CHAPTER 7

Who Signed the Painting?

You are now through with the preparations for buying and ready to buy. Instead of concentrating on yourself, as you have been doing, you are going to start looking at the art and at the artist.

The Name Is Crucial

On the average of once a day, the phone rings in every art gallery and someone somewhere offers an oil painting for sale. It's a great picture, in full color, a typical caller claims, a mounted cowboy galloping right at you, and it's very well done, the central figure filling the whole 24 by 18 inch canvas so realistically you want to duck.

Up to this point in the conversation, however, the caller has failed to evoke any interest. Why? He has omitted something. It is not the price, as you might think, but the name of the painter, the crucial part of the purchase.

Who signed the painting? This question is the essence of a transaction in art for investment. The answer all by itself determines whether to proceed into an exploration of the subject, date, size, condition, and price.

Finding and researching the signature is the key, because you must restrict the art you will consider for purchase to works by professional artists who are listed in the art reference or source books mentioned in the discussion of "touch." These listings mean that works by the artists were exhibited, sold, or publicly collected either in the artists' lifetimes or after. Just as the father's advice to his son was to associate only with rich girls so when the son married, he would choose a rich girl, you must associate only with art done professionally so when you buy a piece it will have been created by a listed artist and be defensible as an investment.

If there is no signature, that is the end, as a general rule for works of the nineteenth century and later. There are a few painters, however, who had periods when they did not sign all of their paintings. Georgia O'Keeffe (born 1887) is one, and her authenticated paintings are investment grade, signed or not. A pleasant part of appraising is when an unsuspecting owner brings in an unsigned painting for evaluation and a painter like O'Keeffe can be verified as the artist and a value suggested in a full five or six figures.

3. Nick Eggenhofer. "Navajo Woman." Gouache on board, 11 by 14¼ inches.

4. *Thomas Hart Benton. "Prayer," 1920. Oil on masonite, 16½ by 18½ inches.*

A more commercial example than O'Keeffe is Nick Eggenhofer (born 1897) who omitted the signature on scores of his illustrations. The customary dealer practice is to forward the unsigned illustration to the painter to have the signature added, if the painter is living, but signatures applied after the painting was completed often cause complications. For one thing, some good-natured illustrators have signed more drawings this way than they made.

Other artists like Percival Rosseau, the great American painter of field dogs, did not sign a work until it was sold. When Rosseau died, many of the paintings in his estate were unsigned, and this omission could be remedied only by the lesser authentication of a stamp affixed by the executor of the estate.

Paintings that Rosseau had signed during his life but at the time of sale rather than when he painted them produced a different problem. As you will see, black light investigation usually shows when a signature has been added to a painting, either in the course of a career as with Rosseau or as a signature applied as a forgery. Most ethical dealers assume that a painting that could have been a forgery is a forgery, so a Rosseau painting not signed until its sale might be rejected as not authentic years later.

Painters like Thomas Hart Benton who understood the problem penned a note on the reverse of the painting, explaining the circumstance of a later signature.

Misspelled Their Own Names

In this emphasis on signature, the oddest difficulty concerns the number of artists who misspelled their own names in signing their work This would not include Frederic Remington, although his forgers some-times added a "k" to the given name. The Remington bronze "Stampede" was cast posthumously, and there is said to be a casting signed "Frederick."

The eccentric Louis Eilshemius (1864–1941) occasionally dropped the last "i." The Hudson River School's Samuel Colman (1832–1920) also signed Coleman. Alex Compera (1856–1906) gave up Comparet as his name because of mispronunciations in Denver, and Maurice Prendergast (1859–1924) omitted the "s" at least once.

Wood Gaylor (1883–?) who was a studied primitive painter exhibited six paintings in 1920 that he had left unsigned because he did not expect to sell them. When a collector bought all six, Gaylor was flustered. In signing his name, he ended by spelling Gaylor two different ways and he later apologized by saying that as an artist he concentrated on the esthetics of the capitalized lettering in the signature and not on the content.

The Artist as a Professional

Art works to be purchased have to be by a listed artist, and the appearance of the name in an art reference book means the artist was recognized. He was a real professional. The requirement that the artist be a professional is fundamental enough as a ground rule for investors to justify casting it in concrete.

The point is not that the artist was a major figure or even well known, but that he was a professional. Previous books on how to buy art have dealt

5. Wood Gaylor. "The Automobile," 1914. Oil on wood panel, 6¾ by 8¾ inches.

with the manner in which wealthy collectors acquire major works by famous artists. Instead, this is an exploration of the mass market that has opened for 20,000,000 American art buyers, not just for a couple of thousand of the "proud possessors," the elite collectors. New buyers who are being addressed here cannot afford the famous and simply want to be directed toward enjoyable, secure, and profitable works by the second- and third-tier artists who are investment grade.

Not that there is anything wrong with sticking with the well-known artists, ones with international reputations. They are the best bets for the greatest profits in the long run, if their costs are within your budget. At most, though, the famous are only five percent of the listed artists, and everyone who hangs around galleries knows their names. Reference books are not needed for them, whereas it is the next 45 percent of the listed artists

6. *Hayley Lever. "Cape Cod." Oil on board, 14½ by 20 inches.*

who are the less familiar group where the most available investments come from.

As the supply of art by the famous diminishes, these lesser known artists are the ones whose work will increasingly be sought by all buyers, both the elite and the rest of us. When the paintings of The Ten American Impressionists reached a premium price, aggressive investors looked to the works of Hayley Lever (1876–1958), F. Luis Mora (1874–1940), and George Herbert Macrum (c. 1870–c. 1940).

The trick is to get there first, or at least early on.

Symbols of Recognition

The earmarks usually identifying the investment-grade artists start with the symbols of recognition by their peers. These are the insignia of the National Academicians, the Associates of the National Academy, the American Watercolor Society, the National Sculpture Society, the American Academy of Arts and Letters, and so on.

Currently, honorary groups also extend to artists who work in specialized subjects. In contemporary Westerns, for example, there are the Cowboy Artists of America, the Northwest Rendezvous Group, and the National Academy of Western Art.

Another indication of recognition is whether the artists' works are in public collections like museums. Also look to the relative importance of the particular museum, and whether the work in the museum was acquired by purchase or gift. Whom the artists studied with, and where, tells a story, as well as where and when they exhibited and the prizes they won.

Artists' memberships are a key, including the clubs and associations like the Salmagundi Club and, back at the turn of the century, The Players or the Century. Illustrators can be rated according to the prominence of the publications commissioning their work.

Inclusion in auction catalogs is significant for sparsely listed artists when the price realized is comparable to prices realized for widely recognized artists. Such a price would be tantamount to a listing for an otherwise unlisted artist.

Having an established track record of sales at national public auctions is a plus for any artist. A single sale is not as significant as a spectrum of sales to demonstrate that the artist is a bankable commodity. The point is not entirely the level of prices realized at the auctions. It is also the fact that the artist's credentials have been established as suitable for auction. His work brings enough return to make him worth handling.

The second-tier artists you are seeking are likely to be in the standard art reference and source books. Mention in the art history books is properly reserved for the famous, although sometimes there are unexpected additions or omissions. In the June 19, 1981 Sotheby auction sale, for example, Waldo Pierce who was mentioned in *Art and Life in America* brought $950, while Charles Sprague Pearce who was not mentioned brought $225,000.

Who the Artist Is Controls Value

Thus, who the artist is controls the investment value of his art. The name is all important. The identity of the artist determines whether his work is investment grade, and buying only the work of listed artists becomes the firm rule. Even when the collector has adopted a specialization that is extraordinarily tight, he is still bound to these listed artists for his purchases. These are the artists who are likely to show greater increases in value, while the investment qualities of the works by unlisted artists are suspect and speculative.

It may appear that this restriction to listed artists severely limits the pool of artists the collector can buy from, but it does not do this at all. In Western art alone, there are more than 1,700 professional artists catalogued in our *Biographical Encyclopedia* who were working before 1950, and there are at least another 1,000 who worked after 1950. More than 700 living Western artists are listed in our *Contemporary Western Artists*. A total of all the American artists who are recorded in all the books would run into the tens of thousands. There is no shortage of professional artists to choose from.

The function of these listings is to separate professionals from artists who never made the grade, the Sunday painters, the students who worked a la their masters, the copyists, the locals, the practitioners of arts and crafts, the whittlers, and the amateurs. In Las Cruces, New Mexico, half the homes have paintings of the region's geologic attraction, the Organ Mountains, but almost all the paintings were done by amateurs. The paintings have no value for investment. In Portland, Oregon, the paintings are of Mount Hood, but surprisingly, many were done by professionals.

There are of course some paintings by amateurs that do have value, for particular purposes. Paintings of the Civil War done by amateurs at the time would be an example, for a narrow market and not for a routine investment. There are also paintings by amateurs that are accepted as primitives, and there are amateur artists whose work has value because of the identity of the artist—for example, a painting by former President Dwight Eisenhower.

Decorative Pictures Are Precluded

In addition to the amateur paintings that are verboten, there are paintings manufactured on an assembly line. These are not appropriate for purchase, either. Some of these paintings were done for wall coverings, as a premium with sales of furniture. The paintings are commercial products, although they may be signed with catchy names to add luster.

These are in the category of "furniture paintings," decorative pictures the collector is absolutely precluded from buying, regardless of how cheap the price may be. There is nothing to be gained from beginning by buying wrong. You cannot buy a painting that is just a decoration. The moment you take it home, it has no value.

If there is a market for decorative paintings, it is not the investment market. All dealers get inquiries for a picture in a specific color, style, and size, to fit over a particular couch. Dealers generally refer the caller to an interior decorator, because few decorators are concerned about investment values.

A few years ago, a casual visitor at a gallery asked to see paintings of kachina dolls she wanted to suit the current style of her house. The reply was that the gallery showed art by listed professional artists exclusively. Some of them painted Indian still-lifes including kachinas, but paintings are sold by the names of the painters and only secondarily by subjects. While kachinas would indeed be a superb specialization for investment, it is not a valid subject unless you start with the requirement that the painter be professional.

You have to concentrate on the listed artists. One way that seems a little extreme at first blush is to get to know the artist himself, if he is alive, or his family. You could then consider buying directly from the artist or from his estate.

Most people respond to letters and most artists are glad to invite callers, particularly if the purpose is investment in their art. You would get details of the artist's life and his works that are not common knowledge. You might see a body of his pictures and perhaps have a unique chance to look at the results of a lifetime's effort, to observe for yourself what made this one artist professional.

The opportunity is especially available with the illustrators of the 1930s and 1940s who have retained many of their paintings because until recently there has been no great demand for their work.

Not all meetings with a professional artist or with his family are productive, but if you do make such a contact, you will at worst have touched the man behind the pictures, have known the real thing, and have given yourself an extra reason for exploring the sidelights of investment in art.

The Probability of Value

All of the oeuvre of a listed artist is likely to be investment grade. It all has the probability of value, the drawings as well as the largest oils. Without yet getting into the question of price, there are of course gradations in value. In general, a drawing is worth less than a watercolor which is worth less than an oil painting. In general, an unsigned painting is worth less than a signed painting, even where the painter signed few paintings, or where the painting was purchased from the artist's estate, or where the provenance is impeccable.

The careful buyer not only sticks to listed artists, he investigates pricing factors by finding out whether the artists had preferred periods, sizes, subjects, or media of special value. He researches the range of the artist's work to see how one piece that is for sale fits in. Prices for the best pieces are much higher in relation to lesser pieces than you might expect.

Conversely, none of the work of an unlisted artist is likely to be investment grade. If the artists working before 1950, for example, managed no listing in the books, it was because they did not behave in a normal manner for a professional artist. They did not exhibit or sell paintings through conventional channels during their careers and they were not discovered later by museums, historians, galleries, or auction houses.

In the last ten years, source books and catalogs have been issued on virtually every aspect of American art before 1950. There can only be rare exceptions left of those artists who were trained professionals rather than amateurs and who are still available for meaningful discovery.

There were few closet artists of quality. Not many fit that category in art, compared to major poets like Emily Dickinson who were undiscovered in their time.

CHAPTER 8

Judging Current Artists

To this point in exploring the significance of "who signed the painting," the discussion has been primarily about the American artists who were working before 1950. The same principles that apply to those artists also apply to current American artists, although it is the fashion for dealers who handle works by the older artists to be deprecatory about the living ones.

New York critics claim, for example, that a Julian Schnabel "plate" painting which sells for $60,000 in his gallery ranks with the best of contemporary art, but there are debunking dealers who say that if you offered such a painting at public auction without dealer support, the painting would "be just a piece of crockery." That is, it would not bring nearly as high a price as it does in the artist's gallery. The proof of the pudding was May 1983 when the price of a Schnabel at auction in New York City was $93,000.

Similarly, Eastern critical opinion calls contemporary Western art "95% dreck" (ARTnews), "mostly dung" (The Wall Street Journal), and "derivative" (Rudolf Wunderlich of Kennedy Galleries). The reference is to some of the living Western artists who follow the Remington-Russell approach.

No Worse and No Better

Despite these critics, however, it is clear from even a casual examination of contemporary art that works being created today are on a par with the past, no worse and probably no better. Opportunities for collectors are as they always have been.

The problem for the collector, though, is that only about 20 percent of the professional artists now working are listed. How then do you tell which contemporary works of art to buy?

The answer is that you check for the same indicia of professionalism—honorary memberships and such listings as there are, the quality of the galleries representing the artists, and the published biographical and critical material on the artists.

Look to memberships in organizations like the National Academy and to listings in books like *Who's Who in American Art*, as well as to the large number of other associations and references that are possible. Send for the galleries' exhibition catalogs showing the artists in question, and read the reviews. Buy prize winners among the works of the artists in juried shows. Go beyond the one piece offered to you, and examine a quantity of the artist's work, to verify what his usual level of accomplishment is.

Consider asking the dealer to hold a work for you for a few days while you ascertain whether the memory of the work grows stronger in your mind. See whether art publications have done articles on the artists. Find out whether the artists are listed in specialized books like *Contemporary Western Artists*.

For artists who are professionals, you will discover that no one of the factors of memberships, galleries, and publications is more important than the others. Some artists who are elected to honorary groups like the Cowboy Artists of America, for example, may soon quit their gallery representations. They have collectors approaching them directly who offer to buy more than the artists can produce, so they no longer need to pay gallery commissions. Some even quit the groups.

Other artists shun memberships and publicity, and their work is available only through galleries. They belong to no association and they are not written up.

Art periodicals may not be entirely reliable either, as a single guide to professionalism. Some artists advertise directly in magazines, without the sponsorship of a gallery, and the magazines do not refuse advertisements from artists just because the quality of the work is relatively poor. In fact, publications feature artists who are popularly accepted, regardless of the editors' judgment of the quality of the imagery.

A question that always comes up at this point is, How does a new artist become listed? The answer is, he must earn the necessary memberships, representations, and write-ups.

He begins by showing every place he can, and then as he progresses, he shows in juried and national exhibitions. He accepts the galleries he can get, until he can secure the more prominent. When he believes that he has achieved professional levels, he seeks publicity. Some of the art publications are "vanity press," which means he pays for the editorial space, until write-ups are possible in the major magazines.

By then, he will be listed.

The Collectors' Group

A new wrinkle for museum acquisitions of contemporary art that emphasizes popular acceptance over honors and publicity is the formation of a collectors' group among a museum's wealthy patrons. Cash donations are pledged by members of the group which then travels to New York City with the museum director and curator.

Appointments are made with a dozen galleries pre-selected by the museum. The group tours the galleries and nominates for purchase the pieces appealing to it, based on the members' reactions to the individual galleries and on what they like. Museum officials review the list and delete the pieces considered unsuitable. From what is left, the patrons choose the works for actual purchase.

The procedure is said to be highly successful for museums, which thereby obtain modern art work supplementary to museum budgets. Also, the patrons are involved in the process of acquisition. Any problems that arise will be similar to the conflicts caused by Booster Clubs in university athletics—questions of ethics and misdirected enthusiasm. The animals may end up running the zoo.

The same procedure is adaptable to purchases by a single collector. All that is involved is for the collector to make up a list containing more pieces than he intends to buy, and then review the list with experts to determine which should be excluded. It is commonplace for major private collectors to have such discussions with museum curators.

Not All Listed Artists Are Equal

Similar to determining which artists who are not listed are investment grade is distinguishing the varying levels of investment grade among those who are listed. That sounds harder to do than it is.

The answer is not just how high an artist's prices are, because price is someone's else judgment, made at one moment, for some purpose other than yours. In the course of time, prices for the same art work will rise and fall. Henry Golden Dearth (1864–1918) commanded high prices during his career, but then his work slumbered for 60 years before being resurrected recently. The paintings of Rosa Bonheur (1822–1899) were priced high while she was alive, fell to almost nothing by 1950, and today are higher than ever.

As a starting point in distinguishing among the listed artists, it is clear that not all artists who are professionals are equal in accomplishment. There are artists who are first-tier, just as there are artists who are second- and third-tier. The tests are the same ones that have been used before. Among the honorary organizations artists belong to, some are more prestigious than others, just as some galleries representing artists are more selective than others and some of the periodicals featuring artists are more significant than others.

The trick is to avoid buying the work of artists who are only marginally investment grade. Make no discovery of such an artist, even if the price is low and you have the opportunity to acquire a holding as large as an estate. Discoveries take promotion and time and money to provide a chance of making a profit. Making a discovery is the province of an aggressive dealer rather than a collector, although even then, it would be the rare dealer who would participate in marketing an artist who is low on the investment grade scale.

A Connecticut dealer once bought 200 paintings by a professional artist who had seldom exhibited or sold, although he had painted alongside a famous neighbor. Because the artist had picked up a similar style, his works were confusing to the public, hindering sales. Nevertheless, the dealer was able to sell enough of these paintings every year to make a profit over the small amount he had paid for the collection.

Eventually, however, it occurred to the dealer that the sale of a score of these paintings was producing no more income than would the sale of one work by an important artist. He was bogged down in the wasteful task of mass merchandising a product of limited value, so he disposed of the remainder in one lot, again at a profit, and he was rid of them.

Art You Do Not Like

Some veteran art dealers debunk the use of listings of artists to influence their own buying and selling. These dealers tell customers that lists are surplus because they already know all the names they need to know.

This is a put on. Currently, artists' lists are highly volatile. Artists of the past are being researched continually, so there is no such thing today as dealers "knowing all the names they need to know." These dealers simply want to avoid demeaning themselves by having to prove to their clients the professionalism of the artists they offer.

The worth of the art starts with the signature. Professional workmanship is something the buyer can trust, although there are some fine artists who take longer to like than others. Marsden Hartley (1877–1943) painted mountainous landscapes in a blocky style. Many collectors think Hartley was crude. At the same time, John Marin (1870–1953) saw the identical mountains as planes and colors. Other collectors find Marin's levity to be an unreal version. You might have to look at a lot of Hartleys and Marins to learn to appreciate their points of view.

What it comes down to is this. If you do not like a given work by a listed artist who is investment grade, do not buy it. On the other hand, if you already own a work by a listed artist and you do not like it, your first step should be to get an opinion concerning its authenticity and condition. The piece may be a fake or it may have been altered, providing understandable reasons for your dislike.

If the piece proves to be authentic and is in original condition and you still do not like it, you will at least have the consolation of being able to sell it, although the price may not be as high as it would be for a more attractive work. A large Frank Boggs (1855–1926) landscape that was oddly composed still brought $2,800 at auction, if not the $12,000 the usual marine scene would have fetched.

Actually Determining Listings

The actual technique of determining which artists are listed, and on which tier, is just good library practice. You need access to the art reference and source books and persistence enough to try variations in names because art books are not copyread as well as dictionaries.

For example, Benezit used to list the turn of the century American painter Van Dearing Perrine (1869–1955) under "Dearing," not under "Perrine." You have to be confident enough of Perrine's ability to try to locate his listing under "D" and even "V" when "P" doesn't work out.

Similarly, the good California landscapist, Jean Mannheim, (1863–1945) is listed in *Mallett's Index of Artists* with the transposition Mannihem. That's pretty close, but John Young-Hunter (1874–1955), the English portrait painter who moved to Taos, is properly a hyphenate. Yet, *Fielding* has him under "Hunter," and Benezit has added a cross-reference to "Young-Hunter" only in its latest edition.

7. Will Crawford. "Steer Riding Contest." Pen and ink on paper,
6 by 6 inches (sight).

The First Book Is *Mallett's*

The easiest way to explain how art research is done is to run through some uncomplicated examples. Suppose you are offered a little pen and ink drawing by Will Crawford of a cowboy riding a steer. Crawford's title is "Steer Riding Contest" and as provenance the seller shows you a 1928 rodeo program illustrated with this drawing. Is Crawford a listed professional painter? Is the line drawing investment grade?

The first book to turn to is *Mallett's*. Crawford is listed there as Crawford, Will (Illustrator), but the only reference is the unpromising one to Mallett's own library, the lowest level of reference. Because the art work is Western, you also look at the *Biographical Encyclopedia* as the key to professionalism. One reference there is to his obituary in *Who's Who in American Art* for 1947, and full treatment like that is the sign of a prominent illustrator because not many commercial painters were accepted into the ranks of the serious artists.

Crawford's biography in the *Encyclopedia* starts with negatives. He was self-taught, had no exhibitions, won no award during his life, and there is no auction record to indicate public sales of his work. On the other hand, he is recognized as a friend of the major Western artist, Charles Marion Russell. He was a pen and ink man, so a line drawing is what you should expect to buy. His pictures originally appeared in leading magazines and books of his day and are also reprinted in newer source books for illustrators such as those by Walt Reed, Jeff Dykes, and Henry Pitz.

As has been observed, contact with Crawford's home community produced an intriguing tale of a Socialist hunchback vividly remembered after 40 years, the subject of MacKinlay Kantor's "My Most Unforgettable Character." Crawford was thus a professional illustrator whose work is certainly second-tier investment grade, and his bohemian life provides a real potential for promoting him into the first tier.

First-Tier in His Day

Suppose you are offered a large oil painting of a lovely woman seated at a table, done in the Post-Impressionist style and signed H. Dearth. *Mallett's* identifies the artist as the American Henry Golden Dearth who died in 1918.

The references provided are those of an artist who certainly was first-tier in his day: *American Art Annual*, the rare citing of *Dictionary of American Biography*, Fielding, Benezit, and the German international listing Thieme-Becker. Dearth was a National Academician and also a member of the Society of American Artists. He was in *Who's Who in America*, in art history books like Isham, in major museum collections including the Metropolitan Museum of Art, and has 105 paintings in the John Herron Art Institute.

Surprisingly, there are only low-level auction records for Dearth. They were for his early Barbizon landscapes that would also be good investments, but this painting sounds special, similar to one that was in the collection of a predecessor of the Brooklyn Museum. *American Art in the*

Barbizon Mood states that Dearth's memorial exhibition was shown in 19 museums and his late works featured "elegantly dressed women in bright, broken colors." Like Crawford's pen and ink cowboy, Dearth's woman is typical of his ultimate style. This Dearth picture is thus a high order of investment grade, despite the poor auction results.

Suppose you are offered a 20 by 15 inch pastel portrait of an unnamed Blackfoot chief, signed W.L. Kihn (1898–1957) and dated 1924. *Mallett's* lists W. Langdon Kihn as born in Brooklyn and refers you to the *American Art Annual* and to Fielding which names "Wilfred Langdon Kilm" as having specialized in painting American Indians.

The mention of Indians keys you to the *Biographical Encyclopedia* where you find the full story. Kihn is listed in all the primary references and in Canadian source books as well. He painted North American Indians for *National Geographic* illustrations for 15 years. All his work is investment grade.

8. *Henry Golden Dearth. "Sublimity." Oil on canvas, 32 by 42 inches.*

9. W. Langdon Kihn.
"Blackfoot Chief,"
1924. Pastel on paper,
20 by 15 inches.

One Time the Book Misses_____

Suppose you are offered a 42 by 26 inch oil signed H. Rasmusen (1909–c. 1966) dated 1940 and titled "How Hard the Furrow." *Mallett's* in its supplement identifies Rasmusen as a painter born in Utah and refers you to *Who's Who in American Art* and to the IBM colleciton.

The mention of Utah sends you to the *Biographical Encyclopedia*, but this is one time the book misses. Although the painting involved is re-

10. *Henry H. Rasmusen. "How Hard the Furrow," 1940. Oil on beaver-board (flakeboard), 41⅜ by 26 inches.*

gionalist in subject and style and Rasmusen lived in Utah in 1941, the Utah source books never included him. Consequently, he does not show as a Western artist.

He did, however, exhibit nationally, win prizes in Utah, write on art, and teach. The clincher is that the painting, "How Hard the Furrow," is the same one that was in the IBM exhibition, according to *An Index of Reproductions of American Paintings*. The painting is certainly investment grade.

Suppose you are offered a large ship portrait signed James Bard (1815–1897). Bard is not listed in *Mallett's*, or in Fielding, or in Benezit, or in the *American Art Annuals*. That makes the search more difficult, but there is a full listing in Groce & Wallace for artists working before the Civil War, referring you to the Karolik Collection, to the New-York Historical Society, and to the Mariners' Museum in Norfolk. From this, it is easy to infer that Bard is investment grade.

The Listings Can Be Found

These have been simple examples. You just follow the procedure through the books and ignore misspellings like Kilm. Equally easy would be establishing the credentials for Hayley Lever who exhibited frequently in the 1930s, for Van Dearing Perrine who exhibited in the prestigious Armory Show in 1913, or for Junius Brutus Stearns (1810–1885) who was a National Academician in 1849 and is in Groce & Wallace.

All of the inquiries start with *Mallett's*. If the artist is not listed in *Mallett's*, try the other references and sources that are indicated by the circumstances. If the artist does not show in any of the books, that is a minus for the value of the art work.

That's how it goes. Given the books, the listed artists can be found. A lot of books may be needed, to cover the reference and source materials for some painters, but Groce & Wallace is definitive for artists working before 1861. Fielding is incomplete, compared to the *American Art Annuals*. The old exhibition records reprinted for the National Academy and for the Boston, Philadelphia, and Brooklyn museums help, too. You have to remember that mistakes are possible in all of the books.

Whether a work of art is investment grade is thus relatively easy to decide these days. You look to the listings. Before the *Biographical Encyclopedia* was published in 1976, however, there were hundreds of Western artists who worked before 1950 but who could not be proved to be investment grade because they were not in the reference books and there was no key to the sources.

Similarly, there was no key such as the *Contemporary Western Artists* until 1982. Some of the more important living Western artists like Michael Coleman (born 1946) or Fritz Scholder (born 1937) have had retrospectives, are listed in *Who's Who in American Art*, and so are relatively easy to research, but hundreds of their peers could be approached only through their galleries, their honorary associations, or the magazines that have done articles on them.

There are professional artists in other specialties, too, who have been catalogued only recently. Some American marine painters would be examples, and so would many illustrators.

In the nineteenth century, there were American painters who made series of realistic ship portraits to order, finely detailing the subject for the owners, less for the officers, and sparsely for the crew. These paintings bring significant amounts at auction today, despite the omission of the artists' names in older reference and source books.

Investment grade artists working before 1950 are mainly those whom the new painting dealers euphemistically call the "deceased" rather than the "dead" artists. You look for their work in galleries' "vintage rooms." Confining yourself to them for investment lets you look at values with the perspective of at least 30 years, a period long enough for thorough analysis. You can judge by hindsight, as has been said, whereas the living artists are judged by foresight.

When you are about to buy a work of art, you have to temper your pleasure with an eye to what the situation will be when the piece is to be resold. Achieving a sale means finding a buyer, at a time when the decision is not just the seller's. Rather, the seller has to contemplate the scenario where he holds out his prized piece for a detailed examination by unknown faultfinders who can be turned off by factors that might be quite surprising.

That's when the help you received in buying will come in handy.

CHAPTER 9

Buy the Best

By this time, you have a good idea of the rewards and the risks in collecting art and of the collector's role in finding his touch, in specializing, and in managing his money. You have also been introduced to the artists, particularly to the professionals, and exposed to procedures for researching old and new signatures. These are basic preparations for informed dealings in art.

The next step is to look at the works themselves, to put to rest that old humbug, "I don't know anything about art but I know what I like and that's what I buy," and to scrutinize the injunction that replaces it, "Buy the best."

I Know What I Like

"I don't know anything about art but I know what I like" is a know-nothing refrain, the claim of an arrogant debunker of the thoughtful qualities the insider in art stands for. It is an announcement by the braggart who relishes his act of uninformed acquisition, made without sensitivity to risk or reward.

"I know what I like" is the unreasoning justification for an impetuous purchase of the wrong work of art, a 1930s copy of a medieval religious masterpiece, or a portrait of an unnamed and unpleasant looking old man by an amateur, or a sketchy river landscape on thin fabric that is representative of unsigned oil paintings given in 1900 as a premium with the purchase of a suite of furniture.

Secretly, the know-nothing buyer hopes the product of his uncultivated taste buds will prevail over the touch of the educated, but his purchase is doomed. He has allowed an eagerness to buy to precede the desire to understand.

Art bought under the banner of "I know what I like" is the junk food of the shortsighted collector. The purchase guarantees that such an uncritical

85

collector will never have the kind of touch he needs, simply because he is incapable of making the effort to develop a pattern that is personal and yet objective.

Even dealers catch the sickness. A Connecticut auctioneer, for example, had the walls of his home hung with pictures he had culled from sales because the pictures pleased him. None of the pictures was worth $50. He didn't mind. He had what he liked, and he was not interested in learning the difference between paintings that were wall coverings and paintings that were worth holding on to. His ignorance was a disservice to his consignors.

Similarly, an antique dealer in New Jersey brought home from her shop the art she really liked. All of the pictures she hung in her house were attractive to her, but they were all defective as investments—unsigned pictures, cut-off pieces of pictures, amateur pictures, and so on. The good things had been picked out of her shop quickly, at low prices. Her own specialization was silver. That was where she invested, and pictures were just decorations she enjoyed. Auctioneers and antique dealers, however, are supposed to be more knowledgeable, in order to obtain full value for their consignors.

Every Piece of Value

When a collector is buying from a reputable dealer, he can in theory safely buy whatever pleases him. Every art work in stock is supposed to be of value, and he can buy what he likes.

Unfortunately, however, some dealers and a chorus of acquiescing aesthetes are actually encouraging the know-nothings to "buy what they like," from any source and under any circumstances. One such cheerleader is The Print Council of America which recommends that you start your buying "with something that appeals to you for any reason whatever. . . . Then go on to buy others in the same way. Have the courage of your own tastes. . . ."

To buy what "appeals to you" is following self-serving advice, though, given for the benefit of the dealers themselves. Casual buyers who take what they like may well be acquiring the dealer's mistakes, the pieces he cannot sell to a collector.

The advice fails the moment you need to fix a value on what you have bought. The casual buyer who makes a poor purchase from a suspect source will have problems. If he brings the valueless piece to an established art dealer for resale, and he justifies having bought the work somewhere else under the excuse of it "appeals to me," the situation can be enough to raise an ethical dealer's hackles. Faced with the collector's expectation that every work of art must bring some price, however low, the dealer still cannot buy the work, at any price. Generally, he softens the refusal with the ploy of asking whether the owner really likes the piece, and when the owner replies in the affirmative, as he must, the dealer advises the owner to keep it.

Instead of indulging his whims, a collector is supposed to confine the buying of works of art to those of investment grade. Then the hop is a short one from investment buying in general to its refinement, "Buy the best."

Quality, Quality, Quality

Governor Connally's three rules for purchasing art, "Quality, quality, quality," set the right tone for "Buy the best," but they leave a fundamental gap. The definitions are missing. What are the criteria of quality in art? How does one know what is the best in order to buy it?

To find the answers, it is necessary to start by outlining the aspects of "best," and then to develop the concept more fully.

For some, and this includes part of the Governor's Texedo generation, the best is the highest priced. If it costs the most, it must be the best. You get what you pay for. Price, however, is generally set by artists, dealers, or bidders, not necessarily by innate quality, and the highest priced art may not be the best for you as a collector or investor.

Actually, the lower priced can sometimes turn out to be the best. A few superior artists like the painter and printmaker Gene Kloss (born 1903) have made a practice of selling their pictures at artificially low prices in order to assure a wide distribution and to keep the demand steady. Such prices should zoom to more realistic levels when the artist stops working, and meanwhile, less expensive may be better.

Even calling a work of art the "best buy" may be a condescension, implying the existence of another work that was better qualitatively but not purchased because it cost relatively more. "Best buy" is a consumer's way to distinguish between substantially identical items of manufacture like brands of detergent, not a term to be applied to art. You may well want what is the "best" for you at a higher price rather than what is second best but a cheaper "best buy."

Best Is Personal

"Best" is initially personal, the excellence your touch inclines you to, within your area of specialization—and your budget. When your taste has become trained enough to let you choose from a group of paintings the one that has to be for you, the best is what you actually do pick, in the exercise of your own judgment. "Best" is your individual best.

Alternately, "best" is a snapshot taken at an instant, the highest order of art for you at the moment you are ready to buy. It is the best at the time. This timely best should be leavened by the caution that you wait for the objective best. Unfortunately, when the funds available for purchase and an opportunity to buy are in the same place at the same time, impulsive buyers tend to make the purchase. Objective standards fade, as in the old joke about the love bug and the bed bug biting at the same time.

The objective "best" is a judgment from the standpoint of the usual marketplace indices, such as the analysis of the artist's work by size, medium, composition, complexity, subject, period, and so on.

Connoisseurs say that Charles Russell, for example, had definite periods: before 1900, between 1900 and 1910, between 1910 and 1920, and after 1920, and some periods are preferred to others. The objective best is the best by test, the best painting from the best period, as well as by the best painter. This would be called the statistical best if art happened to be a product subject to mathematical analysis.

"Best" can be weighed by purpose, too, and by trappings. If you are buying with the purpose of quick resale in mind, for example, best is the work of art most appropriate for the type of customer you expect. The trappings that would help to influence a resale might include knowing the complete history of a bronze or having a letter from the artist calling the piece "one of his best."

Professional "best" is the work of the artists who have had the greatest impact on American art. Winslow Homer (1836–1910) is certainly one, as are Thomas Eakins (1844–1916) and Frederic Remington. It is the best talent, judged after the phases and vogues of a generation have survived the testing of time.

Best Is Singular

"Best" is typically singular, the one prime example more meaningful than all the rest put together, the one that by itself can outweigh an entire group. It is the one that is the best.

Then there is the scarcest best. Charles Schreyvogel (1861–1912) created less than 100 paintings, for example, although he lived longer than Remington. Collecting rarities might be a goal, as long as you keep relative values in mind.

Finally, there is the expert "best," the one the authorities kowtow to, that the hoopla is directed at, and that is hung for optimum exposure. This is the "best" that is controlled by the bogey of authoritative criticism.

That is a bevy of "bests," so we will expand them, one at a time, to make them more comprehensible.

Keep in mind that a faultfinding attitude is more appropriate for a collector than is a willingness to accept. In art appreciation, the genteel approach may be to excuse a painting that fails to please by emphasizing attractive parts. This is not so in investment. You deal in dollars, not propriety. You must settle for only your best picture, the one that provides a sense of well-being whenever you think of it. Any unattractive part of a picture may negate the whole. It is not then likely ever to be your best.

Best as the Highest Priced

If you were to look just at price, the best would by definition be the most expensive. On that basis, lot number 34 "The Icebergs" by F.E. Church (1826–1900) was the best at Sotheby's auction sale no. 4290 held October 25, 1979. It brought $2,500,000, more than ten times the next highest priced lot.

This Church painting could also be regarded as having been the expert best in the sale. It had the highest pre-sale estimate, $750,000 to $1,000,000, set by the expert appraisers. It had the best trappings in the sale, too, having been reproduced as a full color fold-out in the catalog of the sale, provided with an extensive provenance, and promoted with great fanfare in the press. "The Icebergs" could even be said to have been the objective best. The picture was by far the grandest art work in the sale, a whopping 112 by 164 inches.

Was, however, "The Icebergs" really the best painting in the sale? Perhaps not, for most investors. Church was not the highest order of talent in a sale that included watercolors by Winslow Homer. It was thus not the professional best. If the purpose of the purchase was resale, you would have to note that the auction price was two and a half times the experts' top pre-sale estimate. It was implicit in the opinion of the appraisers that considerable time might pass before the market catches up with the price paid.

From such contradictory possibilities, it may appear difficult to identify the "best" picture for the investor to buy. How does he know whether one picture is better for investment than another? He cannot think that what he bought at auction was necessarily the best because he outbid the world to get it. Auctions are erratic. He would have to know such secrets, for example, as who the other bidders were. They could be dealers or collectors, agents or the owners.

Similarly, if the art work under consideration as "best" is offered in a gallery rather than at an auction, the investor cannot ask the dealer for advice without suspecting the dealer of a tendency to sell from the bottom of his stock, to describe his worst as his best.

A Lot of Bests

What does it all mean to the investor? If he wants to "buy the best," and thereby follow universally recommended advice, what does he do?

First, as we have seen, he has to recognize that there are a lot of bests to be sorted and rated as to how they fit him before he can make an informed purchase.

Otherwise, you may get the image of this discouraged person slowly making his way around an art gallery, trying to learn how to buy pictures from general principles in an old book. He is unable to bridge the chasm between what he should in theory buy as best for him and what is actually buyable. Encircled by the brilliant pictures and intimidated by the lighting, he is increasingly uncomfortable and then he leaves. If he had penetrated beyond general principles, however, in order to relax to a personal pattern, he might have been able to acquire his own "best" picture, without the anguish.

Clearly, the highest priced picture is not always the best for the average individual, if only because it might not be comfortably within his budget. On the other hand, quality, as the Governor said, should be the index.

Thus, the investor should buy the best he can afford, even if the price is at a premium of as much as 150 percent of value. There are paintings dealers buy for which they are willing to pay retail prices because they are certain that trends will force new and much higher prices in the short term. They are seldom wrong when they stick to the work of the best artists, in the artists' forte and in their own specialization. As an example, landscapes by California artists like Guy Rose (1867–1925), J. Bond Francisco (1863–1931), Jean Mannheim, and Julian Rix (1850–1903) that were bought at retail in the East in 1977 had quadrupled in price in the West by 1979.

We are not yet ready to consider the dollar amount of the price. That will be a later chapter. Here, we are saying only that if the investor does manage to decipher what the best is and he acquires it, the fact that he paid through the nose to get it will probably correct itself in time. It is likely at some point to prove to have been a good investment, although the act of overpaying does not by itself mean he bought the best.

The next concept, the best at the time, is primarily cautionary. Be patient while waiting for your best picture. It could be one of the first pictures ever offered to you, but it is not likely to be. When a veteran dealer thought back to the first important paintings he might have bought, one was a huge Thomas Hill (1829–1908) of Yosemite that was relatively inexpensive, but from present knowledge it was perhaps too modern looking to have been authentic. There was a large William Keith (1839–1911) of a forest interior, but the picture is still around, without a permanent home and without having increased much in price. Keith is frequently forged. There was a small A.B. Davies of bobbing boats, but Davies has not yet brought big money and if he did, it would not be for boats. There was a batch of Julius Rolshoven (1858–1930) pastels, but when they flash on memory's screen, the signatures don't appear. There was probably nothing missed in not having bought any of those paintings, though they seemed compelling at the time.

When You're Hot

You should not buy until what you see gives you confidence. Then be aggressive and act without hesitation. As we have said, the most dangerous period is when you are ready to buy and nothing offered to you qualifies for purchase as your best. The urge to buy intensifies as time passes. Pressure mounts, and you have to resist buying pieces that are less than your best, just because they are available when your stance calls for action. You have to slow yourself down and realize that opportunities come in cycles. When you're hot you're hot and when you're not you're not. Wait until you're hot.

There are auction catalogs coming to you that will contain no picture you have to own, and the next catalog may list two. When you are versed in your specialization, there will be offerings only you will appreciate. A New Mexican dealer glancing through the catalog of an unimportant Sotheby auction found the title of a famous Taos painter's favorite painting, estimated low and not even illustrated. He entered a nominal absentee bid, discounted for the problems he anticipated, and won. Most remarkably, when he received the painting it was in original condition, in the original frame, with the original exhibition stickers.

There is no way to predict when the best art work will be offered to you, or how, or at what price.

CHAPTER 10

Your Personal Best

There are more "bests" to come.

To start with, the extension of knowing "the best at the time" is knowing "the growth best," the capacity to see ahead, to supplement what is with what will be. If you are specializing in nineteenth century representational paintings of the Grand Canyon, you might decide to extend your field to the explorer-artist Frederick Dellenbaugh (1853–1935) who overlapped the turn of the century, or even to a contemporary like Wilson Hurley (born 1924).

If you are specializing in nineteenth century American still-life paintings and you fail to find a Harnett or a Peto, the very best may not be available to you at that time. You might then consider where your specialty will be taking you in a year or two. What will your direction be? Perhaps it might grow into still-life examples by painters known for other subjects as well, such as Junius Brutus Stearns the Academician doing fish or John J. Enneking (1841–1916) the Impressionist doing fruit. These artists might have the potential to be your future best, for growth.

The Objective Best

Another aspect of the painting you are waiting to buy is the objective best, optimally a large oil in the right subject for the prime period of a major artist's career. If the artist is museum quality, his big pictures are likely to be his best.

Why did "The Icebergs" bring top dollar? It was a huge oil, recognized as a winner when it was painted, and then dramatically rediscovered after having been lost for more than a century. In addition, the picture was certainly fresh on the market rather than shopworn from having been bandied among galleries. The subject was the Arctic, a new frontier in art that is now as collectible as a Western. A lot of objective pluses were concentrated in the picture.

When you are looking for the objective best, though, don't ask the artist. He is seldom an authority, even on what is his own objective best. Frederic Remington was famous as a Western illustrator before he became known as a fine arts painter. Late in his life, he came to believe his easel paintings would win him national recognition, and he burned his unsold illustrations because he felt the illustrations detracted from his chances for academic honors.

In contrast, his friend Howard Pyle (1853–1911) called illustration the highest usage of his own abilities. A little later, Pyle's student N.C. Wyeth (1882–1945) worked almost totally as an illustrator but he sided with Remington in envying easel painters and he disparaged illustrators.

The question for the investor, however, is not what the artist thought but what the market indicates. Some of Remington's illustrations bring as much as his fine art today, despite Remington's beliefs, while Wyeth's easel paintings have substantially less value than his illustrations. It is part of the objective best to buy the subject and style the artist is known for, regardless of the expressed feelings of the man himself.

Many artists have owned important collections of the work of their peers, but it usually was not because they recognized intrinsic value or economic worth. The collections came about because artists habitually traded with each other and also acquired the work of their teachers. Like Remington and Wyeth, artists tend to be poor judges of what is best for an investor.

Critics are the same. Both artists and critics talk in terms of preconceived theories of line and color and chiaroscuro, not the practicalities of value. Critics choose pictures that are beauty perceived by them, sometimes at the expense of work like genre pictures telling a story, despite the high prices genre pictures might bring. An art teacher may stop to marvel at the composition and light in a small watercolor by an unheralded artist while ignoring a painting by a master that is a thousand times more valuable.

Perfection to Your Eye

Objective standards do change to broaden the investment area when art prices rise, calling for new evaluations of sizes, subjects, and media. The value of a watercolor used to be thought of as ten percent of the value of an oil, while a drawing would be perhaps half as much as a watercolor.

As big oils are grabbed off the market, oils of smaller size are more in vogue. As all oils become less available, watercolors and drawings are more sought after. The ratio of their value increases. At a 1981 auction, a 4¼ by 3½ inch pencil drawing on the back of an envelope that was just Grant Wood's (1892–1942) conceptual sketch for the painting "American Gothic" brought $19,000 from a dealer.

Whatever the objective criteria, however, buy perfection to your eye, or don't buy at all. If a defect in an art work repels you to any extent, it is likely to repel the next guy, too. Reject any flaw that might bother you later. Defects in art grow more noticeable the longer the work is around.

If a bronze figure looks out of proportion to you, or if the piece is unsigned, or if the subject of a picture is religious or a nude or cruelty to animals like dogs mutilating a trapped bear or Indians stoning a mother and child, and this bothers you, don't buy the work, regardless of price or provenance. Some mechanical flaws like tears and discolorations in pictures are repairable and some are not, but you can never change the subject.

The director of a leading Western art museum once turned down a large and valuable painting by Charles Russell solely because the subject was a frontier fight scene he called "too bloody" to show to the general public. He was looking for peaceful pioneering subjects at the moment, although he did not object to pictures like "Custer's Last Stand" which may be the bloodiest of all.

As another example of how personal preference can control a museum's policy, another director praised Charles Schreyvogel as a Western painter and bought his work because he said Schreyvogel's hand-to-hand combat never resulted in blood from an open wound or in maimed limbs. A similar approach favoring peaceful Indian, cowboy, and mountain man scenes has also been required from the higher priced contemporary Western artists, as we have seen.

The Best as the Easiest

Relatively speaking, the "best" talent is the easiest to discover. Theorists and critics talk about accuracy of detail, draftsmanship, perspective, color values, method of application of the paint, the number of figures shown, and so on, but this is usually an analysis made after the artist's fame has been established.

In fact, the top painters in any specialty are known to all who follow the specialty. Along with memberships, galleries, and documentation, money also remains one of the tests for quality of investment, which takes you back to the high-priced best.

Another test is whether the artist generated a school of followers, as Remington and Russell did—followers who carried on the technique after the artist was dead. Russell enjoyed having imitators and called them his friends. Remington began to hate being copied when the leader of his imitators, Schreyvogel, was declared by some to have surpassed the master in painting the real West. He responded to the challenge by becoming a distinguished Impressionist and elevating his personal "best" beyond the reach of his imitators.

The Best for Resale

If your purpose in buying paintings is to have a secure investment, then using your touch to buy the "best" talent you can afford provides positive results in good times and also protection against loss during declining economic conditions.

If your purpose in buying is to secure the best picture for immediate resale, however, be careful. Buy only when the quality of the picture serves your own collecting needs, and not just because you have resale in mind. Looking at an art work through someone else's eyes may not be possible. You cannot always judge what another buyer would call his best. In the absence of an explicit commission, even dealers buy only for themselves and not for any specific customer because they are likely to fool themselves if they try to wear someone else's hat.

A customer who specializes in the works of one remote illustrator, for example, might not accept a large oil painting by that illustrator if he felt the sky was wrong for the man's technique. This might be an arcane difference a specialist could claim to know but one you might not perceive.

Another customer who needs only one canvas to complete his collection of the Taos Ten might still not take a painting bought for him if the faces of the Indians in front of the pueblo were insufficiently detailed, even though all of the artist's other pictures of that size and period were equally Impressionistic.

The literature is full of tales like the one about the expert who found a $250,000 Renoir for sale while traveling in France. He called his American customer six times to be certain of the resale, and discovered when he delivered the painting to Cincinnati that the size was too big for the intended spot over the bed.

Dealers have learned to buy only if the painting qualifies for their own stock. They never buy expressly for the purpose of a specific resale, unless it is tied down in advance. They apply their best judgment, not their concept of someone else's judgment.

The Better the Trappings

For any buyer, though, the better the trappings accompanying a picture, the likelier the resale. As a part of its provenance, the best picture may well come from the best source. When a Missouri dealer was offered a major Thomas Hart Benton painting from a prestigious museum, where the chain of title ran from the artist to the museum's founder, an important customer asked for permission to sit in the next room while the dealer completed the purchase from the museum. The customer then entered and immediately acquired the painting from the dealer. With reinforcement in the form of provenance like this, the entire transaction of buying and reselling a major picture took 15 minutes.

Trappings that help are quite varied. The art work may have been exhibited and listed in a catalog either when created or later, perhaps by a major gallery or in the auction of a meaningful estate. It may have been referred to or reproduced in a book or an article.

The complete chain of ownership may be available, with names, addresses, and dates, and may include famous links. You may know the date of the work, and have the artist's title for it. The artist may have described the work, on its reverse or inside its base or in his papers. The painting may be in its original frame with descriptive labels on the back of the frame.

This is all part of the provenance, the historical record, and should be established at the time of purchase. You may even find that the work fills a niche in art history, as by discovering a fish still-life by Junius Brutus Stearns when an article in *Antiques* magazine said that the one in the Toledo Museum was the only one extant.

The subject or the use of the work may also serve as trappings. A painting may tell a story, a scene in American history, for example, of identified troops crossing a named river in a specific Civil War engagement. Knowing the place helps. A visitor from San Francisco may identify a California landscape as Mount Tam in Marin County.

You might learn the name of the sitter in a portrait. Percival Rosseau's papers may indicate that the dogs in one of his paintings were his own. A painting reproduced as an illustration is aided when a tear sheet of the reproduction is attached to the backing, in a manner that does not damage

11. Junius Brutus Stearns. "Striped Bass with Creel," 1848. Oil on domed wood panel, 13 by 34 inches.

the painting. All of these elements are part of what comprise the trappings of the one best art work.

You must keep in mind, though, that it is natural for any seller to seek to enhance his property by puffing. This is especially true for a professional seller. He may come to believe what could be possible is possible, and he may say so, as by describing a picture that could be of a particular place as actually of that place.

You must be aware, too, that before offering an art work for sale, the seller will have done whatever restoration is cosmetically beneficial. He will also have considered reframing and adding a nameplate. You should expect to be looking at a refurbished product, tarted up to sell.

In addition, dealers may seek to inflate the aspects of quality, by advertising, issuing circulars, publicity, and giving private viewings. When the dealer is successful in enhancement and promotion, prices rise, and it is up to the buyer to distinguish between the art work and the cosmetics.

The One Best

Buy quality over quantity. With what you can afford, buy one major work rather than a number of minor things. First-rate pieces are always in short supply and are getting scarcer. In a depression, top quality works remain salable while lesser pieces may be more difficult to sell. This

12. *John Steuart Curry.* *"Frontiersman."* *Oil on canvas, 30 by 20 inches.*

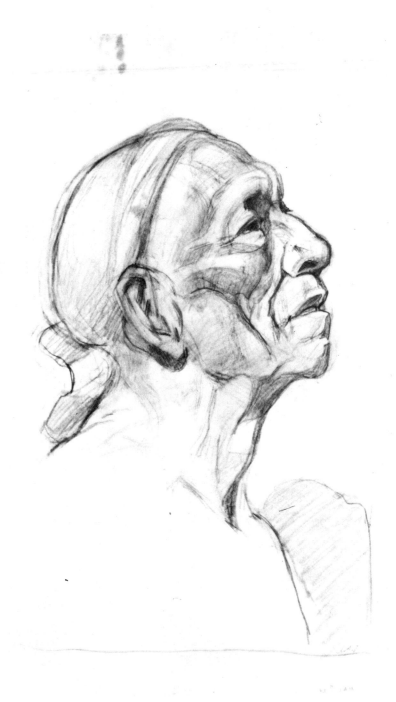

13.
*Joseph A. Imhof.
"Taos Indian."
Pencil on paper,
18 by 11⅝ inches
(sight).*

approach of buying one over many is the ultimate extension of specialization, the riskiest act if not taken with deliberation, but the one that definitely promises the greatest protection and gain.

The concept of the one best is a key requiring emphasis. As in any other activity, investors in art can be divided into nibblers and gobblers. There are dealers, for example, who stock 500 works of art, all marginally investment grade but none that is anyone's best except for new collectors and casual buyers of decorations. There are other dealers who stock 50 works, all capable of being some insider's personal best.

This restrictive tendency in buyers toward an excess of caution is a widespread failing. What happens is that most investors start as nibblers, perhaps as treasure hunters. That is appropriate in the beginning, but some of them never grow to be gobblers.

At least once a year, every investor should stop to analyze his direction. He should realize that after he knows enough in his specialization to trade up to his one best, he should shed himself of what he will perceive to be lesser things when judged by his current touch. From then on, he should refrain from buying lesser things.

Among dealers, trading art work is a constant practice, to get rid of a piece a dealer has not sold in return for one he might sell. The goal in trading is always to try to give several minor things in return for one that might be a best. Seascapes, for example, are not hot sellers in New Mexico. A Taos dealer traded four seascapes to get one painting of a frontiersman by John Steuart Curry (1897–1946).

There are exceptions to the singular best. Joseph Imhof painted relatively few oils in Taos and the ones not in collections are generally of poor quality. As we have seen, however, his drawings of Indians are fine. Buying a quantity of good Imhof drawings as one grouping might be regarded as preferable to purchasing a pedestrian painting.

The Expert Best

The expert best can be explored by looking again at the 1979 auction catalog containing "The Icebergs."

For specialists in ship paintings, with budgets under $20,000, lot number 24 might have seemed like the best. It was J.E. Buttersworth's (1817–1894) "Yachts Racing Out of New York Harbor," an 18 by 24 inch oil that was large for this marine painter. The experts accurately provided a pre-sale estimate of $15,000 to $20,000, and the painting sold for $16,000.

There was an identical estimate and selling price for the next lot, J.F. Cropsey's (1823–1900) "Figures on the Hudson River," a 12 by 20 inch oil painting that would fit several specialties as a best. Neither painting is likely to be worth less than those selling prices. By 1981, just two years later, the auction price for a Cropsey of similar quality, size, and subject was $33,000.

The "best" painting in the sale, however, may have been one for the Western specialist. This was lot number 88, "The Judith Basin Roundup," an authenticated oil 30 by 48 inches signed C.M. Russell and dated 1889. Old time Western art is now accepted by most Eastern critics and museums, partially because it has become a favorite at Eastern auctions.

The expert pre-sale estimate was $200,000 to $300,000, a reasonable value as an example of the early Russell period. The painting actually sold for only $185,000, although it was an oil of major size with cowboys roping a steer, a typical subject for the artist. Russell was as we know a leading Western painter, and his realism in this picture extended to the recognizable brand on the horse in the foreground. The chain of title ran back to the artist himself, and an additional embellishment was that Russell had traded this "best" painting for an ordinary violin.

What more could an investor in Westerns ask for from an auction?

I Know What Is Best for Me

What "buy the best" comes down to is buying your personal best, in line with your own collecting philosophy and your own temperament, in terms of your age and your finances. All of the other "bests" are modifying factors to help you make up your mind.

These other bests do provide you with a check list, too. Can you acquire your best at an acceptable price, they ask, one within your budget? Will your principal be safe in inflation and deflation? Is the artist a leader in his field, long established, with an unbroken string of rising prices? Is there a strong potential for appreciation? Will you be free from the worries about fads? What will your obligations be in portfolio management? What will the marketability of the piece be?

In the end, it would be most appropriate to hear the collector proclaim, "I buy what I like because I know what is the best for me." Then, once he has acquired that best art work, the next step for him will be to go forward to concentrate on his new best—after reevaluating where he stands.

CHAPTER 11

Physical Condition Versus Cosmetics

In these days of volatile art prices, there are art dealers, dedicated investors, and major collectors all over the country who avidly subscribe to the catalogs issued by the leading auction houses. Three weeks or so before a given auction, these art buyers get the illustrated catalog with pre-sale estimates, and three weeks after the sale they get the list of prices realized.

For those who cannot attend the viewing or sale, the catalog is a crucial link to trends in the art business. The list of prices realized is all there is to use in evaluating what those dealers buy and sell who live outside the big cities where auctions are held.

A Photograph in a Catalog

How helpful, though, are the prices realized at an auction sale of paintings that the catalog subscribers have not actually seen? The answer is, not much. The condition of a painting is a factor in its value, and looking at a photograph in a catalog cannot provide a true analysis of the condition of the painting illustrated.

As an example, assume that an auction lot in a 1980 Sotheby sale was a huge 25 by 53 inch Oscar Berninghaus (1874–1952) oil on canvas, commissioned as a mural for a private home. The Remingtonesque subject was four Indians galloping across the plains in profile, a strong presentation except that the Indians were drawn small in relation to an amorphous landscape.

The pre-sale estimate was $20,000 to $30,000, a low appraisal for such an active Indian subject by a Taos master. It would not have been surprising if the price realized had been $50,000. Instead, the bidding at the sale did not even meet the reserve or minimum upset price that presumably was less than $25,000.

The unresolved questions became, why was this Berninghaus painting given the low pre-sale estimate, and, why did it pass? The answer may be one that would never have been apparent just from the catalog photograph. Suppose the Indian figures in the focus of the composition had been generously retouched. Rumors of this might have spread along the dealers' grapevine, so the professional bidders were turned off. What would then appear on the record as a serious drop in Berninghaus prices would in fact be nothing of the sort. The condition of this painting would have affected its value.

It is common knowledge that auctions are dumping grounds for doubtful art as well as legitimate sales agencies for sound pieces, with no disclosure in the catalog either way. Some auction houses will on request orally reveal what they believe the condition of a painting to be, but no guaranty of condition is made.

Moreover, many dealers will not even admit to a knowledge of condition. They may put paintings on exhibition in their galleries without any black light examination at all, as long as the cosmetics of the surface of the painting are visually satisfactory.

Condition Is Ignored

Thus, the physical condition of the art is being ignored, rather than treated as the foundation of the business. As a result, the casual buyer may never learn how to see condition because his eye goes only to the beauty of the surface.

When a collector phones a dealer with a painting to sell and the signature is professional and the price fits the circumstance, the dealer will ask what the condition is. "Good," the owner may reply. "Beautiful. Not a mar or a mark on it. It's clean as a whistle." "Good" is likely to be describing just the externals, the cosmetics, though, and not the basic physical condition that should be the dealer's concern. In the reality of the art business, price means little without a statement of physical condition, and this statement is hard to come by.

In dealing with any ethical seller, then, you can learn anything the seller knows, assuming you are experienced enough to ask every question required to obtain a full disclosure. Sellers, you see, are not expected to be volunteers. If they do agree to guarantee one quality like authenticity, for instance, it does not mean they also guarantee condition, a different quality.

In addition, sellers can only disclose what they know. If they shield themselves from learning about condition, or if they are not qualified to judge condition, you cannot scoop from the pot any more than is in there.

The Kinds of Pictures

Consequently, you can protect yourself only if you do your own homework on what a painting really is and on what the variations in condition can be. The place to start is to distinguish between the different kinds of original pictures.

Physically, a painting is a work of art comprising a surface laid on with pigment. In an oil painting, the pigment is dispersed in oil before application. In an opaque gouache, the pigment is in gum arabic with chalk. In a transparent watercolor, the pigment is in gum arabic alone. In a pastel, the pigment is dry, like chalk. In a drawing, there is no pigment.

Starting from the back of an oil painting, the structure begins with the stretcher, which generally is an adjustable wood frame capable of being keyed out to keep the canvas taut. Twentieth century stretchers are machine-made products with mitered corners. Older stretchers were handmade and square cut on their ends. A stretcher without provision for keys is a strainer.

A painting may look to be microscopically thin, but it is composed of different structural layers. The first layer is the painting support. This is usually a linen canvas folded over the outer edge of the stretcher and tacked or stapled into place—ergo, the tacking edge.

The second layer is usually the ground, a coating on the canvas to provide an even surface for the paint. Then comes the film of paint itself, the pigment in a medium such as linseed oil. The fourth and final layer is the varnish, the transparent skin that seals the complex package while heightening colors and adding the illusion of depth.

What you see when you look at a painting from the front is the paint viewed through the varnish film. When you look from the back, you see the stretcher and the canvas. From the side, you see the tacking edge.

The moment a painting is completed, its condition starts to deteriorate. An oil painting on canvas looks to be inert, but each of the separate layers in its structure is subject to continual pulls and stresses from changes in temperature and humidity and from handling. The wood, fabric, ground, paint, and varnish all move independently of each other.

The canvas may distend and sag on the stretcher, pulling the paint apart, or the canvas may shrink, decreasing the area of the support for the paint and causing it to crack and to cup. The ground may separate from the canvas and crumble, taking the paint along. The paint may part from the ground, fissuring or flaking. The varnish may darken or turn a color. Foreign materials from smoke or grime or flies may adhere to the surface of the varnish.

And, besides the built-in destruction and the effect of the elements, there is man.

Categories of Condition

To provide simplified descriptions of condition in art, paintings in oil on canvas can be classified into five categories:

Fine Condition.

The painting is in its original "mint" state, as completed by the artist, with no paint loss or addition or canvas damage. Not cut down or overpainted. May have been cleaned lightly and revarnished but not otherwise restored. Paint surface may be dirty but only if simple cleaning is assured.

Very Good Condition.

The painting is in better than average shape, substantially in its original state, as completed by the artist. Insignificant paint loss or addition is acceptable if not in focus of composition or in signature area. No canvas damage. May have been lined by a conservator, but not cut down. Not damaged in restoration, as by overcleaning or excessive repainting. If restored, conservator's report is required. Painting may be unrestored if state is as above and complete restorability is assured.

Good Condition.

This is the average shape in which paintings are offered for resale, so the seller's description of the condition of a group of paintings could be "good or better unless noted." Minor paint loss or addition or canvas damage acceptable if not significantly in focus of composition or in signature area. May have been lined and retouched professionally, but not cut down. If restored, conservator's report should be available. Painting may be unrestored if state is as above and if complete restorability is assured.

Fair Condition.

The painting is in less than average state, to the extent that seller is ethically required to make disclosure because value may be affected negatively. Paint loss or addition or canvas damage may be sizeable, or may be in focus of composition or in signature area. Signature must still be original at least in part and may have been supplemented. Painting has not been cut down. Heavy restoration may be required, if painting is unrestored.

Poor Condition.

The painting is in an unacceptable state, to the extent that seller is ethically required to make disclosure because the value of the painting may be appreciably reduced. Paint loss or addition or canvas damage is substantial in focus of composition or in signature area. Signature may be wholly in a retouch area. Painting may have been cut down and may not be worth restoring, from an investment standpoint.

Not Apparent to the Naked Eye

These classifications of condition come from the descriptions of antiquarian books, but the application is quite different. Ordinarily, books are inspected visually, by the cosmetics, which is precisely what should be unacceptable in the examination of paintings. In art, we are concerned with the basic, inherent state of the physical object, something that may not be at all apparent to the naked eye. Only after assured of that do we turn to cosmetics.

When the seller specifies that his paintings are good or better, he means there has been no significant paint loss or addition in the focus of the composition, on the face of a portrait, for example, or in the signature area, that there has been no large paint loss or addition elsewhere, and that the painting has not been cut down in size. If a painting is "fair" or "poor," the seller should disclose the actual deviations from mint condition.

When a professional seller of art professes to be unable to characterize condition because he claims to know nothing about conservation, he should be required to make a statement to that effect when offering art for sale. He of course has the option of retaining a conservator to do the characterization.

The Best Is the Simplest

The easiest way to look at condition is by example, and the best condition is the simplest to describe. A little oil on canvas board of Taos Pueblo in New Mexico is signed J.H. Sharp (1859–1953) at lower right and is dated '13, the first full year Sharp made Taos his residence. The painting is immaculate both visually and under black light. If the surface was ever

14. Joseph H. Sharp. "Taos Pueblo," 1913. Oil on canvasboard, 10 by 13 inches.

cleaned, there is no trace of it. There has been no paint loss. Even the frame was Sharp's own.

The painting is in mint condition, classified as "fine."

Alternately, a big oil on canvas signed W. Schumacher (1870–1931) at lower right and dated 1911 was purchased in a difficult physical state where most of the tacking edge was broken. The painting was flopping over the stretcher and frame until the canvas was secured for travel. The surface of the varnish was exceedingly dirty, obscuring the scene. Nevertheless, the condition was classified as "very good," a short step below mint because only relining was needed.

The paint was all original, easily cleanable with a simple solution, and the frame was original. Schumacher was an American in Paris, and his title for the little girl saying goodbye to her mother as she was leaving for a walk with the governess was "Le Baisir (The Kiss)."

15. William Emile Schumacher. "Le Baisir," 1911. Oil on canvas, 25½ by 36 inches.

Classification of the painting as "very good" helps to distinguish condition from cosmetics. A painting in very good condition can probably be restored so as to be cosmetically perfect, but not all paintings cosmetically perfect are in very good condition.

The Poorer the Condition

In handling damaged paintings, the uninitiated may feel that a badly torn and soiled picture can be thrown around because the picture needs heavy repair. The rule, however, is the opposite. The poorer the condition, the more the care required to transport the painting to the conservator. You simply cannot judge condition without expert advice. What looks to you like severe damage may be easy to fix, but carelessly extending the damage may be fatal.

A 22 by 29 inch painting "San Francisco in 1849" attributed to Joshua Peirce (active 1841–1850) was purchased from a famous old California family. A miniaturist's view of the traffic in the streets and on the piers, the painting had been restored about 1930 with a glue lining onto canvas tacked back to the original strainer. The varnish had since discolored, but the underlying paint was bright, despite considerable cracking and cupping. Retouch was minimal, limited to some peripheral foliage. The frame was gilded wood rather than the gold leaf over gesso the original would have been.

Removal from the frame showed that the painting had been cut from the strainer with a knife, a common practice in 1930. The tacking edge of the original canvas had been discarded. When you look at the edge of the painting now, you can see that the existing tacking edge is part of the lining canvas. Clearly, though, the painting had not been cut down in restoration. The strainer was original and its inner edge had over the years made a line through the paint. The composition was complete visually and it conformed to other views of San Francisco in 1849.

In spite of the painting's problems, the condition was "very good." After arduously taking off the old lining, relining would be required, under pressure to correct the cupping by putting down as much of the paint as possible. Restoration should return the painting substantially to its original condition. The age of the picture and the uniqueness of the subject as a basis for geographical specialization would tend to make a buyer more accepting of the physical problems.

Turned Down and Tacked On

A portrait painted about 1915 of an elegant woman seated at a table, signed H. Dearth at lower right, is 31 by 46 inches. The only paint missing is an irregular strip ten inches by a half inch at the bottom center, amounting to less than one percent of the painting area.

Removing the painting from its new frame exposes an old glue lining, with the original tacking edges retained on both sides. The presence of the old lining indicates that there had to have been damage because conservators did not then practice preventive maintenance. At top and bottom, the tacking edges were gone, and the painting itself had been turned down and tacked on.

The stretcher was original, with a horizontal as well as a vertical support bar, and all three vertical sections of the stretcher had been sawed and reglued to accommodate the shortened picture. The sections of the stretcher were square cut and there were long tapered keys with rounded backs.

Black (ultraviolet) light showed no retouch paint, so the condition would be classed as very good. The painting would be relined to restore it to the original size, with the relining canvas serving as the tacking edge in the manner that the first lining should have done.

Where the tacking edge of the original painting is retained in lining, rather than cut off and thrown away, the process is more time consuming for the conservator. He must take extra steps. Tacks have to be removed carefully, edges of the canvas straightened, impacted dirt scraped from crevices, and the edges held to the painting in lining and then held down when the painting is mounted to the stretcher. The tacking edge is part of the body of the painting, however, and deserves retention despite the extra trouble.

Repainting by the Artist

A 25 by 40 inch painting of two Conestoga wagons crossing a brook, escorted by armed men, some mounted and some on foot, was signed E.F. Ward at lower left and dated '24. On the reverse was a later but undated reference to book rights.

The painting was purchased from the artist in the 1970s. It appeared to be in original condition, not lined or repainted. Black light, however, indicated the presence of a modern synthetic varnish pigmented with tints of different colors for different areas of the painting. The tinted varnish blocked the usual penetration of the black light and over the years had darkened the painting itself. Removal of the varnish allowed the black light to show retouch of faces and foliage.

Investigation disclosed that the reproduction rights to the painting had been sold to the magazine trade in 1924. In the 1950s, the artist was offered a second sale, this time for a book jacket. By then, his style had changed from romantic to realistic and he retouched the painting to fit, before varnishing with tints.

Now, careful removal of varnish and repaint will restore the picture to close to its original state. This example is the exception, where heavy retouch in focal areas will not preclude the painting from being classified as in "very good" condition. The addition was by the artist himself and the original state was recoverable.

Despite this example, paintings by living artists are generally safe as to condition if the work is acquired from the artist or his primary gallery. At any later point in the chain of title, though, condition may be a problem.

You do have some artists who are inveterate fiddlers. As long as a painting remains in their possession, they continue to touch it up. They see how it can be improved and they go ahead and make changes. Sometimes this continues over many years. The buyer of such a piece can have a problem in resale, so he should have the artist describe both the condition when the work was acquired and the changes made earlier. The artist can put this on the reverse of the work or can note it separately in a letter.

16. *John Young-Hunter. "Purple and Gold." Oil on canvas, 35 by 30 inches.*

Rosy Tones Rather Than Black

A 35 by 30 inch portrait of a dark-complected nude woman kneeling in profile, wearing gold Victorian jewelry against a purple drape, was signed J. Young-Hunter lower right but not dated. Titled "Purple and Gold" on the reverse, the frame chosen by the artist was medieval with gold leaf markings on dark wood. Also on the reverse of the frame were English exhibition stickers dated in the 1950s.

The back of the picture was hidden by a sheet of corrugated paper tacked to the stretcher. Removing the paper revealed another exhibition sticker noting a juried award made to this picture as Southwestern art in 1945 when Young-Hunter lived in Taos, New Mexico.

The artist's autobiography had reproduced "Purple and Gold" in color, with the nude painted in rosy Spanish-American tones rather than black, making it appear that the black body tones were added subsequent to the artist's death in 1955. "Purple and Gold" was classified as in "good" condition, subject to restoration of the warm body tones by removal of the added black tint.

An oil painting on plywood 19½ by 30 inches was signed with the monogram "W" for Frederick Waugh (1861–1940) and was not dated. Showing ceremonial Art Nouveau figures, the painting was titled "Mothers of Pearl" on the reverse. The paint was all there, although soiled, but the basic plywood support was severely rippled.

Handling wood might be an unusual restoration for a painting conservator, requiring consultation with a furniture restorer. Shrinking the ripples would stress the paint. Consequently, "Mothers of Pearl" was classified as in "fair" condition, pending the outcome of the repairs.

An oil eight by six inches showing the head of an Indian in profile was signed E.W. Lenders (?–1934), "101 Ranch" lower right. Lower left was the inscription "Iron Tail/Sioux." The painting was cosmetically fine, but it had been lined with glue onto a new canvas and then tacked to a stretcher with tape over the sides.

Black light revealed that a triangular tear one and one half by a half inch on the cheekbone had been repaired. The condition was "fair." Damage to the face should be disclosed, even though not visible to the naked eye.

Poor as a Fixed Condition

A new dealer in the art business bought as an exercise in restoration an oil portrait of the *Brig Carib* that was lacking half of its paint in a wide stripe

17. Frederick Waugh. "Mothers of Pearl." Oil on plywood, 19⅝ by 29¾ inches.

right down the center of the ship. A conservator replaced the missing ground, leveled to the oil paint surface, but this was as far as he could go. A leading painter of historical ships was induced to repaint the missing half of the vessel.

His repainting was so fine that for years the picture was used as a prop in lectures. To the eye, the painting was cosmetically perfect, but under black light the audience was blinded by the mass of purple that was the repaint.

Regardless of any repair, however, the condition of the painting could never be improved from the "poor" state it was in when it was acquired. Eventually, the *Brig Carib* was sold at auction without provenance.

Finally, there is the tale of the two Balinks. Both were 1930s portraits of Indians by Henry Balink (1882–1963) of Santa Fe. Both were oil on board 14 by 11 inches. One was physically and cosmetically perfect and was classified as "fine." The frame on the other indicated that the picture had been in a fire. The paint was flaking in unobtrusive spots, calling for the classification of "good" condition.

The conservator's report, however, stated that the bond of the remaining paint to the board was weak, so the probability of a satisfactory restoration was in doubt. The classification of condition had to be revised to "poor," leading to the pessimistic thought that classification of damaged paintings before the conservation reports are completed should perhaps follow a "worst case" diagnosis.

Putting paint back down on board is generally much less successful in conservation than lining a painting on canvas, although in this instance, the restoration proved to be perfect.

The physical condition of art is thus a critical factor in value that may be concealed from the inexperienced buyer. Methods for ascertaining and disclosing condition are simple and are available, but they will never be used until buyers demand them.

CHAPTER 12

Condition in a Buyer's Market

We have been paying a lot of attention to the physical condition of art. Why, though, should condition matter to a collector or insider? Condition is certainly not a hot topic in the trade.

A Cavalier View

A dealer in California bragged a few months ago that he walked into an auction in process in New York City and "stole" ten pictures he had never seen before and did not have the opportunity to examine. He hung the pictures in his well-advertised gallery and sold every one at a substantial profit, without ever ascertaining their condition. His customers were not told about condition when they bought, and to this point, they have not been concerned with condition because they have not tried to resell. After all, they bought from a reputable source.

Dealers like this one offer cosmetically repaired pictures as equivalent to gilt-edged securities, and their casual customers accept this. There has been no complaint.

In a seller's market, such a cavalier view of a painting's condition may get by for awhile, with some buyers, under some circumstances. It would not be advisable, however, to own a painting in poor physical condition when analysis of soundness becomes more crucial and when experienced buyers get pickier. In a buyer's rather than a seller's market, the more evidence of restoration the lower the value.

Value attaches to the original art, and a conservator's work is not the artist's work. There are cities you might visit where one conservator hogs the restoration commissions. In gallery after gallery there are unrelated paintings he has restored extensively, and you would swear all of them were originally painted by the same hand. Pictures with heavy restoration are worth less than equivalent paintings in better physical condition.

117

The Concept of Conservation

The whole current concept of conservation is new, American in origin, and increasingly scientific. Old sins in restoration are as passé as the Neanderthal age.

The type of framer who cut a painting down to a stock frame size is, we hope, extinct, along with turn-of-the-century restorers who disapproved of Impressionism and added hard outlines to everything they retouched.

So should be the Victorian restorer who repainted a nude Grace Hudson (1865–1937) Indian boy into a girl to hide the exterior plumbing and the 60-year-old restorer and her mother who accidentally removed the signature of E.H. Blashfield (1848–1936) in cleaning a mural and then put it back misspelled.

Extinct, too, should be the dealer-restorer who painted out a church steeple to make it into a sailboat on a lake, in order to avoid any religious connection, and the restorer who had trouble matching the color of a spot of lost paint and so repainted a large area.

Years ago, a local artist repaired a Gilbert Stuart (1755–1828) portrait that had suffered many small paint losses in the background. The artist cleaned the area with a strong chemical fortified with a caustic. He then smeared the entire surface with a filler compounded from gelatin and he bladed the surface flat, creating huge islands where the original paint was obscured.

The overpainting was a pleasure for him. He loved to paint, and as a professional artist, he considered himself the equal of anyone, including Gilbert Stuart. Today, a trained conservator would have to remove all of the local artist's labors before beginning again with the respect due to the shade of Mister Stuart.

For most of us, choosing a professional conservator on our own is impossible. Serious dealers say they are meticulous in commissioning conservation, but when pressed, many of them have no idea what restoration actually involves. They judge by the cosmetics of what they get back.

In an extreme case, a well-known conservator who teaches restoration finished off his work on a painting with a white museum board backing that was eyeletted and screwed to the back of the frame to protect the painting. When the board was removed by the collector, a piece of masking tape was exposed, stuck to the reverse of the painting to hold together a slit in the canvas, like a band-aid covering a child's scratch.

Conservation Is a Science

Restorers used to be people who liked to paint but who did not have the skills to be artists. Nowadays, many experts consider it unethical for a creative artist to do restoration because his ability to paint might, as we have seen, soften his resolve to avoid removing original paint in the cleaning.

Conservation is a science, not an art. There is a code of ethics and a set of standards. You pick a conservator by his education, training, and experience, as well as by museum references and memberships in trade associations like the American Institute of Conservators.

Professional conservation can be costly. To start with, there are the basic expenses of the conservator's documentary photographs and preliminary reports, so a minimum charge for examination alone may be $100 or more. Most conservators estimate jobs by time, at $35 an hour for example. Others may also judge by size, estimating a simple cleaning at one-and-a-half hours per square foot. The cost will always increase when the art work is particularly valuable.

Buying a painting needing restoration becomes an economic question. If you can purchase for $200 a damaged painting that could be worth $1,000 when restored, should you go ahead when the restoration will cost $500 and the framing $200? Probably not, as opposed to buying a painting in "very good" condition. Any significant repair may be a problem in your resale, and some paintings in "poor" condition may turn out to be ethically unrestorable, although a dealer might make up his mind based on rarity, condition, and on how the painting would fit into his stock.

The function of the conservator begins with the examination. Some tests are simple. For example, the conservator may look at the front of the painting under strong direct light, and then with a raking light from the side. The painting may also be held in front of a strong light so the conservator can look through the back. If the painting proves to be opaque, there may be an unobserved lining. If the light penetrates, bare canvas can be noted and may indicate the painting has been stripped in an overzealous earlier cleaning.

In addition, there is a battery of mechanical aids available to the conservator. Black ultraviolet light induces a fluorescence that may contrast new paint with the original, by showing the new as dark purple or black while the original is recessive. Infrared film may disclose what is just below the surface of the paint, for an analysis of the painter's technique. When there are two paintings on the same canvas, X-ray film may show both paintings in one photograph, like a double exposure.

The Preliminary Report

As in most organized activities, the next step for the conservator is paperwork. First, a written preliminary report is made, describing the painting and explaining its condition in detail. Treatment is recommended and cost is estimated.

The following preliminary analysis is excerpted from a four-page conservator's report on a painting on millboard that had split parallel to the bottom after being moved from an island to a desert atmosphere.

The examination (the comments in brackets are added) listed "1. Title: *Westward Bound in Utah.* 2. Artist: Harvey Young. 3. Signature/Date: Lower right, 'Harvey Young.' 4. Medium: Oil on panel. 5. Size: 19" x 29½" x ⅛". 6. Owner: Peggy and Harold Samuels. 7. Owner's #: 7333. 8. Date Examined: 8/9/81. 9. Frame: Burled Wood. 10. Labels (or inscriptions): Reverse of panel, a. In pencil - #4 'Westward Bound in Utah.' b. In pencil - '31.' c. In pencil - '49795.' d. In pencil - 'ECS 146' [These numbers probably indicate that the painting was published as titled].

"Support: Wood pulp board laminated with wood pulp paper on both sides ["wood pulp" means that the paper self-destructed because of its acidic content, but it was the customary artist's board of the time]. There is a crack and tear in the panel. . . . There is a patch on the reverse. . . . There is a 26" break in the support which does not penetrate through to the reverse. . . . Manipulation of the break does not result in realignment. . . . The lower left corner is partially crushed and broken away.

"Ground: No ground layer is readily discernible.

"Paint Film: When viewed microscopically, the extreme vertical edges exhibit two layers of paint film and a varnish layer between the two. In other words, it appears that there is another painting beneath *Westward Bound.* . . . This circumstance is undoubtedly the reason for the current condition of the upper paint layer. The upper paint layer is cracked, cupping, tenting, and erupting throughout which in turn has resulted in extensive small losses throughout. Many of these losses have been filled and/or retouched previously."

The conservator then listed 20 of the small losses, beginning with "Losses *not* containing fills or retouch (filled or retouched losses are not listed because it is not possible to accurately measure these losses): 1. Measuring 3/16″ x 3/32″ and located (through 'H' in signature) 4½″ from the right edge and 7/8″ from the bottom. . . . There are numerous other losses measuring less than 1/16″ x 1/16″ throughout. . . . The signature has been partially removed through some previous cleaning.

"Surface film: There appears to be a synthetic resin surface coating [varnish]. There is extensive discolored retouch throughout . . . . Some of the retouch is delaminating. . . .

"Solvent Tests: [##1 and 2 chemicals - the names of the actual chemicals have been deleted as it is not advisable that would-be but untrained restorers use such chemicals to try to clean a painting, risking damage]—no reaction to surface coating; no reaction to paint film [which means that the chemicals did not penetrate the varnish to the paint]. [#3]—removes resinous surface coating; no reaction to paint film. [#4]—removes old retouch very slowly; no reaction to paint film.

"Recommended Treatment: 1. Photograph before and after treatment [this would include the pencil inscriptions on the back, plus an X-ray photograph to find out about the buried painting]. 2. Clean painting. 3. Set down flaking from front. 4. Remove patch from reverse. 5. Laminate original panel to new panel with wax. 6. Fill losses. 7. Inpaint compensation [the missing paint]. 8. Apply new surface coatings. 9. Properly install in frame."

In the letter of transmittal, the conservator concluded that "I feel that I can return this painting to you in good shape. . . . The overall condition of the paint film really concerns me more than the crack in the panel. . . . I think that with the treatment I have outlined, however, we can pretty much arrest this condition. . . . All of the steps listed are essential to insuring the good condition of the painting."

The conservator's examination report is reproduced at length in order to give you an idea of the technology you are entitled to when you buy a painting restoration. You must not settle for the ministrations of an unqualified neighborhood artist, framer, or dealer. If all the European immigrants who claim to have been painting conservators for the Metropolitan Museum of Art in New York City had actually worked there, the Museum walls would have had to expand like an accordion.

After restoration, the Harvey Young painting was classified as in "fair" condition. All of the spots of lost paint do not amount to much compared to the 560 square inches of painted surface, but part of the signature was touched.

Cleaning a Painting

Cleaning a painting can never be performed by the untrained, yet the quaintest nostrums in art attach to this process. One that is widely accepted among otherwise learned art experts is rubbing a dirty painting with a forefinger moistened with spit to test whether the painting can be cleaned. Such a test might work if the expert could spit detergent or solvent, but not otherwise.

A second and worse quack recipe is to saturate the painting with linseed oil. The oil will never come off completely. A third is to wipe the surface of the painting with a slice of raw potato or a ball of wet bread, a technique for vegetarian restorers. A fourth is to break up the old varnish physically with a scalpel and brush off the debris. A fifth is to wash the picture with soap and water, an easy way to cause the paint to pop off the canvas, producing irreparable damage.

In reality, the process of cleaning is scientific, critical, and chancy. What is needed is knowledge of chemistry and of painting practices over the ages, plus experience and knack. When the cleaning becomes hazardous to the painting itself, for example, it is wise to underclean because overcleaning is not reversible. The trained conservator recognizes that some parts of some paintings cannot be completely cleaned.

After proper cleaning may come lining, which is the backing of the original canvas to a second and stronger support by means of an adhesive like heat-softened wax penetrating both canvases from the back. Current prophylactic practice also calls for lining a weak original canvas, even though it may be in mint condition, for safety in handling. Old stretchers and tacks may be discarded, as long as descriptions are recorded in the conservator's report. Lining is followed by the cosmetics of replacing lost ground, paint, and varnish.

A basic principle in conservation is that all steps must be reversible. There has to be a barrier between old paint and new, for instance, so the picture may be recleaned as necessary without going deeper than the barrier. Any lining which is added must be removable.

Art on Paper

Conservation of watercolors, drawings, and prints on paper is a separate science, even more esoteric than the conservation of paintings on canvas.

If you are buying a picture on paper that is framed behind glass, the framing should be opened unless you know the framer and his practices. The reason has nothing to do with the old joke in the trade about finding a cache of valuables hidden in the old framing, although a dealer once found a second watercolor behind the one he bought. Rather, there may be latent damage that could be halted by following the newer concepts in reframing paper, and, sometimes there is information written on the hidden part of the picture.

Art on paper must be protected from humidity and heat, from contact with wood pulp materials, sun and fluorescent light, and rough handling.

The Black Light

The black light is an important tool in examining oil paintings. Where there is a power source and a darkened room, you need only a shielded two-bulb electric fixture with 17-inch black light fluorescent bulbs and a long cord. This is more powerful and more revealing than the typical commercial product.

For all the experience dealers have accumulated in examining thousands of paintings, they still should never take in a picture without a black light examination, if black light is at all available. This is not to say that black light is absolutely reliable. Sometimes, the residues of recent cleaning of an old painting may make the old paint look new. Conversely, low temperature oven heating of new paint can sometimes accelerate aging to simulate old paint.

The black light is, however, invaluable. Some careful dealers even avoid purchasing a picture with an opaque varnish that prevents examination by black light. Other types of varnish than opaque are available to the conservator, so use of opaque varnish is a conscious choice that might suggest a desire to hide the extent of the repaint. At the least, opaque varnish is applied without regard to the investigatory needs of a later buyer.

Forgeries

The use of black light is not limited to an examination of condition. It is also to check for forgeries. On the illegal market, the traffic in forged and stolen art is said to be second only to that of narcotics in criminal activity. While Thomas Moran was so protective of his reputation he stuck his fingerprint alongside his signature on some of his paintings, other artists were not as careful.

Forgeries of paintings generally take one of three forms—copying an original by a famous painter, creating a new picture in the painter's style and signing the painter's name, or subverting a painting by a lesser artist by substituting the signature of a more well-known painter.

Copies of originals come up frequently. You may for example see four Remington copies for one painting or drawing that is real. Many copies were done as exercises, without fraudulent intent, by young artists seeking to learn by following successful techniques, but there was also a little basement factory in Chicago in the 1930s, set up by the son of a famous

18. John N. Marchand. "Prospectors." Pastel on board, 19 by 17 inches.

poet to forge Remingtons. Some Remington bookplates forged there are still in the collections of important museums.

Forging a wholly new picture is the most difficult. The subject is usually a combination of elements taken from several genuine pictures, but once in awhile an adventuresome forger is moved to compose a painting the famous artist could never have conceived, like a Remington still-life.

Changing signatures is the easiest forgery. A signed J.N. Marchand (1875–1921) painting of a cowgirl turned up as a signed Charles Marion Russell, reappeared as unsigned, and then finally metamorphosed into a signed Marchand once again, guaranteed to be authentic. Marchand's work is also a typical origin of Remington forgeries, as is George Varian's (1865–1923) work.

Occasionally, signatures are added when the painting is not a forgery. There is a notorious instance in the 1960s of a lecturer in a conservation class at a major museum demonstrating how to clean a painting. He accidentally wiped off a Corot (1796–1875) signature, and then claimed the painting must have been a forgery because the signature was fleeting. The painting was real, however, and the signature was reapplied by another hand, thus ending with a forged signature on a good painting.

There is even an instance where an untrained restorer cut off a damaged area in a painting, including the signature, and then glued the signature fragment to the reverse instead of forging the name on the front as might be expected in such a botch.

Fakes are funny. There are ingenuous collectors who cannot believe a forger will go to great trouble for a small return, failing to understand that there are forgers who just relish deception. Forging can be a compulsion.

A dealer once bought tens of thousands of dollars of museum-grade paintings from the agent for an outstanding estate, and then saw on the agent's table a beautiful piece of antique whaling scrimshaw which the agent said came from the same estate. In addition to the paintings, the dealer bought the old scrimshaw for a couple of hundred dollars and marvelled at its aura until a casual visitor proudly declared that he was the man who had carved and aged the scrimshaw for the agent.

As another example, a dealer had a customer who bought a large number of paintings of good quality. He did not connect the fact that all the paintings were unsigned until the customer's associate was arrested for forgery.

The reverse of the coin is the collector who says he can't afford an original Norman Rockwell painting, for example, so he knowingly buys a forgery because it is as close as he can get to the real thing.

Distinguishing the Fakes _____

Fakes can be hard to pick out. Infrequently, one piece of the work of a listed artist is so bad, you think it must be counterfeit. At other times, the work of a forger is so good, you think it must be real.

The muddy area in the middle is the hardest to pin down. If you doubt the authenticity of a painting you want to buy, contact the appropriate curator of your local museum. Museums say they help collectors, and important collectors state that they rely on curators for "informal opinions." See what your museum will do for you.

Independent experts are also available. If your museum curator won't give you the same kind of attention that a major collector gets from him, he should at least refer you to the one expert who covers your field. Ask the expert in advance what his fee is, and then furnish a color transparency, black and white glossy, provenance, and all other details you can think of.

Your own specialization, however, is your primary protection. It at least lets you know the names of the artists who are frequently forged.

If you do buy a forgery and can prove it, some auction houses will refund your money as long as your claim is timely. Some allow five years, some five days. Ethical dealers will stand behind what they sell—forever.

Those are the guaranties of the trade on authenticity, but as we have seen, the volunteered guaranties of neither the auction house nor the dealer yet extend to condition. To protect the collector, auction houses and dealers should publish the condition report which is recommended here for every picture, classifying the state of the work from fine to poor.

Otherwise, collectors must take it on themselves to demand that a guaranty of condition be incorporated in every bill of sale. If buyers do not protect themselves as to condition, they cannot properly be called investors because they may be buying art with hidden defects that has no investment value at all.

CHAPTER 13

The Theory of Appraisal

This chapter is about appraisal of works of art, and how appraisal relates to price. Price is the amount of money asked for or paid in a sale. It is what makes the art business go. It is a fact.

Compared to the reality of price, appraisal is the theory that precedes or succeeds it. Price and appraisal are thus different, yet linked as opposite sides of the same coin. Appraisal is a function of the experts who provide advice about art in terms of money, whereas price is a function of money itself. If the art business was a horse race, appraisers would be handicappers and investors would be bettors.

Informal Evaluations

Determining when you need an appraisal is like any other occasion for deciding about engaging a professional service. If you are considering purchasing a work of art and you are not yet confident of your own ability to determine its worth, you may want advice concerning the reasonableness of the price. Such advice can be of different kinds, informal as well as formal.

Suppose you are buying from a gallery, and the price of a bronze you want is $3,000. The dealer could for all you know be asking $3,000 for a $300 piece, particularly if the condition of the work is not disclosed. For that reason, you might start your exploration of worth with an exercise in informal evaluation, by enlisting the dealer to tell you how he arrived at his asking price. After overcoming his professional reluctance and discounting his commercial bias, you may learn something of the appraising/pricing process.

If you are considering buying an art work at auction, you should have the pre-sale estimate as a guide. Like the dealer's asking price, this is also a self-serving evaluation, but you may proceed with some confidence because pre-sale estimates influence sales prices, even when they are wrong. To check on the process of appraising for auction, ask the house staff how they arrived at their estimate. Auction houses keep elaborate price records and can swamp you with data.

Needing an Appraisal

There may be a time, however, when you have had this informal explanation from a dealer or an auction house and you still have doubts. This is when you can properly call a professional appraiser for advice, assuming the piece involved is worth the expense. The Berninghaus painting that passed at an auction where the minimum pre-sale estimate was $20,000 was soon re-offered through a gallery at $50,000. What will the auction house then say about value? What will the offering dealer say? What was the painting really worth? An appraiser might tell you, if he is qualified.

As a simple example of when you might need an appraisal, every valuable work of art that you own should be insured. For fine arts protection, however, the insurance carrier will initially prefer to cover no more than the amount you paid, as shown on your bill of sale, rather than conforming to an appraisal giving the higher value you might prefer. A purchase is an actual event. An appraisal is an opinion, and insurance carriers are aware of the practice of doubling retail value for an insurance appraisal.

In a couple of years, however, the worth of your art work should be reviewed to determine replacement value. That worth can be determined only by appraisal.

You also may need an appraisal when a jointly owned work of art is to be retained by one of the parties, as in a family facing separation or in a partnership undergoing dissolution.

In addition, when you want to dispose of a work of art, an auction house will provide a tentative written estimate for the piece or a dealer will tell you what he will pay or what consignment value he will set. You might wish to have an appraiser check these.

Alternately, you may need an appraisal for tax purposes when you make a gift of art. If the recipient is an institution like a museum, the curator will probably furnish you with a high valuation by an appraiser to induce you to donate the piece. If you are making the gift to a member of your family, though, you may be looking for an appraisal on the low side, as would your executors, for any estate tax evaluation which might be required.

As you can see, the appraisers are likely to get you at some point, either when you are coming into the market or when you are being carried out. They might even get you more than once, when the prices of art you own are volatile.

Finding an Appraiser

If you are bringing an appraiser into your home to show him your valuables, it is obvious that you should be careful about disclosing where you keep them. There are always rumors of burglaries following visits by unprofessional appraisers.

To find a reliable appraiser, you can ask for recommendations from museum curators, conservators, auction houses, or galleries. Curators and conservators are ethically precluded from appraising and so may make unbiased references, while many dealers are themselves appraisers. So are auction house employees.

You should also get lists of local members of the American Society of Appraisers and the Appraisers Association of America, although these members can be dealers too rather than full-time appraisers. Auction house staffers usually avoid such memberships.

There are about 120,000 active appraisers in the United States. There is no federal or state regulation of them, but 30 percent of the appraisers belong to professional societies. Half of these members have demonstrated the qualifications necessary to be certified by their societies. Being certified, however, does not mean the appraiser is an expert in your specialization in art.

Authenticity and Condition

In making your choice of an appraiser, be certain you pick one who has the correct background for you. Many appraisers are so broad in their scope they cannot tell a painting from a print. Some will not disclose their inexperience voluntarily. There are appraisers who are members of professional associations who advertise themselves as experts on buying, restoration, selling, and even on teaching you how to avoid unqualified appraisers, when they themselves are not experts on much beyond how to advertise.

Be sure, too, that your appraiser is willing and able to provide an opinion on critical issues like authenticity and condition. Some appraisers will not, and most appraisers could not. Although one appraisal society has claimed "it is important that the appraiser be knowledgeable in counselling the client to avoid poor investment and to recognize sleepers," such a claim is pretension as well as a conflict of interest.

Ethical and legal problems abound. Auction houses may make high initial estimates, to induce the owners to sell at auction. Appraisers who are dealers could have an interest in buying the works they appraise. There are estate appraisals where the dealer has valued a highly salable piece at a low amount and a piece with little commercial interest at a high amount, hoping to be able to buy the salable one from the estate.

There are also possibilities for fraud. The director of a Southwestern museum of art, for example, recently publicized the circumstances surrounding a gift of three modern paintings and a Degas bronze to the museum in 1974. The donor had bought the pieces from a New York City dealer for $101,000, along with an appraisal of $265,000 the donor had used for his tax writeoff.

The dealer himself was the appraiser, giving as credentials his senior membership in one of the leading appraisal societies. Unfortunately for the museum, the three paintings and the bronze all proved to be forgeries currently worth a total of about $120 for the frames. The donor had died in the interim, so no civil claim was made against the dealer or his alleged supplier in Lichtenstein.

Even legitimate appraisers are practical men. If the insured has paid a substantial amount for an unsigned art work he attributes to a famous artist, an appraiser will normally go along with the amount paid as the starting point for insurance coverage. He would not question the attribution.

After the owner dies, one would expect the picture to be reexamined for authenticity and then perhaps classified as an unsigned picture of just decorative value for any estate purpose. That kind of investigation is not likely to happen, however. It is easier for the appraiser to stay with the attribution than it is to come forward with bad news.

In recent years, the resolution of the appraiser's fee has become an ethical question. Auction houses usually provide either a free informal oral estimate or a formal written appraisal for a fee. The informal estimate tells you only whether an employee of unknown competence believes your art work has any value. The formal appraisal is more precise, and there lies the basis of the quarrel about the computation of the fee.

By long practice, some auction houses have based their fees on a percentage of value. One percent is usual, with a minimum. It is then in the appraiser's interest to set high levels to justify the appraisal process, elevate the fee, and titillate the owner.

For that reason, some appraisal societies have stated that percentage fees are improper and should be replaced by hourly charges or flat fees. These might range from $50 per simple item brought to the appraiser, to $1,000 per day per appraiser. There may still be a minimum charge.

You should negotiate in advance the type of fee most fitting for you.

Is Value Value?

After you have established the basis for the fee, you must acquaint the appraiser with the reason for the evaluation. Theoretically, value is value. Fair market value, retail value, and replacement value might be pretty much the same amount, even if arrived at by different routes.

Evaluation for a conventional auction could be less, though, with evaluation for a foreclosure sale or a liquidation one step below. An appraisal to justify a price in buying from a dealer would not be the same as arriving at a price to sell to a dealer.

The appraiser is necessarily a theoretician. A work of art generally has no raw material or hourly labor cost to be computed. Instead, putting a value on a work of art comes down to who did it and what did he do, compared to what he has previously done.

This makes appraising works of art more subjective than appraising real estate parcels, for example. In contrast to land sales, there is no comparable public record of art dealers' asking prices or selling prices to use as guidelines. In a few areas like Santa Fe, dealers do mark asking prices on pictures hung for sale, but you never know whether the picture sold at all, or if it did, what the difference was between the asking and the selling price.

Using Auction Prices

On the other hand, auction prices are published records, regularly available to appraisers as their primary data source. Since these auction prices are pretty much all the appraiser has to go by, he is forced to use them, but the problems are numerous.

If past records show only one sale of a work that is comparable because it is by the same artist of a similar subject in the same medium, for instance, that one price will be less meaningful than an array of prices would be. Also, unless the appraiser had attended the exhibition, he didn't see the art itself. He doesn't know condition. Moreover, unless he attended the sale, he can't know whether the work was bought by a collector at full value or by a dealer for resale.

To do his job, a professional appraiser of art should have Mayer's annual *International Auction Records* or its equivalent for five years or so, as well as both the individual auction catalogs referred to in the annual records and the catalogs for current sales not yet annualized. Hislop's *Auction Prices of American Artists* takes you from 1970 to 1982 in three volumes.

The appraiser should be recording any bit of data that might help him later. Where dealers disclose asking prices in galleries and in advertisements, for example, he should list the amounts on a blank page interleafed in his copy of the annual *Auction Records*.

Also, an appraiser must be able to interpret the prices realized. The annual *Auction Records* does not disclose whether a picture was signed or whether authenticity was guaranteed—two major factors—and the books don't list the works that were passed. This is why he needs the old catalogs summarized in the *Records*. In addition, he needs the current catalogs to keep abreast of trends.

Equally important, an appraiser must be able to project values. When prices are rising or falling rapidly, an appraiser has to make estimates that will be correct for their future use. The only appraisers likely to have the data and the knowledge needed are those with the galleries and the auction houses, both of which may have conflicts of interest.

Oversimplified Examples

Let's try some oversimplified examples of appraisals based on comparable auction prices. Suppose you are asked to appraise a 14 by 8 inch Frederic Remington wash drawing of a posed Canadian soldier, not signed or dated but illustrated in an 1890s magazine where it is reproduced exactly. There is no question of authenticity or condition.

To begin with, a wash drawing is worth more than a line drawing, but less than a watercolor, gouache, or oil. A Canadian soldier is worth almost as much as an American soldier, even in the United States, but lack of action in the pose is a severe limitation. A soldier is not as valuable as a Remington Indian. The absence of a signature removes about a third of value, even where authenticity is clear.

To apply these principles, look at the annual *Auction Records* and then at the catalogs named there. Despite the mass of Remington sales at auction, there isn't much that is relevant. In 1977, a signed 20 by 9 inch wash drawing titled "My Comrade" was described as a portrait of Charles Russell. At the sale, the auctioneer recanted on Russell as the subject, inasmuch as Remington never met Russell, but the denial does not appear on the records.

The pre-sale estimate was $4,000 to $6,000, a fair value, but the drawing sold for $8,000, elevated perhaps because of the Russell connection. By 1982, its real value would have increased from about $5,000 to about $12,000. The picture of the Canadian soldier is smaller and unsigned and thus is worth $6,000 to $7,500 in comparison.

As a second example, a signed 10½ by 8 inch Remington wash drawing of the head of an Arab sold in 1979 for $3,500, a little above fair value, and would be worth $5,000 to $6,000 in 1982. Although unsigned, the Canadian soldier is bigger and twice as desirable a subject, substantiating about $7,500 as its relative worth.

As a third and more remote comparison, a 14 by 8 inch Remington oil on canvas called "Infantry Officer" sold for $19,000 in 1981. The pre-sale estimate was a fair value at $8,000 to $12,000 for this painting in color, but the auction catalog did not reveal that the officer appeared to be German, a subject worth far less than an American or Canadian soldier.

To an appraiser, this data for the three comparisons taken together might justify a figure of between $6,000 and $7,500 for the unsigned drawing of the Canadian soldier, with the leaning toward the higher amount.

Until You Sell the Picture

Obviously, the conclusion is subjective, an opinion, and not hard fact. Until you have actually sold the very picture, you don't really know exactly what the picture is worth, and even then, you can't be absolutely sure.

As another example, suppose you are appraising a 10 by 12 inch oil on board of a horse in Taos painted by Oscar Berninghaus, a 1920s artist of rapidly growing stature. A small oil by Berninghaus is about twice as valuable as a watercolor and five or six times as valuable as a Berninghaus drawing. A sketch of a horse tied to a rail is worth much less than an action scene or an Indian.

There are plenty of recent sales of Berninghaus pictures at auction. In 1979, a pair of small oils sold for $1,800, so you might expect they would at most bring $1,800 each in 1981. Instead, small Indian oils sold for $12,000 in 1981, small watercolors with Indian action for $6,000 to $7,750, and small drawings including horses for $1,500 to $2,200.

Because these prices seem so remarkably high, and unidentified passive horses have historically been such weak subjects, an appraisal would be modified to a conservative $6,000 to $7,500, depending on the quality of the actual painting. This is again a subjective judgment based on experience, and one that flies in the face of data that could be read as justifying $12,000.

Continuing with small sizes, a dealer has a 10 by 14 inch oil on paper signed Bierstadt, a field sketch for a well-known painting of a named Colorado mountain in a museum collection. The dealer thinks the painting is worth $4,900. A Bierstadt oil on paper usually brings about a third of an oil on canvas done in the studio, and the higher values go to paintings with figures. A named place is a plus, as is a sketch for an identified painting.

Bierstadt oils on paper have been selling in quantity at auction. A painting 4¼ by 7½ inches titled "Sunset on the Prairies" brought a remarkable $22,000, while a 9 by 11¾ inch painting called "Hills" brought a paltry $900. Eliminating these two aberrations,—you should normally delete the high and the low amounts where there is an array—the remaining range is $2,800 to $4,250. The appraisal would be about $4,000, not too far below the asking price if this could be your "best choice."

The Formal Appraisal

The appraisal itself should be a formal document, on a business letterhead, made out to the owner of the art work at his address. The piece should be described in enough detail to preclude confusion with any other piece, giving size, medium, description of subject, signature, date, condition, title, frame, and distinguishing marks.

After the statement of value and an outline of how, in general, it was arrived at, a listing of the appraiser's qualifications should appear. In our increasingly litigious society, appraisers are being sued for malpractice resulting from error and omission so the appraiser might want to take a long last look at his document before signing and dating it.

For the benefit of their clients, appraisers should be independent professionals, preferably not dealers or auction houses, who are willing to specialize in the way that collectors do. The expert on Charles Marion Russell might also know a good bit about Frederic Remington, if not as much as the Remington specialist would.

He would be less likely to be qualified on the American Impressionist Childe Hassam (1859–1935) who painted at the same time. He would probably know even less about European artists of the period, and should not appraise their work if the undertaking is at all complex.

Instead of being all things to all objects, the appraiser needs to limit himself to one field of art where he can really specialize, and perhaps then function nationally. Local appraisers should be willing to call on such an expert for help.

One reason why appraisers do not specialize more is that they don't have to. Insurance companies, for example, will take the word of any nominally qualified professional appraiser. They will not accept your own appraisal, however, regardless of your qualifications, so you should feel free to let your professional appraiser have the benefit of your experience, whether he willingly accepts your advice or not.

He may have less expertise concerning your things than you do.

CHAPTER 14

The Reality of Price

Appraisals are a paradox. They are based on broadly comparable past prices, but not on appraisals, even though an examination of how prices are arrived at may lead you to believe that appraisals can be closer to real value than prices are. Appraisers adjust haphazard facts to try to find truth in pricing, because the processes determining prices may be untidy and sometimes even fly in the face of value.

Appraisal and Pricing

When a dealer sets an asking price for a painting, he starts with the equivalent of an appraisal, but from then on, actual selling prices may take a random course.

Dealers' asking prices set their own maximum levels. Dealers can't get more than they ask for. In contrast, their minimum levels are what they paid for the objects they own. Although the prices they paid may be unrelated to value, dealers cannot regularly charge less than they paid and stay in business.

In addition to what the dealer paid, dealer pricing is also an informal reflection of relevant recent prices—their own, other dealers', and auction prices. These establish comparability. For true comparability in pricing, some of the prices of pieces bought at auction may have to be marked up because many dealers buy stock at auction. Auction prices are their costs.

Within the range of prices so calculated, the dealer's ultimate selection of the final asking price is by gut feeling, a kind of pricing by the seat of one's art-conditioned pants. If the work is a very good one in the opinion of the dealer, it will be offered at the top of the range, a modified version of whatever the traffic will bear. After all, the price can always come down. Poorer quality pieces will be priced low, to move them.

When the dealer holds art on consignment, the same pricing factors should apply, except that they may be judged from the consignor's viewpoint of what he paid and his analysis of comparability.

Left to himself, the dealer will tend to price consigned merchandise on the low side, to sell it quicker, particularly if the consignor is willing to accept a lower price to get prompt action. To the dealer, his percentage of $1,000 is not much different from his percentage of $1,200.

Auction Houses Influence Prices

Auction houses are aggressive in their operations, able not only to recognize the economic factors of supply and demand but also to influence them. With respect to works done before 1950, you would expect the supply of art to be limited. Nevertheless, the auctions gather a large number of pieces for sale.

The houses tend to hire employees with family connections which may put them in contact with important art collections. They scour the country to join with local charities for "discovery days." In good times, the houses advertise the high prices that will accrue to the greedy. In bad times, they sell for the needy. They also emphasize beneficial tax changes such as the easing of levies on transfers.

The houses do get some of the finest art works to sell, and they are experienced in making the most out of what they get. They issue elaborate color catalogs and turn their major evening sales into newsworthy social events, to reward the consignors and to entice the buyers. The houses insist that the merchandise for sale be prettied up, restored, and reframed as necessary to show the best face to the customers. As the auctions get to be more sophisticated, the catalog descriptions become more creative in their promotional aspects.

Even then, though, the quantity of fine art at auction may not meet the demand in a seller's market, expecially when influenced by concern about inflation. The individual collector is persuaded that art prices will never come down, because the art market is said to be insulated from business cycles. Top quality art, he has been told, will never lose value.

In addition, we are in an American era of conspicuous consumption, evidenced by the newly rich who equate the acquisition of art with social standing. There is also the beginning of foreign buying of American art, even when economic conditions abroad are weak and the American dollar is strong. Moreover, there is an unpublicized wave of art buying by funds, trusts, and businesses. And finally, dealers are always forced to buy at auction. They need stock, and auctions get many of the best works. All of these factors push auction prices up, in good times.

High prices bring still more works into the market. Even the dealers sometimes sell special pieces at auction when they expect to derive more money from competitive bidding than they can get at retail in their galleries.

In turn, the auction houses capitalize on the high prices by announcing the setting of price records as if the price levels were art news. Sotheby claimed to have set 26 price records at its October 17, 1980 sale and another 26 on November 13, 1980, all to huzzahs from the press. The promotion fans flames, so works that have recently sold at auction soon come back up on the block again to let the new owners get their shares of snowballing profits.

Protecting Buyers on Price

The auction houses are thus cultivating the supply of quality art work and at the same time stiffening the demand. The question is, then, how does the collector protect himself on price during such a feverish period? With restraint, of course, in the exercise of his knowledge and experience, employed within the framework of his specialization.

The serious collector understands what quality is for him personally, and isn't afraid of price, within a reasonable level above fair value. As an example, five years ago a museum held a silent auction to de-accession a Homer watercolor. The director solicited closed bids from known dealers and collectors. When all the bids were opened, the highest would take the watercolor.

A doctor who asked a dealer to bid for him was told that the probable value of the watercolor was $35,000. It was recommended that he bid $51,000 to be sure of winning, because a picture of such quality and provenance was not likely to be offered again soon. The watercolor would surely be the doctor's best.

The picture is now worth about $150,000, and the doctor owns it. The price he bought at merely determined how long he had to hold the work to make a profit, not whether a profit could be made. When he bought high, he had to wait longer, but he gained more.

Painterly and Commercial Factors

In general, however, the scenario that some sellers describe of a constant price rise in the art market is fictitious. The buyer should be aware that while some people say anything old has value and will be worth more tomorrow than today, age alone doesn't make value in art. Otherwise, American portraits from the end of the eighteenth century would be worth relatively more than American Impressionist paintings from the end of the nineteenth century, instead of much less.

The art market does fluctuate with the national economy, as we have seen, within a modified format and on a delayed basis for downturns. Every work of art, though, is unique, and apart from fluctuations due to the economy, individual prices vary because of both objective and subjective elements.

The objective elements affecting price are of two types. The first is the intrinsic or painterly factors such as quality, size, shape, medium, subject, period, condition, and the identity of the artist. These are the usual bases for appraisal.

The second objective element affecting price is the external or commercial factors such as provenance, exhibitions, promotions, fads, auction sales, and chance.

As an intrinsic factor, a child with a cat is usually a more valuable subject than a solitary child, who is better than a young woman, who is better than an older woman, who is better than a man.

In period, you want an early Corot and a late Twachtman. You want Bierstadt's American scenes rather than European. In Sotheby's June 19, 1981 auction, for example, lot 278 was a resale of C.C. Curran's (1861–1942) "Cloud Drama." The painting had sold at auction in 1977 for $1,500. A later cleaning of the painting exposed a seated figure, and the 1981 sale estimated at $3,000 to $4,000 brought $12,000. Figures add value.

The next lot, Hayley Lever's "Landscape with Tilling Machine," was estimated at $2,000 to $3,000 and brought only $1,200, the lowest relative amount of all the Levers in the sale. The shape was 33½ by 17 inches, too long and too narrow. Difficult shapes depress prices, an evidence of the impact of intrinsic factors.

As an example of an external factor, the second of these objective elements, a dealer who can get a reference to a painting he owns into the text of a landmark catalog has made money, and an illustration of the painting in the catalog is a virtual guarantee of more money. A dealer can promote the quality work of a second-tier artist into high prices within three years, if he can upgrade the artist's reputation through exhibitions and with publicity.

And on top of all of these intrinsic factors and external factors realistically affecting price in a relatively predictable fashion, there is this random psychological determinant, the feeling in your gut. What else explains the variations you find that can increase prices to 20 times reasonable expectations?

Estimating Auction Prices

The best exercise for learning how real prices are arrived at is to take an auction catalog, say that same June 19, 1981 Sotheby sale. Pick an illustrated art work of interest to you. Study the picture and the catalog entry, and guess what the lot will bring at auction.

For example, lot number 104 is a pair of marine watercolors by Edmund Darch Lewis (1835–1910) with guaranteed authenticity. One of the pair is medium in size, the other large. Both are what a Lewis watercolor should be, scenes of sailing, and they are done competently, as near as can be learned from the illustration.

According to the *Auction Records*, similar appearing Lewis watercolors have recently brought about $1,000 each. Consequently, a safe estimate would be about $1,500 for the pair, and if you agree, you should record this amount alongside the illustration.

Next, look up the pre-sale estimate and write it above your guess. In this instance, the Sotheby pre-sale estimate is only $800 to $1,200. Should the pronouncement by the experts change your mind? There is nothing in the data at hand to suggest that. This seems to be an estimate for one watercolor, not two. It may be the house estimator did not notice that lot 104 is a pair, or perhaps the physical condition is poor, but in an exercise like this, you have to assume that estimates fit facts and condition is average.

If you accept $1,500 as your safe bidding level for the pair, the next step is to decide what these pictures mean to you. If they are not within your specialization, forget them, although they might be a profitable venture for a generalist.

If these watercolors could be among your best, however, then perhaps you should consider a higher bid in order to make a serious stab at buying them. Although a pair like this one usually brings less than the sum of the paintings sold individually, these seem to be worth at least $2,000, and one bid above that could be your personal buying level.

The final step in your practicing the technique of pricing art at auction is to check the actual selling price. It was $2,100, so you appear to have been on target.

If you were not close, however, it will be necessary for you to re-examine your first guess. Check the factors given in the catalog. You might for example have missed whether the painting was signed. Look to see how close to the house's pre-sale estimate you were. The house's estimates may well be truer than the prices. The question is, how do you explain the difference between your guess and the actual price? What can you learn from the exercise?

Lot number 73 in the same sale is "Study of Rocks" by Asher B. Durand (1796–1886), signed with initials and dated '69. Provenance is a New York Gallery and reference is made to the Durand *Catalogue* in which this painting was presumably listed. That seems great. The *Auction Records* indicates a level for this sort of Durand at $4,500, and if you agree, this is the guess you should write down for fair value. The pre-sale estimate is in line at $4,000 to $6,000.

Just a minute, though. A little star precedes the painter's name in the catalog, and this means that authorship is "ascribed" to the artist, not guaranteed by the auction house, despite the provenance from the gallery. The fact that the lot finally sold for only $3,000 is an obvious indication of weakness.

The amount of the price, however, is irrelevant. If the auction house in its capacity as selling agent would not guarantee authenticity, why should an investor buy the painting at any price? A painting not supported by the house or its gallery of origin is not usually appropriate for an investor.

An Incredible Price

Lot number 130A is "Reading by the Shore," an 11¾ by 18 inch oil on canvas signed Charles Sprague Pearce (1851–1914) but not dated. The picture is illustrated in color on the cover of the catalog, showing a fully dressed young woman reclining on the beach while reading.

Pearce was a second-tier painter of the 1890s, an Associate of the National Academy but not an innovator. Before this sale, his paintings had seldom appeared at auction. In 1974, a painting called "The Grape Harvest" that was three times the size of "Reading by the Shore" sold for $1,100. In 1978, a masterwork called "Tea Time" sold for $13,500.

The use of "Reading by the Shore" as the cover of the catalog was bound to influence the estimate, and our figure of $15,000 seemed appropriately high. Sotheby's pre-sale estimate was $10,000 to $15,000, a range in line with past prices.

The actual sales price, however, was $225,000, almost 20 times the estimate. There is no obvious explanation for this incredible amount, but the price realized will certainly influence the appraisal of the next similar Pearce that comes up.

Price Is a Funny Cat

The Pearce painting is an extreme example of the process of "doubling" in buying art, where your specialization can lead you to an especially undervalued field you can concentrate on. That way, you can not only obtain the benefits of the growth in art values that are available to everyone, but also you can secure an extra return as a bonus for your insight. You can double your profit.

Pearce was a predictable star, if not of the magnitude that developed. Superb paintings of his were featured in the illustrated books of the Columbian Exposition in Chicago in 1893, and might have led you to him years ago.

As another example of doubling, paintings of the American West are a field of art investment that has proved to be very profitable. The question for doubling is, where within that field will the greatest upward movement take place?

You might decide the top Western illustrators will make the largest gains, relatively speaking, and that painters like N.C. Wyeth and Harvey Dunn (1884–1952) would be typical. If you are right, buying their pictures will give you the profits that Western pictures in general are getting, plus a special reward for your perspicacity about illustrators.

A second Western investor might analyze the field and take doubling a step farther, buying Ed Ward illustrations of the 1920s in the belief that Ward was as good as Wyeth or Dunn and is particularly undervalued today. Ward's pictures would not only gain as Westerns and as illustrations, but they would also gain because Ward has not yet had his full rise compared to his peers, Wyeth and Dunn. When you choose the right picture by the right painter in the right category, doubling offers rewards in art not quite like other investments.

You can even be an art detective and seek out the estates of these listed painters with promise of doubling. The works of good listed artists are still out there, waiting undiscovered in forgotten places, and you can join the ranks of the researchers who are looking for them.

A young researcher discovered a reference to the estate of the Civil War illustrator Alfred Waud (1828–1891) and located a whole batch of Waud drawings. With them, he found an even more important group of

19. Edmund F. Ward. "Prairie Child," 1921. Grisaille oil on board, 32 by 40 inches.

paintings by the explorer-artist Frederick Dellenbaugh (1853–1935), along with the personal papers and libraries of both artists and Dellenbaugh's personal collection of paintings of fine artists of the period like Helen Turner (1858–?), the American Impressionist. This one find launched a career.

Doubling in art investment is like betting on a long shot in the horse racing analogy, in that the winnings can be substantial. The distinction is that in racing, you are likely to lose your whole stake, whereas in art, every knowledgeable buyer with patience wins. Only the amounts differ.

If Ed Ward paintings do not take the huge rise in price that you expect, they will at least give you the big increase most good Western art works are finding. Art handicappers have it all over the horse race touts.

As we have been saying, price is a funny cat. Only five of twenty-five Winslow Homer paintings were sold at his Knoedler exhibition in 1909, despite the $300 price his work commanded then. Homer died in 1910. By 1918, Knoedler had sold a Homer watercolor for $1,500 and his oils were bringing $20,000. Today, his top oils are priced at more than $1,000,000, and you can bet that one or two of the 1909 buyers of Homers predicted what has happened, and profited by doubling.

20. Frederick Dellenbaugh. "Kadiak," 1899. Oil on millboard, 5⅝ by 9⅛ inches.

CHAPTER 15

Auction
–A Classic Confrontation

Viewed simplistically, an auction is a classic confrontation between an auctioneer and his audience, the bidders. The word "auction" is from the Latin "to increase," and increase is the name of the game.

Acting for the seller who is his client and for himself, the auctioneer makes every effort to raise the price of the object "on the block," while the bidders, who are sometimes acting in concert, seek to dampen the action. In essence, the auctioneer cajoles, reads bids off the wall, changes tempo, and threatens, while the buyers resist opening the bidding, stall, combine, and try to halve the bidding jumps. Even in the high-class auction houses, this fundamental conflict between the auctioneer and the bidders is the gist of the action, although there the roughness is glossed over with camouflage and refinement.

Auctions over the Years

Auctions are one aspect of the art business where the process of selling is generally older than the product, which is the art work sold. Sales to the highest bidder were conducted in antiquity. Four thousand years ago, the Babylonians auctioned maidens for marriage. The Roman quaestors auctioned war booty including captives: In England, there was "candlestick" bidding in the eighteenth century, the winner being the one making the highest offer before the wick fell.

Over the years, the English practice that was the basis for the American system evolved into an advertised event with a printed catalog listing the conditions of sale. The auctioneer was licensed. At the sale, he stood on a platform and "put" the "lots" up on the block in sequence. Lots are generally one item, but can be a group. He took bids on each lot from the bidders, in increments varied by him to attain the highest ultimate bid.

Misrepresentation by the auctioneer was illegal, and he was forbidden to "run up" the price through fictitious bids.

The owner could not bid unless expressly permitted to do so by the conditions of sale, while a bid from the floor was only an offer and could be withdrawn until accepted by the auctioneer. Where the sale was without a stipulated minimum amount called the "reserve," which was not disclosed to the bidders, or where the reserve had been met, the auctioneer was compelled to sell to the highest bidder. He "knocked down" the lot, ending the bidding, with a tap of his gavel, at the "hammer" price, the amount of the winner's bid. A lot that had no bidder or that did not meet the reserve was "bid in" or "passed."

A Shady Proceeding

The auctioneer's chief personal risk was that he might knock down property stolen or otherwise not owned by the consignor. While the auctioneer does not guarantee good title to the lots he sells, questionable ownership diminishes the house's credibility.

For many years, the auction bore the stigma of a shady proceeding, particularly in the sale of personal property. The cheating that occurred led to a loose regulation in England and in states and cities in this country, by imposing license fees, limiting frequency and hours of sales, controlling obvious fraud, and barring transients from the business.

In order to overcome their immoral image and take on the trappings of legitimacy, the auction houses assumed the appearance of gentility. The most successful auction houses in America became impeccably British.

Today, New York City is the world's auction capital. Most of the major international auction houses are represented, along with many local houses. Anything of value is accepted for the block, from Napoleon's penis to Queen Victoria's knickers, but the most important market is in fine art, particularly Impressionist paintings.

The auction house employees who are up front to meet the public are former debutantes, the younger sons of wealthy families, and poor nobles, or at least they act that way. Bryn Mawr and Columbia art history majors do the work.

As the cleverer employees learn where the art, the sellers, and the buyers are, they go on to open their own shops. They become independent art dealers because no salary can compete with entrepreneurial rewards.

The Motif of the Sale

The motif of the auction sale is streamlined elegance on plain pipe racks. The setting is free theater where high drama plays before an audience that is either social or wealthy or both. A revolving turntable on the stage moves the lots in and out quickly. On a screen above the auctioneer, bids in dollars are electronically converted into six foreign currencies. Out-of-town bidders are plugged in via telephone.

The hoopla is hell on collectors. The auction houses conduct classes in how to bid, with practice sessions using play money, but nevertheless the emotional pressure at the actual sales is so intense that many amateur buyers run the danger of giving in to that "just one more bid" syndrome. In addition, at every sale some inexperienced bidder is so anxious to purchase a particular lot that any prolonged pause after his bid startles him into instinctively bidding again without waiting for the competition, thereby bidding against himself if the auctioneer permits it.

John Howat, who is a curator at the Metropolitan Museum of Art, has recommended that you "beware the theater of the auction house. You may wake up Monday morning having had a Saturday romance that didn't wear well."

Getting good merchandise to sell is the heart of the auction business, and the houses are quite successful at the task. Procurement is a reason for hiring employees with connections to the old art collecting families. The newer collectors and investors, however, are the monied class, not necessarily high society, so the auction houses' art hunters have had to use more aggressive approaches while spreading a wider net.

The art hunters know who bought at auction over the years and who exhibited. They pay finder's fees for names disclosed to them by knowledgeable tipsters, and they travel the country on regular routes to meet with art owners who might be willing to sell at auction.

Beyond soliciting the sale of collections, teams of auction house experts beat the bushes around the country on "Heirloom Discovery Days" to turn up individual items worth putting on the block. It would have to be a remote town which would not have had its newspaper announce that on a given day, an auction house staff would be in a nearby public building to appraise any private person's treasured objects for a nominal five dollars each, to benefit a local charity and indirectly to flush out "pigeons" for the auction block.

Appraising for Auction

If you think you might want to sell art at auction and no auction house has been in touch with you, make the contact on your own. Before you do, though, you should have a good idea of what your art work is worth.

A few years ago, a Long Island dealer in Western art had an appointment with the experts in the Old Masters department of a major auction house to bring in a German painting by Angelica Kauffman (1740–1807) that had been acquired as a "throw in" on the purchase of a Thomas Moran (1837–1926) oil.

On the way to New York City, the dealer stopped in a shopping center parking lot to meet clients who had a pair of Old Master still-life paintings he had also agreed to buy. He paid for the still-lifes, although he was not sure of their authenticity, and took them along.

In the city, he did not want to leave the still-lifes unwrapped and unprotected in the rear of the car so he brought them into the auction house. The Old Master expert who came out paid no attention to the Kauffman at all but promptly gasped at the sight of the still-lifes and asked if they were for sale. Well, to a dealer, every art work is for sale, so he said yes. The expert wanted the pictures for an Old Master auction and offered an estimate of $3,000 for the pair.

Happily, the dealer had read the *International Auction Records* to learn what the pictures would be worth if they were genuine, and now the expert had implicitly established the authenticity. The only question left was money, so the dealer replied that $3,000 was insufficient.

The expert then offered $4,000 to $5,000. The dealer refused this estimate as well, so the expert went to his superior, who offered $8,000 to $10,000. The dealer refused that, too, and suggested a look at the records of their London office. They then offered $15,000 to $20,000 as the pre-sale estimate, and the dealer accepted that amount as consistent with the *Auction Records*.

As you can see, knowing the worth of what you have is essential. Otherwise, the inexperienced consignor could accept a pre-sale estimate at 20 percent of value. Apologists for the auction house would say that pre-sale estimates are just indications of value and the paintings would have found their own level at the sale. This is not likely to be correct, though, particularly when the variance in the estimates is so extreme.

An estimate far below the anticipated value would signal to the knowing buyer that there might be a flaw in the offering—perhaps something wrong with the condition or the quality of the pictures. Such a suspicion would survive any explanation.

Choosing the Auction House

Choosing the auction house to contact is a question similar to every other professional selection you have had to make. You will have to talk again to the museums, conservators, appraisers, and dealers to get specific recommendations to fit your situation. Try other collectors, too. Their requirements are more like yours than a museum's would be. What you have to decide is where you will be most comfortable, and which house will do the best job with your art.

This selection process may sound a bit like your travel agent's booking a flight to meet your time and destination requirements. There is no equivalent figure in art, however, to ease you into an auction house. You must make the arrangement on your own.

If your art work proves to be worth less than $300, there are auction houses that make a practice of getting inexpensive pieces onto the block within three weeks by eliminating the selling catalog in favor of a computer printout. An auction like this might be the one for you.

Or, when you check the recommended auction houses, you might find one with a sale coming up within three months that will just suit your art work. Your piece will fit right in.

Then, once you have settled on the auction house, the next step is for you to contact the appropriate division of the house, like nineteenth-century American paintings.

If you live nearby, phone and set up an appointment to bring the piece in. Otherwise, write a letter fully describing what you are offering and enclose both a glossy photography and a color slide or transparency, along with specifications and any other data you might have. The specialist assigned to you will tell you whether your work will be accepted for auction and if so, what the preliminary pre-sale estimate will be and approximately when the sale will take place.

Questions to Ask

You are entitled to ask any question that occurs to you. What you should know would include such matters as, first, how the specialist's estimate was arrived at. The auction house will say only that the amount is preliminary, but the real answer usually is that at this early stage, the figure was a high guesstimate, subject to review downward.

Second, which sale will include your art work? You should avoid an off-season or summer sale, a sale concentrating on lesser works than your own, an Americana sale that does not feature the kind of work you have, or any other "mixed bag" sale. In contrast to your goals, the auction house may be trying to fill the lists of the more difficult catalogs like the ones you should avoid.

Third, what will your lot number be? The opening and closing sections of a sale are the least desirable because bidders may be settling in or leaving, and a morning session is assigned lower estimated lots than the evening.

Fourth, will your art be illustrated in the catalog? If not, the sale will be less beneficial for you.

Fifth, will the authorship of your art work be guaranteed by the auction house? If not, why not? If you believe your piece to be authentic, it should not be offered in a sale where the authorship is not guaranteed.

Sixth, what title will be used for your work in the catalog? A title that "sings" helps sell, whether the idea was the artist's or yours.

Seventh, what provenance will be given?

And so on. While catalog copy is supposed to be strictly descriptive, you may prefer some forms of description to others.

The Amount of the Reserve

As you can see, there are many kinds of issues you ought to resolve, and you must be prepared to raise them. One of the most important is the amount of the reserve to be placed on your art. The auction house may give you the standard pap about your piece finding its proper price in a free market, regardless of the reserve, but if the pre-sale estimate is more than $1,000, you need the protection of the minimum selling level that constitutes the reserve. Without that, you might get only the liquidation value of your piece, or less, instead of the fair value that is your due.

The calculation of the actual reserve is a matter of negotiation. The auction house would prefer to have the lowest amount a consignor will permit, or no reserve, so that everything sells. The reserve is strictly for the benefit of the consignor.

In turn, the consignor wants the highest amount that will protect him, without impeding the sale. The usual reserve is about 70 percent of the mid-point of the range that is the pre-sale estimate. If the estimate is $1,000 to $1,500, then 70 percent of the mid-point is $875. The maximum reserve would usually be the top of the pre-sale estimate.

On higher valued art, consignors may shop from auction house to auction house to get the reserve that suits them. The auction houses have so far been hostile to each other, preventing them from establishing a "ring" to fix a ceiling on any one reserve, but this will change. Competition on reserves is bad business for auction houses because the higher the reserve the less the certainty of sale.

In an expanding economy, an elevated reserve is an important consideration, as we have seen, but not a tragic one. Rising prices cure high-side errors in setting reserves, simply through the passage of time. In a recession, though, the auction houses are beset. The articles they auction —apart from art—suffer quickly from lessened demand and put the houses under pressure. After awhile, art auctions are affected, too. The lesser works slack off, and the prices for major works may cease rising.

Then, errors in overstating reserves do become critical. Some of the major pieces do not sell because of unrealistic reserves, and the auction houses themselves lose strength. A few reduce their operations and others fail, until the house experts can negotiate more reasonable reserves with those consignors who become aware of the impact of the economic times on auction sales.

Double Agents

The auction house was exclusively the seller's agent until 1977. The seller generally paid about 20 percent commission on lots bringing less than $500, 15 percent up to $5,000, and 12½ percent over $5,000. Dealers could negotiate for a smaller fee.

Now, the seller and the buyer both pay approximately ten percent on most items. This is a boon for sellers who receive about seven percent more for their goods, and for auction houses which receive an increase of about a third in fees, but it is a new burden on the buyers. Dealers, who saw a conflict of interest for the double-agent auction houses, considered a boycott in protest of the change in fees but could not bring it off because they would have starved for merchandise.

In practice, an important seller may negotiate in advance the fee he is to pay, and on high priced lots he may pay little or nothing, if he is in a good bargaining position. The buyer must always pay the posted buyer's fee in full, however, because he has no relationship with the auction house on the lot he purchases until the sale to him is concluded.

The Printed Provisions

When you do take your art work in for auction, the printed conditions and recommendations concerning the auction sale will be handed to you by the house specialist. These provisions have grown from one page to four in recent years. They are in flux as they tip slowly in the buyer's favor.

The conditions of sale used to provide only that the auction house did not warrant correctness of description, genuineness, authenticity, or physical condition of the property, and that consignors reserve the right to bid. That was a complete disclaimer.

By the 1960s, the main change at more progressive auctions was that buyers' claims as to authenticity would be recognized, if made within ten days after the sale. Even by 1970, the only additional protection for the buyer was that he had 21 days to claim he had purchased a counterfeit.

By 1981, however, it was evident that a buyers' revolution was in progress, fostered by governmental investigations of the auction process in some states. The changing conditions of sale now guaranteed authorship under some circumstances, although the auction house was not required to guarantee the authorship of all art it sold—only of those pieces where it elected to specify that guaranties would exist. Other representations in the catalog including physical condition, size, provenance, etc. remained expressly excluded from the guaranty.

The term of any guaranty of authorship was spelled out as extending for five years, when applicable. After five years, the guaranty expired. Lots subject to reserves and lots owned by the auction house were to be so marked in the catalogs. Finally, oral condition reports on the art works were to be made available to bidders on request.

Terms Favor Sellers

The printed terms of sale are not negotiable. You have to accept them in order to sell at auction, although you can shop terms from auction house to auction house. Unless you are totally satisfied, you do not have to leave your art for sale. To this moment, you owe nothing to the auction house and you are free to take your piece and go.

Generally speaking, the terms are in your favor as a seller. After you sign the agreement to sell, though, the auction process is under way. In addition to the fee, you will have agreed to miscellaneous charges as they may be incurred for photography, crating, cartage, storage, insurance, and so on, and you may not be able to remove your art from the auction house before the sale without paying a cancellation charge.

You should also have received a receipt for your piece that spells out any defect or breakage, to protect you against what might happen to your work while it is in the custody of the auction house.

Closer to the date of the auction, you may receive a call from the house expert, seeking to revise the reserve downward. The reason you will be given is that other experts who have looked at your art work have expressed doubt about its marketability at the original amount. You do not have to agree.

This call can come at any time prior to the moment of sale because the reserve is not published in the catalog the way the pre-sale estimate is.

The Actual Auction

Before the auction is held, you will see a copy of the catalog, but you will probably not attend the actual sale. The seat you would occupy might keep a bidder out.

About one-third of the bidders will also be absentees. They will have left "order bids" with the house in advance, just as you have established the reserve as the counter step. The amounts of these order bids are written into the auctioneer's catalog, along with the "secret" reserve and the pre-sale estimate, so all of the house's data concerning both sellers and buyers is available to him.

The auctioneer asks the audience for an opening bid in an amount within his discretion that fits the monetary facts he has. Most bidders resist any opening, but there is generally a friend of the house to aid the auctioneer from the floor. Alternately, the auctioneer may read bids off the wall—that is, announce make-believe bids as real—until he reaches the order bid or the reserve, whichever is higher. When the bids do not make the reserve, the lot passes and is not recorded as a sale. As the consignor of the unsold lot, you pay a partial commission, unless the auction house volunteers to find you a private customer.

The gossip is that in the better sales, important buyers do not just raise their hands to bid like ordinary folks. They have secret signals prearranged with the auctioneer so the competition will be ignorant of their moves.

Stories like this are the basis for the old expert in the audience telling the tyro to take the tip of his index finger away from his nostril because that signal means he is raising the bid when the amount is already $55,000. Touching your left ear lobe with your right hand can be said to be dangerous, too, but it is all part of auction folklore, as far as you are concerned.

It is also claimed that at the smaller auctions, the house has a shill in the crowd to pump up the bidding. In reality, the man the old hand points to as the shill often turns out to be the new curator at the state museum.

When the hammer falls, though, the lot is sold. Before picking up the art work, the ordinary bidder pays the hammer price plus the buyer's fee, although favored buyers can charge purchases and extend payments. In 30 days, the seller receives the sales price less the auction fee and the charges he incurred.

If the buyer reneges on the purchase, however, the auction house as the seller's agent can cancel the sale or try to force payment from the buyer. The onus is really on the seller, who may get the art back and have to re-offer it at a later auction with the burden of the unexplained previous offering. Alternately, the consignor can pursue the buyer, or have the auction house sell the piece privately as it might when a lot is passed.

None of these choices is pleasant for the seller, but they do happen. When the house makes such a private sale following a reneged bid or a pass, there is always the suspicion that the house is playing footsie with favorite dealers. There was, for instance, an auction house expert who was engaged to be married to a dealer who also received referrals from the auction house, but the marriage did not last.

CHAPTER 16

Everybody Follows
the Auctions

Much of the publicity issuing from the auction houses stresses how their sales benefit sellers. These statements are mostly true, particularly concerning those consignors who know how to protect themselves.

As Edward Munves, President of the National Antique and Art Dealers Association, has said, "The auction room is the only way that masses of merchandise can be liquidated."

Exposure and Competition _____

Because the auction house wants the highest price possible for the property it sells, the whole slant of the auction is pro consignor. The underlying reason is that the house's fee is a percentage of the sales price.

Consequently, when the "best free show in town" is put on to draw the monied crowd to the sale, the consignors gain from what can be the widest possible exposure of the art works, especially when compared to consignment to a single gallery. Everybody in the art business follows the auctions, and most people who go to auctions intend to buy.

Art works that sell at auction might not sell as well—or even at all—elsewhere. Percival Rosseau painted field dogs which are very popular. These works can be sold any place where there is an interest in sporting subjects. In addition, he painted portraits of his own pet Boston Bull, paintings that need to be seen by a multitude of people in order to reach those Boston bull fanciers who will pay the extra money Rosseau's name calls for. Rosseau's pet portraits sell best at auction because of the exposure.

Similarly, some good art brings more under competitive bidding than it would privately. A dealer who specializes in European paintings bought a nineteenth century Belgian marine painting at a price higher than his European customers would pay him. He put the painting on the auction

157

21. *Percival Rosseau. "Boston Bull portrait," 1916. Oil on canvas, 19 by 17 inches.*

block, convinced that at auction his customers would bid against each other instead of vying one on one with him. He was right. The winning bidder paid a third more than the dealer would have asked his customers in his gallery.

When bidders go head to head this way, they create the legends sellers dream of. At an auction that included a picture by an artist whose estate was owned by a dealer, the agent authorized to bid for the dealer was outbid by a stranger who also had the same dealer in mind as his customer. The price was three times the estimate, much more than the dealer would willingly have paid, so he was lucky his agent had been sensible enough to stop bidding when he did.

At another auction a decade ago, a little Hudson River School painting by William M. Hart was obviously in a damaged condition. The bidding opened below the $200 estimate but was soon joined by two Madison Avenue dealers who did not like each other. The price went to $2,400 before one dealer recognized how unprofessionally he was behaving and gave up the bidding.

Act of Last Resort

There is also a seller's advantage at auction that the house does not brag about.

For one thing, the auction house can manufacture diamonds out of glass, if it chooses to. A picture bearing a famous signature, for example, can bring a large sum if the auction house guarantees the authorship despite questionable authenticity or condition. The picture could be one that has been wholly painted over by an unknown hand, with the authentic version buried underneath, detectable only by X-ray. The amount of the sale can be more than $100,000.

Again, the sellers can rig the bidding if they are discreet and if the auction house looks the other way. At one country sale, a dealer and his silent partner who jointly owned the bronze on the block were sitting on opposite sides of the room, bidding spiritedly against each other, hoping that the auctioneer would not stop them before a stranger got caught up in the action and joined in. One bid by a collector would have silenced the owners.

Sometimes, too, consigning to an auction is the seller's act of last resort. An art work with a cloudy history of signatures added and erased that has been offered over a period of years to most of the dealers in the specialization has no place to go but to the closet, to the junk pile, or to auction.

The end of the line for the seller at auction is the work that is so questionable as to authenticity, he would not offer it for sale under his own provenance. A dealer who bought an F.E. Church landscape that was atypical thereafter began to have nagging little doubts about the authorship. He could not ethically sell the painting to a collector in the gallery. The way out for him is to put the painting up at auction without disclosing his ownership.

Getting Rid of Mistakes

Collector Eric Martin Wunsch has said that auction houses have been "most helpful" in de-accessioning erroneous purchases. Dealer Robert H. Ellsworth added that "occasionally I make a mistake and without the auction house there would be no way to get rid of it." The loyalty of the auction house to its important consignors may sometimes be excessive.

For the experienced seller at auction, the risks and the burdens are few and generally minor. When the casual buyer seeks to sell at auction, however, even dealing with arrogant house "experts" who are learning on the job may be disconcerting.

As an example, a young dealer brought in to an auction house an unsigned painting clearly in the style of a second-rank American artist who is frequently sold at auction. He told the house specialist the painting had been an illustration in a landmark book. The specialist, who was not familiar with the artist and did not have a library that would include such a book, refused to accept the painting for auction, even without being obliged to make a guaranty of authorship in the auction catalog. The young dealer became so upset that he sold the painting directly to a well-known collector of the artist's work, at a lower price than he had hoped for at auction, rather than to persevere with the auction house personnel.

Of course, the consignor is always subject to freak events that may influence the sale, although they happen rarely. A storm or the word of a stockmarket decline can eliminate bidders, or the sale can be assigned to an auctioneer who alienates the bidders. Also, the art work can fail to bring a full price because of a lull in the auction tempo, particularly if the piece is of average quality or less.

Despite these minor dangers, though, the seller does have his reserve to protect him, and seeing a piece pass at auction is not the calamity it used to be when there were fewer houses and fewer bidders. It may actually be better today to have the work pass and be returned for sale another time than it is to have the work sold at a reserve price that might be only 60 percent of the high side of the pre-sale estimate.

Misdescribed in the Catalog

Your item can also be misdescribed in the catalog, although specifications should have been settled with the house specialist in the very beginning.

At the Morgan sale on Long Island years ago, a wood carving of a woman's head was estimated at $10 to $20 as if it were a molded hat stand. When examined, the head proved to be an original mahogany sculpture signed by the famous artist Allan Clark (1898–1950) and there was a receipt taped to the bottom of the base, recording the $800 paid to the sculptor 40 years earlier. Thousands of viewers passed through the exhibition in the Morgan home, but at the sale the valuable carving was bought for the price of a hat stand because that was what the catalog had implied it was.

In addition, the seller at auction can be harmed by the operation of the infamous "ring," a syndicate of dealers bidding as one at an auction instead of competing against each other. Because the operation of the ring cuts down on the number of active bidders, the members generally intimidate other bidders and buy at a lower price.

After the sale, the members of the ring re-auction the lots they bought, in a "knock-out" among themselves. The winner pays the knock-out price in an amount higher than the auction price, and the difference between the two prices is immediately divided among the members of the ring. Some members find auctions to be profitable without any investment because they are being paid to refrain from bidding. The operation of a dealers' ring thus decreases prices and hurts sellers, but since commissions are also decreased, auction houses crack down on obvious combinations.

All in all, the results of selling at auction are good for the consignor, as long as he has acted to protect himself. The interests of the knowledgeable seller and the auction house are similar.

This is true even for the consignor of an inexpensive object. Despite the auction houses' continual claims of higher prices setting new sales records, only one-tenth of one percent of the lots sold go for more than $50,000. Most of the sales are not in the millions of dollars but rather are within the reach of the mass of collectors. In fact, 50 percent of the lots have sold for less than $500, even at the top houses. Auctions are valuable for the average seller as well as for the seller with prime art works.

A Short String for the Buyer

When you list the advantages for the buyer at auction compared to the disadvantages, however, it is almost the reverse of the seller's position. The string is short for what is favorable for the buyer and long for what is not.

The relatively few advantages the buyer has include being able to view a couple of hundred preselected pictures and bronzes in one place at one time. This is certainly good for the experienced purchaser who has done his homework in studying the catalog and making his own estimates to compare with the pre-sale estimates of the auction house.

Moreover, bidding is an informed gamble letting you as the buyer pit your wits against the whole art world, including the auction house itself. If you have the touch, you can buy at auction for less than you can at a gallery, but you take exhilarating chances. The value you saw in a work of art may really be there, despite a low pre-sale estimate by the auction house and a low price at the sale—the Allan Clark carving is an example—or the value may *not* be there.

Your specialization should focus your attention on any sleeper in the group being auctioned. You can catch gaps in the auction pace. The next lot after the dramatic competition that drove the bids on the William M. Hart Hudson River School painting up to $2,400 was a Carleton Wiggins (1848–1932) cow painting with the same $200 pre-sale estimate. The crowd was still buzzing about the two leading dealers facing each other on the Hart when the Wiggins was bought for $35.

The buyer must concentrate on what is best for him in the sale. If his best art work comes up early in the sale and brings more than his preset limit, he should not buy the second or third best work just because he is at the sale.

If he was the underbidder, he should not think that if he had only set his limit a little higher he might have won out. He has no way of knowing what the winning bidder's limit was, any more than a poker player would know another player's hole card unless he paid to see it.

The Cracks in the Sale

For profit or just for the fun of it, you can train yourself to go to a top auction and look for the cracks in the sale. If you have developed the knack, one or more of the lots suited to you will sell for a fraction of what you perceive to be value.

You can then take the piece you bought for less than full value and put it up for sale somewhere else, perhaps at a country auction where your piece may delight the eye in an inferior setting, and with its major auction house provenance let you resell it at a profit. While you are there, you can buy good art to resell profitably at the prestigious auction houses.

A W.A. Walker (1839–1921) painting bought at Sotheby's in New York City for $4,250 was resold for $8,000 at a lesser New Orleans auction house within five months. Taking advantage of regional collecting like this is not an easy way of life, but it's gratifying to do a couple of times and it surely is a test of your development.

Dealers at Auction

Dealers go to auctions mainly because they are paid to go as agents or because there is no other way for them to get the art works offered there. They are inherently hostile as buyers at auction, and sometimes they rationalize the importance of their roles. Dealer Eugene Thaw has said that "if you [as a collector] buy something at auction, it is only because a great dealer didn't want it or didn't want it at the price."

Thaw's statement is partially correct, despite the propaganda issuing directly from the auction houses to the effect that private collectors can win over the dealers every time. The houses claim the dealer is buying for stock he will mark up for resale, so the collector can safely outbid the dealer and always get a bargain compared to retail prices.

Unfortunately, though, the auction houses don't tell you that the dealer may not be quite what he seems. He may even be the seller, or acting for the seller, in bidding up the price, or, the dealer may be bidding for an absentee retail buyer like a museum that doesn't want its identity disclosed for fear of elevating the price. Dealers regularly act as agents for a ten percent fee as well as for themselves as principals, and it is in their interest to inflate their image so they can discourage individuals from competing with them.

Dealers magnify their power, vaunt their knowledge and experience, and cloak their activities in mystery in order to influence collectors into employing their professional services, even at auctions open to all.

CHAPTER 17

Auction Traps

Collectors who are bidders at auction face two sets of dangers, some personal and some part of the auction process.

The personal dangers include the "auction fever" that grips bidders and carries them to foolish heights. For them, bidding at auction can be the manifestation of a sickness that is like compulsive gambling or drinking.

In addition, racism and sexism can enter, to the point that white macho males cannot lose a bid to a woman or to a black. For the fevered and the macho, a "Bidders Anonymous" may be needed.

Built-in Discrimination

Besides the emotional problems a bidder may bring to an auction, there are all of the ancient, hidden, built-in traps discriminating against the buyer as if his role in the auction business did not count for much.

According to the printed terms of an auction catalog, for instance, a work of art is signed if it is expressly stated in the catalog that the work bears a signature. If nothing is said, the work is not signed. As the result, every bidder who analyzes the scores of offerings in any auction catalog will at least once fail to notice that nothing was said about the signature of a given art work and thus will make the mistake of overvaluing an unsigned piece.

How easy it would be for the auction house to counter "signed" with "not signed." The only reason for not doing so would be the awareness that some unfortunate bidder will not notice a particular lot is unsigned and therefore will bid more than he should have.

Also in connection with signatures, you will recall that some auction houses under some circumstances in some sales do guarantee the authorship of a work of art. Does this mean that the auction house guarantees the signature?

Not necessarily. If the signature was forged to an unsigned painting done by a famous artist, the painting itself was still "authored" by that artist, even if the signature was not. The house guarantees the painting, not the signature.

This is one way of looking at authorship, although the value of a good art work with a bad signature is obviously decreased substantially, to the point that an investor should not buy the work at all.

On some lots the auction house may say "signature strengthened," which should mean there originally was a good signature on the piece that had been weakened in some way and then partially overpainted. In most such instances, however, there is no trace at all left of the original signature and the auction house is simply taking the word of the consignor that the signature was ever there.

The pre-sale estimates bear examination, too. Sometimes the range is so wide as to be ludicrous—$10,000 to $20,000, say. With such spreads, it would be hard for the experts to be wrong very often and equally unlikely for the estimates to be very helpful.

Also, a check of pre-sale estimates versus actual sales prices would seem to indicate a practice of keeping the estimates low to mislead bidders into believing the sales prices will be within their personal means. The pattern is to entice the consignor with the original high guesstimate, and then reduce the guesstimate before the catalog is printed in order to persuade the buyers to bid by raising their hopes and trusting to "auction fever." Consciously or not, pre-sale estimates are figured so they are usually exceeded by the sales prices.

In good times, two-thirds of the selling prices are higher than the top of the range in the estimates. If the estimate is really $10,000 to $20,000, the selling price will generally exceed $20,000. Even where the prices realized were as strong as $40,000 or more, two-thirds of these sales prices were more than the high sides of the estimates.

It is possible to excuse this by saying that when the art market is bullish and the pre-sale estimates are done months before the sale, understatements are inevitable, but there are so many calculated pitfalls for the buyer at auction that suspicion as to the house's intent is invited.

The Catalog May "Puff"

Auctions lend themselves to rigging and to misrepresentation, and even the major auction houses themselves accuse each other of improper practices.

The primary problem, though, is not actual wrongdoing in a legal sense but the result of bias in favor of the seller and thereby in favor of the auction house itself. There are a lot of little procedures that are bent, some of which we've seen. The catalog may include data to puff the value of the lots to the point where these elegant English auction types who operate the houses are making the suit fit by pulling in the jacket from the back like the stereotype of an old-time clothier.

For example, the auction catalogs are starting to flower with the abbreviation "cf," which means "compare" this art work to a collateral reference in a book that is cited, not a direct reference. In other words, the legitimacy is established on the basis of a metaphor, as a kind of circumstantial evidence, not as a reality. That's salesmanship.

Provenance may be no more than a prior auction sale, which is a sort of a bootstrap authentication. Such a reference, though, is only to transactions at the auction house holding the sale. Competitors' sales are not mentioned.

Or, provenance may even be a dealer in the chain of title who is notorious to the insiders because he has been indicted for art fraud. This extends the meaning of an auction house's "trappings" from a figure of speech to the ludicrous.

Also, there are "likelies" that have been introduced into the descriptions, such as "this landscape very likely depicts the area" that is named.

Again, the catalog may specify a title for the work such as "Picnic in the Hay" or "End of the Day," without indicating whether the title was the artist's or the owner's or the auction house's, despite the difference in value to the buyer. A catchy title on a brass nameplate is part of clever packaging for auction, whether the title was the artist's or not.

In the June 29, 1982, sale at Sotheby's Los Angeles gallery, lot 315A was a 10¼ by 17½ inch watercolor ascribed to William Keith (1838–1911). "Ascribed" was the highest category of authenticity in this catalog, but the authorship was not guaranteed despite the fact that Keith is a frequently forged artist.

Provenance was given as a married couple in California who are presumably collectors like you, not connected with a museum or a leading gallery that would add real weight to the authenticity. There was no reference to how the couple acquired the painting.

Under "literature," the catalog then referred the bidder to a page in a Keith biography so rare it is probably not in your public library. If you can find it, the book quotes Keith's lyrical description of a watercolor with the same title, although specifics like size and place of signature are not stated to pin down the relationship. The pre-sale estimate was $700 to $1,000, low for Keith, but the wary bidders would not even meet the reserve. The lot passed.

Provenance and "literature" may both be forms of puffing.

Condition Not Guaranteed

In addition, dealer Lawrence Fleischman has been reported as engaging in a "diatribe" about auction houses not guaranteeing the physical condition of art works put on the block. The response of the auction house is that if you are experienced enough to be concerned about condition and you ask the house expert, he will tell you what he knows. Has a qualified conservator examined the art work, however, for the house and on behalf of the bidders? Probably not.

One dealer was requested by an auction house to consider buying at a new out-of-town auction location. The dealer picked a painting from the photographs in the catalog and was told that the physical condition was "good." When the painting was received, however, there was a wide swath of repaint right down the center of the picture where the original paint and ground were both gone. The restorer had not even brought the redone area up to the old paint level, but the auction house initially refused the dealer a refund because physical condition is not guaranteed and all lots are sold "as is."

As Fleischman said, the auction house should disclose the physical condition of the art works in its catalog and should guarantee the condition it discloses, particularly when the defect is hidden. It does not.

Part of the reason is the mess. Pictures framed under glass would have to be taken apart. Oil paintings surfaced with opaque varnish would have to have the varnish removed, and so on.

Perhaps the auction house should follow a rule of reason and guarantee what it can conveniently inspect. On the remainder, the buyer would be warned in advance so he can take a conservator with him to inspect the picture, if he remains interested after he has been alerted about the possible physical problems.

Careless Handling

Another danger for the buyer occurs when art is subjected to careless handling at the auction house. Labels can be stuck to the face of a painting or to the gold leaf on the frame. When you remove the label, paint or leaf may come off. Damage from uneven stacking is common. Canvases can be dented or torn. Corners on antique frames are broken and lost.

The recourse is to pick up the art as soon after the sale as you can, examine it carefully for damage, and if you find anything wrong, ask to see the incoming inspection report so you can fix the blame, if there is any.

You must remember, too, that different auction houses have different terms and practices in their sales. There is no industry standard. Every one of the traps we have been discussing is relevant to the major houses. The minor houses and the country auctions have practices you would not believe, down to importing manufactured antiques and indulging themselves in any whim they find to be fun. There is no control other than the maintenance of good will.

As a minor example, an auction house in Connecticut set the rule that a minimum of three bids was necessary to buy the art, rather than one bid as in other auction houses. When the bidding was opened and no second bid was forthcoming, however, the house always entered the second bid on its own, claiming to be doing a favor to the opening bidder by enabling him to buy his lot under the self-imposed rules. The opening bidder's winning offer was thus equivalent to his bidding against himself, and the cost to him was two extra bids. This is the sort of favor you should watch out for.

Disclosure of the Reserve

One of the public fights against top auction houses has been to force disclosure of the reserves. According to the houses, however, secrecy concerning reserves is necessary to protect the sellers and must be retained.

These reserves, they say, add to the mystery of the auction process. The auction business is based on the buyer's dream of stealing a masterpiece, and the auction house nurtures this gambling spirit for the arty but reckless souls who might not want to frequent the race track or casinos. Consequently, the houses have declared that the amount of the reserve cannot ethically be made public, in what they euphemistically call the buyer's interest.

As the complaints about the reserves continued, though, the top auction houses have given way in part, for some sales. They have agreed to disclose not the amount of the reserve but whether any given lot has a reserve. Since then, substantially every worthwhile lot in the catalog has had a symbol next to it indicating that there is an operative reserve.

As a result, the buyer is right back where he was. He always did suspect that every good piece carried a reserve, and now he knows they do, except that he still doesn't know the essential fact—how much the reserve is.

This cynical acquiescence of the auction houses on the issue of reserves is an example of how to give without giving.

Conditions of Sale

To provide you with an idea of the conditions of sale presently in use at some of the better auctions, the following is excerpted from the catalog of the June 28 & 29, 1982 sale at Sotheby's Los Angeles:

> "1. We and the Consignor assume no responsibility for the authenticity of the authorship of any property listed in this catalogue (that is, the identity of the creator or the period, culture, source or origin, as the case may be, of the property).
>
> "All property is sold 'AS IS,' and neither we nor the Consignor make any warranties or representations of the genuineness or attribution of the property nor any warranties or representations of the correctness of the catalogue or other description of the physical condition, size, quality, rarity, importance, provenance, exhibitions, literature or historical relevance of the property and no statement anywhere, whether oral or written, shall be deemed such a warranty or representation. Prospective bidders should inspect the property before bidding to determine its condition, size, and whether or not it has been repaired or restored. . . .
>
> "2. However, if within 21 days of the sale of any lot, the purchaser gives notice in writing to us that the lot is counterfeit and, if within 14 days after such notice the purchaser returns the lot to us in the same condition as when sold, and demonstrates that the lot is a counterfeit, we will refund the purchase price. . . .
>
> "9. Unless the sale is announced to be without reserves, each lot is offered subject to a reserve, which is the confidential minimum price below which such lot will not be sold. We may implement such reserves by bidding on behalf of the Consignor. . . ."

As you can see, these are tough terms, and you would think they would give pause to any prospective bidder. After all, this auction house is telling you it expressly disclaims warranting the authenticity of any lot, even if you have the guaranty in writing. The house does not even warrant the language in its own catalog.

If you live out of town, you cannot rely on the staff expert's statement of the physical condition of any lot. You must inspect the property yourself or send a conservator. In addition, if you live out of town you cannot take advantage of the 21 day provision for counterfeits because the procedures of payment and shipment take more than 21 days for an average collector.

Moreover, you must assume that on every lot there is a reserve in an undisclosed amount, and that the auctioneer will read bids off the wall until the bidding exceeds the undisclosed amount of this omnipresent reserve.

That's pretty hard cheese on the bidders.

Buyer Beware

At some point, however, you will feel you have to buy at auction. You may believe the auction house is really your impartial agent, or that the offerings contain million dollar sleepers, or that at worst, you can steal good stuff from the dealers by outbidding them. There will be a singular work offered that is your "best" and you will think you have to own it.

When you do decide to bid at auction, remember that the rule is buyer beware. Be sure you inspect the physical condition of any art work before you do bid on it. There are portable black lights you can use in the auction room, although they do not have the power of the one you should have at home.

You can ask the attendant to take a picture off the wall so you can examine the back, or to lift a bronze so you can see the base. If you have a further question, you can discuss it with the head of the auction department. Reduce the physical condition to one of the five categories set forth in the chapter on condition. Categorizing the art work this way will aid in clarifying your thoughts.

Second, keep the terms of sale in mind, especially the guaranty of authenticity. If you have doubt about how the terms apply to an art work, ask.

Third, don't rely on the auction house's pre-sale estimate. Assume that the actual hammer price may be higher, and act on the basis of your own estimate, as it fits your situation.

Fourth, determine your bid to suit your estimate and then increase your amount by the equivalent of one step in the bidding. The tendency is for bidders to fix limits in round numbers. Set yours one step higher to gain the advantage. If your estimate is $1,000, think about the amount as $1,000 plus one bid.

Fifth, consider the bidding limit you establish to be your absolute maximum and don't go above it, come what may.

Value by Definition

Now that collectors like you are bidding at auction sales, it is clear that more complete and more accurate descriptions are needed in the catalogs, without the puffing, and that better reporting is needed in the books of annual records.

As we have seen, the catalogs don't cover everything. Most annuals not only add nothing, they take data away. The passes are not generally reported, for example, although they may be as important as the sales prices that are reported.

The incongruous thing about prices at auction is that any price actually realized at a sale becomes the fair value of that work of art by definition, regardless of any fumble in the process. It is the only price available for the piece. The auction house is the sole price maker, no matter how the price is arrived at.

Similarly, the auction house is regarded as the barometer of change in art fashions, although the changes may have been taking place in dealers' galleries for months.

CHAPTER 18

The Dealers Were the Cream

A decade ago, Eastern dealers were consistently winning out over the auction houses in securing art for sale. Moreover, many of the "good" art works the auction houses did manage to get were consigned by the dealers themselves, and when art came up at auction, it was bought by other dealers.

The Madison Avenue galleries in New York City were the cream of the art world.

Dealers Paid Wholesale

The price dealers paid for their purchases was by definition wholesale, ready to be marked up 50 to 100 percent or more to arrive at the retail price for resale to collectors.

The collectors purchased only from dealers. Buying at auction was exclusively the dealers' province. It was a rare collector who would trust himself to buy from auctioneers he had been led to believe were shady operators. Among the dealers, curators, collectors, investors, and auction houses, the dealers were the trusted experts, the repositories of the mystic knowledge for the entire art world.

Over the last few years, however, the major auction houses like Sotheby's and Christie's have developed into Goliaths, at the expense of the dealers. The auction houses still sell on the block, as they always have, but the quantities, prices, and grosses have become astronomical. Auction houses also purchase merchandise for their own account, sell their own merchandise at auction, sell privately, appraise, counsel on investments, restore, and even act as real estate brokers, invading others' territories including the turf of the art dealers.

All of these collateral activities interact for the cumulative benefit of the auction house. Counselling on investments produces captive buyers and finds art for sale as well. Listing real property locates personal property to be disposed of. Selling privately greases the channels to privileged dealers who are kept in line by being handed what are only the auction house's crumbs.

The Money of the Badly Informed

One reason for this emerging strength of the major auction houses has been the appearance on the art scene of a growing number of casual buyers who are looking for prestige-building bargains to be acquired under a thrilling spotlight. Without awareness of the hazards or of the dealers' historic role, these new purchasers tend to buy at auction rather than in galleries.

In addition, the dealers' old private customers have been solicited by the auction houses to bid in direct competition with the dealers, a step that could result in raising auction prices to close to the retail level paid at galleries.

Instead of dealer versus dealer, buying at auction is becoming dealer versus collector and may turn into collector versus collector at the lower price levels. Like a variation of Gresham's Law, the money of the badly informed drives out the good. When one artist's painting brings $20,000 at auction, another painting by the same artist must appear to the inexperienced to be a bargain at $12,000 if it resembles the first.

The new collectors are sustained by an aura at auction that gives them confidence to buy what appeals to them. There is no guide to the pricing levels other than the pre-sale estimates, but the collectors feel that anything they buy is bound to go up in value.

The elixir is the auction mystique, the illusion concocted by the cool and impartial-appearing auctioneers in order to lead consignors into believing that chance might bring them 20 times the apparent value of their goods, while in the next moment persuading bidders that they can steal goods on the block for a twentieth of value.

The rationale in the fantasy is that once in the thousands of lots that are auctioned, the illusion becomes real. The high price in the sale of the Charles Sprague Pearce painting of the girl on the beach must have gratified the consignor, as the purchase of the Allan Clark "hat stand" must have pleased the winning bidder.

Small Dealers as Absentees

Because of its appeal, the auction market has spread. There are major auction houses in Toronto, Washington, Maine, Massachusetts, California, and so on. Dealers and private buyers from all over the world attend New York City sales.

The number of absentee bids has increased. Small dealers from small cities buy by mail and phone, without knowing much more about art than new collectors do and without seeing the pieces until the crates arrive. Other groups of dealers and collectors buy at specialty auctions like the contemporary Western art extravaganzas set up around the country.

Today, most of the veteran dealers are at arm's length from the auction houses. The dealers watch the important collectors, investors, and curators who used to defer to them kowtowing to the auction personnel who handle more desirable works.

Paradoxically, the collectors who are powerful enough to spend a hundred thousand dollars or more on art are not entirely happy, either. They cannot go to the auction houses and simply buy what they want. Instead, they have to compete against the other macho collectors in a bidding war. They end up paying more than they think they should and they take out their frustrations on the once mighty dealers, tendering absurdly low offers at galleries and asking for ridiculous terms.

The Dealers Done In

During the course of this expanded market, however, the dealers made more money than they ever had before. Consequently, they are not yet concerned about where they are going, although it is clear that the promotional devices of the auction houses and the auction chic that is generated have "done the dealers in" as the leading force in selling art.

One evidence of the success of the auction houses vis'a vis the dealers is that 50 percent of the buyers at auction are now collectors or investors. More pessimistic analysts among the dealers put the figure at two-thirds.

As a result, it has become hard to locate the line between wholesale and retail at auction. Appraisers, for example, are finding it difficult to decide how to use auction prices in evaluating art, compared, say, to stock certificates whose published market prices are always regarded as retail.

The question has become whether appraisers should continue to accept auction prices for art as wholesale, the way they used to, or as retail, in view of the buying by collectors. Nothing in the records tells whether a particular auction buyer is a dealer or a collector, and some dealers are even willing to pay the equivalent of the retail price once in awhile to obtain a piece at auction they feel they must have.

Of necessity, then, professional appraisers are being forced to find a different gauge to what is wholesale at auction, and dollar levels of sales have been suggested as the test. An auction sale at a price up to $2,500 is considered by many appraisers to be at retail, regardless of who the purchaser actually was, and sales over this amount are presumed to be at wholesale. In stratospheric price levels, the purchasers are regarded as dealers acting as agents.

Dealers Past and Present

Indications are that the decline in the standing of dealers in the art world will continue, unless the dealers can evolve new ways to upgrade their services, enliven their galleries, and convince the bulk of the art buyers that using them is advantageous. What is needed is a set of recommendations as to how dealers can function better than the auction houses in doing a safer and more productive job for both the seller and the ultimate buyer.

The first step, then, is to look at dealers past and dealers present, to try to figure out what their future may be.

Some of today's leading art dealers are second and third generation experts. One New York gallery which began in the 1920s as a neighborhood frame shop is run by a daughter of the founder. Another which started as a print shop in 1880 is a major gallery currently operated by a grandson with a monied partner.

A third is run by a son of the founder who represented first rank artists a century ago, and the ownership is being passed on to nephews who have served apprenticeships. A fourth began as an art supply store in the Midwest, again a hundred years ago, and now grandsons have separate galleries in New York. A fifth was started in California 50 years ago.

There is a long tradition of knowledge in shops like these, backed by a depth of experience unmatched in American art. What can you add to the expertise of firms which once represented Winslow Homer or Childe Hassam or Frederic Remington? Just the records of the galleries' transactions over the years could serve as a primer on American art. These people have seen everything in their specialties, many times.

The Newer Dealers

In addition, there are thousands of other galleries which have been in business for more than the ten years considered necessary to make their owners into permanent art dealers in this shifting world. The owners have come from every imaginable circumstance, including lawyers, doctors, butchers, engineers, undertakers, bill collectors, piano tuners, and housewives who started by looking for part-time occupations.

These are people whose skills have been sharpened by putting their money or their reputations on the line over the course of a decade. To advise on art is one thing, but to risk money continually in a long series of purchases and sales of art works is a lot more powerful in its educational effects.

Finally, there are the newer dealers. By dint of serious application, some of them are almost as well grounded as the old timers. Others, however, treat art works like any other product to be merchandised. They know as much about art as they would about a computer they might offer for sale.

Among these new dealers are a few who previously had no personal source of funds but who now pay large sums in cash and who can spend a million dollars at any given auction. Because art sales are a favorite means of laundering illegal money, there are always rumors of dealers with "mystery backers," but transactions in cash are not refused by sellers.

Instead, the auction houses go out of their way to compliment the "eye" of these flush young dealers who spend as if they were intoxicated and who can bid tens of thousands of dollars for an object like a desk they have not examined and would not be competent to examine in a field about which they are ignorant.

The Dealer Is the Middleman

Essentially, the true dealer is the middleman stationed somewhere between the initial seller and the ultimate buyer. He is in the business of acquiring inventory, by purchase or by consignment, in order to resell at retail or to other dealers.

Regardless of what he calls himself, dealer or collector or investor, anyone who sells regularly is a dealer, as judged by both the Internal Revenue Service and the trade. A college degree in art is not a requirement, although the dealer is expected to be an experienced professional who knows all about his specialty.

Historically, the fundamentals of art knowledge have resided in the veteran dealer because until recently there has been relatively little formal scholarship devoted to American art created before 1950. A regular forum like the art section of the *New York Times*, for instance, is either mute on the kind of art we are discussing or it is hostile.

Some dealers run galleries with an open door for any viewer to enter. Other galleries are private, with access by appointment only. A few dealers have no gallery at all and put their pictures up for sale on consignment at existing galleries where they can maintain a satisfactory subsidiary relationship.

Some dealers own all of their stock. Others act entirely as agents for consignors. Most combine the two. Again, some dealers rent regular commercial space for their galleries. Others have galleries as part of their homes.

Some dealers operate out of their back pockets where they keep their inventory in the form of Polaroid photographs they flash at prospective buyers. Many of these "back pocket dealers" own nothing and hold nothing on consignment. They merely borrow photographs from dealers and from other sellers, saying that they want to think about buying. They actually do buy only if they have first sold the piece from the photograph.

Galleries usually specialize. Some handle contemporary art as opposed to the antique. Others may concentrate on particular subjects, and stock mainly Hudson River School landscapes, say, rather than the American Impressionists or the American West.

Some dealers sell just to other dealers, at wholesale, especially when they are starting out. They are not called "pickers" because they have a shop. Others price only for retail sales.

Finally, some dealers limit themselves to high priced art while others show work with a range of prices.

Find a "Good" Dealer

When a potential buyer is looking for a dealer to guide him, the usual advice he gets is to find a "good" dealer. With no more instruction than that, the search might be lengthy, but at least the buyer could start by choosing the kind of physical set-up that suits him, in terms of the dealer's location, specialization, hours, and range of prices.

Beyond this, the buyer should be getting recommendations from museums, conservators, appraisers, auction houses, and other dealers, as well as from his fellow collectors and investors. Remember, though, that the dealer a museum endorses is one with museum connections, not necessarily the one most appropriate for you as a collector. Very few dealers are accepted as sources for museums, and the reasons for acceptance are not always the expertise that would relate to your needs.

The same qualifications will apply to references from other dealers. They will send you only to establishment dealers, not to the unpublicized dealers they themselves may actually buy from.

If you reduce what you are seeking in a dealer to the basic factors, you might start with honesty and trust. Thirty years ago, many major dealers were known to be unscrupulous in acquiring art. One device was to get the private owner of the art drunk before taking a receipt for payment along with possession of the work. Dealers also sold by wining and dining, and they may today, too.

Anyone in the art business would love to tell you all that is outrageous about the reputation of any individual veteran dealer, but the gallery atmosphere sought now is decorous and hushed, like a museum or a church. The buccaneering dealers are still around, in their dotage, while their heirs masquerading as curators take over. You can trust them as far as your own experience carries you. Under the recently adopted refinements of the dealers lie interests not exactly yours.

In time, the really bad apples among the dealers will get sorted out of the basket. The dealer who buys with a worthless check disappears, along with the one who refuses to return a consignment or who sells through misrepresentation, misattribution, manufactured provenance and authentication, or forgery.

The dealer who makes a splash buying unsigned paintings on the cheap and selling signed paintings dearly is eventually indicted, as is the dealer who involves his customers in major frauds, while ethical dealers who maintain stolen art alerts, for example, have more of a chance to survive.

CHAPTER 19

Borrowing
the Dealer's Touch

Touch is a readily distinguishable quality in a dealer.

When he has been part of a long-established professional operation, for example, that helps you to recognize his credentials.

The Day You Need Him

The flashy dealers who come into prominence quickly, spending what seem like unlimited dollars, may fade just as fast. Rather than flash, you want a dealer who has been around a decade or more and who will still be there on that future day when you need him, perhaps because you have a question about a piece you bought from him.

While you are learning to develop your own eye, you should be able to borrow the touch of an experienced and knowledgeable expert, to see you through the problems that will arise. Given the advantages of your specialization, you will be surprised at how easy it will be for you to decide which established dealer has the touch to suit you and which doesn't.

Dealers' associations and memberships will not exert much of an influence on your choice, however, because dealers do not generally have professional organizations or standards like those of some of the conservators and appraisers. Anyone can be an art dealer, and advertise himself as such. Some pretty surprising people are dealers, as you may have discovered.

Successful dealers may be listed on the elite rosters of the industry, like *Who's Who in American Art*, but dealers are not usually erudite. They themselves do not tend to write catalogs or articles or books. They can employ people to write them, without giving away the really critical data that took generations to amass. Dealers do not "publish" like academics, although some lecture.

Instead, the dealer is expected only to maintain an inventory of good art priced fairly, to stand behind his sales, to be competent to give sound advice to his customers, and also to respond to inquiries from other dealers, auction houses, and curators. The dealers who now complain that museum experts counsel collectors but not them are reversing the old roles where the dealers had all the practical knowledge and the museum staff had none.

While museum personnel do know more about art today than some of the newer dealers, and it is the curators who have the graduate degrees, the veteran dealers are still the real sages, despite having been self-taught. The big collectors seek out the museum curators, however, because their counsel sounds learned and costs only a lunch or a museum membership while the veteran dealers are savvy enough to limit their counsel to customers.

The paradox is that new collectors who are doctors or lawyers will seek professional advice from art dealers and then be shocked when the advice is not available free.

A Dealer Who Is Solvent

Money is also a consideration in judging dealers. You want a dealer who is solvent enough to be able to make a refund when one is due you. He should be credit worthy. The dealer should also be investment minded, and should sell art at a price where at least some of the value is left for the future.

The quality and extent of the dealer's inventory is always indicative. Just walking into a gallery and looking around should provide a quick estimate of the dealer's general standing. What is said to be gone from inventory because it was "just sold" or what is coming in can be disregarded. Dealers who brag about the superb work they had are not persuasive when all you are interested in is what they have in stock today.

In addition, there is much to be said for the dealer's demeanor and his attitude toward the casual buyer. If he does not concern himself with your questions or if he is rude, you will not feel welcome. Some dealers are indifferent to new collectors and concentrate on the big spenders they know. There are other dealers, however, who enjoy taking a teaching stance with the inexperienced and who will recommend lower priced works as starting investments.

What your reaction will come down to will be a feeling about which dealer will lead you to the best art works for you. Your decision will be based on how the dealer affects you personally, as well as what he offers you in price, guaranties, and terms, factors we will look at later.

Pathfinder and Professor

Thus, the dealer you want is a moral and mature person who has been in the art business long enough to serve you as pathfinder, preselector, and professor. He is someone whose advice you will follow because at this point the patterns are too hard for you to distinguish on your own.

He is not a hard seller. His pricing automatically tells you about the relative investment values of a small Bierstadt at $35,000, for instance, and its look-alike landscape by Feodor Fuchs (active 1856–1876) at $3,500. He should assist you in finding your best picture, at the right price, while helping to develop your touch.

The dealer should also be a seer. He should be able to make an educated guess at the future of the art market. Guaranteeing specified annual growth rate is not possible, but if he is questioned, he should be aware that the art business follows economic cycles, in its own eccentric way.

Business conditions can conceivably turn so sour that years will pass before a piece you have bought will be profitable for resale. A quick fortune cannot be assured. On the other hand, he can state that in his opinion the retail value of the particular piece can be expected to double in five years, or triple, as long as the trend of art sales is strongly up.

Long-term investing is the forte of the collector with time and money, while the reality of the dealer's position is that he is the short-term holder, subject as he is to the pressures of turnover financing.

The Silent Conflict

You should expect to have a silent conflict of interest with your dealer. His first loyalty is to himself or to his consignor. He wants the highest price the market will ethically bear. He is in effect a rival investor, weighing his stake in the art work against making a sale.

He has his tentacles out, using scouts to bring you in as a customer and paying the scouts the ten percent fee that he will have added to your bill.

A bookseller in Manhattan, for example, is such a scout. He knows a doctor in Utah and a lawyer in Iowa who come to New York City to buy art. The doctor and lawyer depend on the bookseller to guide them among the Madison Avenue art dealers, until they acquire experience enough to find their own way. The bookseller collects a percentage of the purchases from both the investors and the galleries, perhaps to the knowledge of each.

Do not be afraid to comparison shop among the galleries, to check out the art in the territory where you are.

If prices are not marked, though, ask only about the few pieces that could interest you. Do not request prices for art you may not want. Prices are a sensitive subject for dealers who do not know you and they may think you are spying for a rival dealer or you are gathering data for a free appraisal of your holdings.

Expect the gallery prices to be generally above average auction levels. A 100 percent mark-up over cost would be common, but it might well be higher, to reflect the actual value the dealer puts on his product. On the other hand, gradations in values will be hard for you to spot. You may not yet comprehend the subtlety of differences between similar works of art that cause vast variations in price.

Or, the subjectiveness of pricing may be confusing. Every dealer has his peculiarities and his short-sightedness. Some downgrade works where the subject is war, or smoking, or snakes, or feminism, and so on.

The old watchword is to beware of bargains in art, but that's baloney. You just have to see farther and clearer than the next guy, and your own touch, tailored to you as an individual, makes bargains possible.

Make Me an Offer

You are entitled to ask the dealer to explain any price.

If he responds by saying, "Make me an offer," the most appropriate answer is to drop whatever it is that you are holding, wave your hands in circles above the dealer's head, murmur arcane incantations, and reply, "Okay. You are now an offer."

Dealers say that every buyer must know what he is willing to pay or he would not be in a gallery, but it is the dealer's function to set the price when he is negotiating to sell to a casual buyer. As the expert, the dealer has all the data and he has an ethical duty to be fair. The buyer has no equivalent knowledge and is being played for a sucker if he responds when he is asked to make an offer.

When the dealer is selling to another dealer, however, he is entitled to assume that the other dealer is also an expert.

Some buyers love to bargain and feel cheated when they cannot squeeze the price. They always want to believe they get the lowest price there is and they have been known to send an ally to the dealer to check on whether the price they received really was the rock bottom.

They practice bargaining as a science. Before they make an offer, they consider whether it is the right time of the month or of the year. The period that the dealer's income tax is due might be favorable, or his rent date. So might late spring and early summer when the art business could be slow, compared to fall when the dealer is happily contemplating the coming holidays. The bargainers probe to discover when the dealer is under pressure to move merchandise.

Actually, most dealers are prepared to come down ten percent for anyone, on their own, if there is no complication in the sale.

Other dealers, however, offer only a firm price, and nagging at them for a reduction may end the whole transaction. These are dealers who follow changing values closely, subscribe to all the auction catalogs, and build their art libraries. They pride themselves on the accuracy of their pricing, and a work of art with any flaw at all is priced down accordingly. When a buyer offers $600 for a $1,000 painting, this kind of dealer may counter by withdrawing the painting from sale.

Making a game out of buying a bargain isn't the purpose of collecting, anyhow. You should want your best picture, and paying a little more, if you really must, is worth it.

Buying from a Dealer

The disadvantages of buying from an ethical dealer in your specialty relate mainly to price and to exposure to relatively fewer works than you would see at auction.

On the other hand, the advantages are manifold, compared to buying at auction. From the outset, the pieces the dealer selects for you to look at may be fewer but they will be limited to your kind of art work. It will be easier if you pick a gallery with your kind of specialization because dealers tend to respond better to buyers who are compatible with the gallery's inventory.

You can ask the dealer about the full provenance of a piece, without settling for what, if anything, is printed in an auction catalog. Auction houses can make a joke out of provenance, listing an unknown consignor by name, presumably to prove that the art did not materialize out of the air.

If you want to avoid works recently on the auction block, because you feel constrained by the fact that the auction prices were published or because the exposure at auction makes you uncomfortable, you can do so simply by warning the dealer not to show you such pieces.

As a client, you have the dealer's knowledge and advice available to you, free. You can lean on his touch, as you cannot lean on the personnel of an auction house. You meet with him one on one and get his undivided attention for as long as you desire.

You work with him in the privacy of his gallery, away from the auction sideshow where everyone learns your business. No newspaper writes articles about what you do with the dealer, and the price you pay is not announced to an audience, disseminated in the list of prices realized, and recorded forever in the annual auction books. Buying a piece at auction is like negotiating under the "sunshine laws," while in a gallery, you can quietly buy whatever you want, as long as you can meet the price.

When you do not see what you are looking for in the gallery, the dealer will act as your personal scout. He will keep your requirements on file and will call you when he hears about something that might be for you. He will actively seek out suitable art if he believes you are a serious buyer.

He may borrow from other dealers for you, adding his cut to the price when he cannot obtain a commission from the other dealer. He may even recommend you to different dealers. The gallery community is small, and he will phone ahead of your arrival to arrange for his ten percent referral fee.

If you do ask a dealer for a guaranty of condition, you can get it in writing, although the same dealers who decry the lack of a guaranty of physical condition at auction do not themselves offer an automatic guaranty of condition. This guaranty of condition means having the dealer disclose the exact extent to which his art work deviates from the original condition.

You can also get a guaranty of authenticity and even of the signature, if you request it. As merchants, dealers are quite aware that a guaranty of authenticity is little help to a collector when the signature may be suspect.

The Fringe Benefits

Besides the nuts and bolts of buying from art dealers where you can resolve the big things like personal service, price, and guaranties, there are fringe benefits, too. These are the homely aspects of collecting that can be critical to you, although they are impossible within the auction framework.

For instance, when you like a piece at a gallery but you need time to complete the purchase, a dealer will hold the piece on approval, with or without a deposit, for whatever reasonable time you require, from a day to a week or more. This is the meaning of half stars you see on a work of art on exhibition, to mark the pieces being held, compared to the full stars on the works that have been sold.

Asking that a work be held for you, however, does obligate you to get back to the dealer within the agreed time, to give him your decision either way. One of the real pains for a dealer is to hold a piece on approval and then never have the customer mention the matter again.

In addition, although auction houses do not permit trial hangings, most dealers will let the buyer take a work home overnight on approval. There can be a shattering difference to a buyer between what a picture looks like in a gallery and on a wall at home. The usual financial arrangement is that the buyer pays for the piece when he takes it, on the understanding that the dealer will hold the payment for 24 hours. If the dealer does not hear from the buyer within this term, he puts the payment through.

For the dealer, the procedure removes the possibility of the buyer trying to return the piece months later because it did not match a changed color scheme or because the size did not jibe with altered hanging arrangements.

Installment Buying

The dealer may also allow an interest-free period during which the buyer may pay in installments. During an inflationary economy, this is an advantage to any buyer and the well-to-do know how to ask for the time.

Payments spread over a period like six months may let the ordinary collector acquire his "best" work of art, rather than the lesser one he could afford only from accumulated capital. While interest rates are high, the savings to the buyer will go a long way toward compensating for the dealer's extra charge for a service that may be built in to his price.

Trades for Art

Most dealers are even glad to take trades for art. Piece for piece is the easiest way, where the dealer can get something more marketable for something he could not readily sell, or where he can get part trade and part cash. The dealer is not necessarily looking for a price advantage, although price helps, but he would prefer a work in his specialization to one that is not, or one good piece for several of lesser quality.

There are dealers who will take trades of anything convertible to money, including gold, jewelry, real estate, or rugs, especially when there is a double profit to be made. Moreover, the dealer and the collector may both find tax savings in trading.

You can also agree with the dealer on a period during which he will take back your art work at the price you paid, for cash or for credit toward another piece, as long as the physical condition of the work is the same.

Some dealers who are confident of a perpetual bull market in art make this a guaranty for your life or as long as you own the piece. Others might give you five years, and then limit the refund to the lower of what you paid or the fair value of the work when you bring it back. These are terms to be resolved.

Most dealers will confine the money-back guaranty to art of consequence to them. Getting into elaborate discussions on taking back the $500 art works that are the hardest to sell would not be productive for dealers, even though one important aspect of the dealer's advantage is the personal service that he offers.

CHAPTER 20

The Standard Bill of Sale

As we have seen, there are advantages and disadvantages to buying at auction and from a gallery. To enlarge these differences in favor of the galleries, and to put a finger on the scale, it is suggested that the dealers should through their associations develop a standard bill of sale for use in the purchase of art from galleries. The reason for such a standard bill of sale is that it will contain provisions not available from auction houses and emphasize both the quality of the galleries' offerings and regularize the selling conditions.

To start with, the dealer should assign a stock number to the art work being sold and mark this number indelibly on the piece itself. The marking on a painting is usually on the stretcher. On a bronze, the marking would be inside the base. The bill of sale should tell the buyer that a stock number is being used, where it is being placed on the piece, and what it is. This number should then be referred to throughout the transaction. It will become a permanent part of the provenance.

The bill of sale should be headed with the stock number, followed by a detailed description of the property. Exact dimensions down to eighths of an inch should be noted, height before width, along with the medium used. For sculpture, the size should be in terms of height, length, and width, and the material and patina should be given.

The location of the signature and the name of the artist should be specified, both as it is on the work and in full as it is in the artist's listings. If the work is not signed, that fact should be stated, along with the name of any artist to whom the work may be ascribed by the gallery.

The date of creation should be noted, if shown. Otherwise, the approximate date should be stated, to the best of the seller's knowledge. Any date or range of dates is better than no date.

The artist's title for the piece, if there is one, should be given, and the names by which the piece has been known should be listed.

Any additional marking or distinctive characteristic should be noted, whether it is on the front or the back or on the frame or the base. An example would be writing on the back of a canvas.

The price must also be stated, along with the terms of the sale, any trade taken, or provision for installment payments, with or without interest.

Provenance should be spelled out, with names and addresses as available for the entire chain of title.

The standard bill of sale should also provide for guaranties of the artist's signature, of authenticity, and of ownership.

In addition, there should be a guaranty of physical condition, in terms of departure from original condition. The physical condition should be characterized as fine, very good, good, fair, or poor, and the factors determining the characterization should be specified. If the signature has been retouched, for example, or if the bronze has been repatinated, the bill of sale should say so.

The right of return, if any, should be described. The duration of the agreement should be given as the period during which the buyer retains ownership of the work, or any other period that might be agreed on, and finally, the bill of sale should be signed and dated by both the dealer and the buyer.

This bill of sale should be in the form of a printed agreement with each of the possible standard provisions that have been named given a separate printed heading so the buyer will know such a provision is possible. Provisions not applicable can be stricken from the form and initialed by both parties.

The purpose of the standard bill of sale is to protect casual buyers, collectors, and investors, whether individuals or businesses. If the purchaser of the work is another dealer buying for resale, however, then the standard bill of sale need not be used. Dealers are expected to protect themselves. One test of whether the purchase is for resale is the payment or waiver of sales tax on the purchase.

More on Dealer Pricing

We have talked about pricing before, but how to price art remains a critical function for the successful dealer.

The most appropriate selling price a dealer can pick for any work is the amount that a knowledgeable customer expects to pay when he sees the piece at its point of sale. As long as this expected amount is not below real value, the canny dealer calculates his price from the customer's viewpoint. The reason is that when the potential buyer considers the price too low, he may think the piece is not any good. He expects to get only what he pays for. If the price is considered too high, the buyer may think the dealer is grasping, or taking advantage, or expecting heavy bargaining.

A few years ago, country auctioneers, through some inexplicable chance, were handed a famous family's estate to put on the block. The auctioneers brought the numerous paintings to a local dealer to examine because the caliber of what they had was stunning. The paintings were all genuine, signed by famous American and European artists, and the authenticating dealer bought most of them at the auction.

One that he purchased for $1,100 had been hung high over furniture at the exhibition and had appeared to show Spanish horsemen with cattle in a European scene. It attracted no real attention from the professional bidders. The local dealer, however, had found the painting to be a rare William Hahn (1829–1887) of California vaqueros that was relatively valuable.

By the end of the auction, the Madison Avenue dealers and their representatives realized what they had missed in the Hahn and offered the buyer $3,500 and then $5,000. He asked $7,500, an amount that the New York dealers would not pay.

When the trustees of a California museum came into the buyer's shop, he raised the price to $12,500 as his approximation of fair value and was stunned to overhear the trustees saying to each other that the picture looked fine, but it was too cheap at the price to be good enough for their museum.

The dealer promptly raised the price to $30,000 and sold the Hahn painting to the next California museum that came through, taking half in cash and the other half in the form of a small Thomas Hart Benton painting. When buyers are amateurs, they expect a top picture to carry a top price and they distrust a bargain at a gallery.

Another example of an extraordinary pricing condition demonstrates that the top dealer prices are not necessarily the highest prices that can be obtained. A scion of an old family like the Rockefellers or the Vanderbilts or the Morgans can take art works on approval from the best Madison Avenue galleries, represent the pieces to be his own collection in a private offering, and sell them to impressed retail customers at prices that include his profits in addition to the already high Madison Avenue prices. Most of the customers would be satisfied even if they learned about the ruse. They would have expected to pay more to a Rockefeller or a Vanderbilt.

In contrast, some dealers claim to have the lowest prices, even underselling the auction houses despite the extra services provided by the gallery. They say they buy from private homes rather than at auction. In that way, they say, they pay less than auction prices and so they can sell for less.

22. Gean Smith. "Buffalo in Winter," 1905. Oil on canvas, 26 by 30 inches.

All dealers have stories about how they acquire investment grade art for very little. One example was of a dealer being called into a middle class home by a woman with a large Gean Smith (1851–1928) painting of a buffalo that was hanging in the den. When the dealer hesitated while considering his offer, the woman became quite direct. The painting had belonged to her former husband, was part of the divorce settlement, and she hated both the painting and the husband. If the dealer would not pay $100 quickly, she was putting the picture out with the garbage that same day.

Of course, some local dealers also have arrangements with the garbage collectors to look at art works that have been discarded, so the dealer who bought the Gean Smith for $100 might well have paid the garbage collectors less.

Other dealers say they keep a three-year room that remains closed. When they buy high, they put the art work away for the three years. At the end of that time, what they paid may have become a bargain they can afford to sell below the market.

You do not need to believe any of these dealer statements.

Recapturing the Initiative

The momentum of the art trade still favors the auction houses. Although in good times the volume of all art sales rises to keep even the inexperienced dealers fat, the dealers' percentage of the art business has fallen, compared to that of the auction houses.

As the art business contracts, however, following the downturn of the economic cycle that inevitably comes, many dealers will lose their galleries unless they learn to recapture the initiative from the auction houses.

Two approaches are suggested.

First, dealers should adopt a uniform bill of sale with its disclosures and guaranties, in order to solidify their hold on their present customers. Publicizing the provisions of the uniform bill of sale would also have an impact on the new collectors who especially need the dealers.

The dealers' associations should provide their members with the copy for periodic news letters to be mailed to customers, noting the general condition of the art market, recommending investment specializations, advising on portfolio management, providing biographical data on artists, reviewing new art books, and plugging the benefits of the uniform bill of sale.

Second, some dealers should introduce into their galleries, at least experimentally, the excitement characteristic of the auction houses, to reach the bidders who are influenced by theatrics.

Today, galleries are designed to look like small museums. Yet, everyone knows that in a museum you can only admire art. You can't buy there. Dealers' galleries should cultivate a warmer image to lure the action buyers, and provide a zippier arena in which to see and be seen.

Reporting Dealers' Sales

Next, dealers should consider asking their private customers to allow prices to be reported in annual publications that would be handled like the auction. Sales would be listed by artist, signature, medium, size, condition, and price. The name of the buyer would not be disclosed.

In those cases where the customer does not consent, that sale would be excluded from the reports, but the exclusions would number no more than the passes at auction. After all, major investors buy wherever they find the best art work, at auction or from a dealer, and they are accustomed to indirect publicity, as in auction records.

And, although dealers' prices might, on the average, be higher than those at auction, that would not hinder dealer volume. Customers at galleries expect to pay for the extra service.

More importantly, though, sellers would see that they might do better financially by putting their art on consignment with dealers. For the dealers, getting fresh works away from the auction houses would change their whole outlook. Dealers would be able to decrease the number of art works they buy at auction for inventory, and thus offer more art in galleries that has not become shopworn through overexposure. Seeing the same art over and over, at auction and in shops, is a drag on everyone who watches the action.

A Mystery Piece

Moreover, it is a mystery how dealers can show a piece for $50,000, say, that was passed at a recent auction for $25,000. The reason can be only that such dealers believe collectors not experienced enough to ask the right questions don't deserve to have the answers volunteered. In fact, though, even a uniform bill of sale would not force the disclosure of a pass at auction.

When the dealers do buy at auction, they could consider tightening their markup for resale and disclosing the source of the art to their buyer as part of the provenance. The point of the disclosure would be the old one: Dealers can recognize quality at auction that new collectors on their own would miss.

Warming Up the Gallery

In addition, as we have said, the more outgoing dealers should try warming up their gallery decor.

Galleries could have new exhibitions regularly, with imaginative backgrounds designed to fit the themes of the shows, like the story-telling decoration in Fifth Avenue department store windows.

Or, the backgrounds could be simplified home furnishings, to indicate how the art would suit its intended usage.

Or, gallery space could be treated like a habitat, hung with artifacts from an artist's studio.

Alternately, the gallery could be subdivided into little arcades, with each mini shop adopting a different theme or specialization. Visualize a contemporary Western gallery with one room showing paintings of Navajo children, the next of wildlife, and so on.

Besides decor, dealers could try to match the gambling action in an auction. For example, a selected art work of general interest could have a posted price along with a box for the purchasers to deposit their declarations of intention to buy. Copying from the similar exhibitions in the Southwest, there would be a lottery at the end of the show and the winner would be that purchaser whose declaration of intention to buy is drawn.

Or, there could be the modern equivalent of the old "candlewick" auction with silent bids to be posted alongside the art. Offers would be accepted for a fixed time like ten days, and at the appointed hour, the highest bid received "before the wick fell" would win. The dealer could even copy the auction houses and have a reserve.

Those Eastern dealers who are still conservatively oriented in marketing art might well take a look at the operations of the galleries that handle contemporary Western art. The vivacity of the Western subject matter has spilled over into the galleries' functions. As we have seen, Western dealers are not afraid to try newer marketing concepts like running their own auctions, using "intent to purchase" boxes, initiating their own print houses, and placing frequent magazine advertisements with lavish use of color.

In addition, these Western galleries enjoy a substantial advantage when they represent living artists. Questions of guaranteeing authenticity, signature, and physical condition seldom arise.

Honor Thy Dealer

One thing about the art business has been proved. The sellers will bring their art work to wherever they get the highest net that is timely, whether the outlet is at auction or in a gallery. Conversely, the buyers will go wherever the good pictures are, even if they have to pay a little more, and it is in the interest of the galleries to provide protected purchasing conditions.

As you might expect, the dealer will do more for customers who are important to him. He will play favorites, so you should determine what his leaning is.

Most dealers cater to buyers of high priced art, especially when the purchasers pay when payment is due and make few demands.

Other dealers, though, may be responsive to flattery, or to young investors, or to eager learners, or to the good looking, or to the knowledgeable and serious, or to the helpful, whatever turns the dealers on.

You would do well to "honor thy dealer."

CHAPTER 21

The Teacherless Schoolroom

Art buyers can be divided into three classes according to how dirty they are willing to get their hands.

When they have money available to spend, casual purchasers will confine their investigations to the slick art galleries or the plush auction houses which add dash to transactions simply because of their fame. There, the selection of art has been done in advance and buying is easier.

Most collectors, on the other hand, want to learn all they can. At the start, they voluntarily confine themselves to smaller dollar amounts of purchases in order to acquire their "touch" safely.

Collectors who want to become insiders, however, must exhibit considerably more dedication. These are the buyers who consciously engage in an educational program of treasure hunting in junk shops, recognizing that these shops can unwittingly act as teacherless schoolrooms in the best practical sense.

The third group of would-be collectors has just modest funds available, too small in any practical sense to buy important pieces of art, so the only way into substantial expenditures for them is to treasure hunt to build a nest egg. These sallies they are then required to take into the world of the used and obscured are the biggest challenges and the most rewarding exercises in the pursuit of experience in buying art.

Dropped in Any City

Collectors who want to go on to become expert will need courage and application, perseverance and luck, but hunting pays. On his first day of looking in low-end antique shops in Baltimore, for example, an inexperienced treasure hunter found two possible purchases to be explored plus one small still-life painting by a listed artist that was priced at $7.50. For safety, he took a guaranty that the still-life was not a print and he paid the $7.50 without bargaining on the price. The picture was worth $400 at retail so he sold it to a dealer for $200, thereby letting him start out with a quick profit of $192.50, two more works to research, and an earned surge of confidence.

Multiple experiences from frequent exposures to art that is not pre-selected make for a forced education, like learning French by immersion in Paris. After he becomes sophisticated, an art hunter can be dropped in any city in the United States or Canada and within a week he will turn a substantial profit on art, without spending a dollar. He will regularly uncover works priced below market that he can take on approval and resell to dealers on a higher level than the junk shops.

In contrast to the trained real estate investor who must first learn local patterns before he can start purchasing land in a new territory, the experienced art buyer is a citizen of the continent who can immediately apply what he knows anywhere. He takes his territory with him.

Treasure hunting is especially productive if you have access to a city of over 300,000. There have to be enough stops that might have good art to let you establish a route so you can return regularly to the likely sources. About once a month is usual.

To cover what might happen in the interim, think about a distinctive logo for yourself and have calling cards printed with your name, address, phone number, and the logo. As one example of a logo for American still-life paintings done before 1900, your card could be designed to simulate a clipping from a newspaper of the period. If you want Western bronzes, you might use a conventional artifact like a buffalo skull or a ten gallon hat as a logo.

Leave the cards everywhere you go. Many shops display cards under the counter glass or on a wallboard. Put yours there, too. You don't have to worry about being overwhelmed with responses. You won't be, but it's a start.

Searching for Experience

You will find two kinds of competing hunters. One kind will be people like yourself, searching for art to gain experience or to generate funds for investment, diffident about what they are doing and welcoming information almost as much as getting a good limited edition print. The day an old dealer tells you that "Heade," as in the painter Martin Johnson Heade (about 1819–1904), is pronounced "heed" and not "head" will be like giving you a pearl.

The other kind of hunter is the picker, the professional buyer who is just experienced enough to skim some of the good things from these shops on the lower levels of quality. Your reaction might well be that if you could only latch on to the route these small time pickers take, you would surely be in the right places. After a few months, however, it will be disconcerting to you to find the pickers following you. They have the experience, but you have the reference materials discussed under "touch," and this makes you stand out.

Unless you conceal your materials, the shop owners and the pickers will call you the "buyer with the books," a description that is not meant to be flattering. Many of the shop owners price their art on a keystone formula. They pay so much and they mark up the merchandise so much, paintings with china and chairs. A chest costing $10 might be priced at $20, regardless of value, and so might an Old Master drawing.

The pickers put down their money based on the savvy they have accumulated over years of picking, with no guaranty that their customers, the better antique shops and the art galleries, will buy what the pickers have paid for. Pickers are risk-taking entrepreneurs in every sense.

Your procedures will be less chic, and it will seem to them to be less sporting, especially since the art you spend an hour considering may be priced at only $5 to $50. For that amount, you are supposed to walk up to a work of art, put your nose in it, and if you like it you buy it. Bargaining a bit on the price is expected, regardless of how low the price may be.

You will stand out, though, because you will not be playing the same game that the shop owners and the pickers are playing. You will be looking only for the sure things.

Years from now, some of these shop owners will still be where they are, continuing in ostentatious disregard of the rule that applies to the expert as well as the beginner: "Buy only when you know what you are getting, not for what you hope to get, and sell only when you know what you are selling."

If the price is low and the art attractive, the tendency of the uninformed is to take the risk of buying even when the art is unsigned. This approach is dead wrong. Buying based on hope is a gamble, and plunking down any amount of money makes you a serious risk taker. Gambles may pay off, but generally they do not, and you will probably end up with a collection of failures that have to be disposed of in another junk shop, on consignment.

There will be plenty of opportunities to buy an investment grade work of art you are sure of, at whatever price you establish as your limit. Wait for the real McCoy. If there is an object you can't make up your mind about and you are determined to buy it, at least ask the shopkeeper to write on your receipt that you may return the purchase within ten days for a full refund in cash. The right to return a purchase for an exchange is not the same thing as a cash refund. The ten days will give you time to decide what to do and to seek help, if you need it.

A Painting or a Print

Part-time treasure hunters prepare themselves with a few art history books and a slim folder of lists, and then are off in a rush of hope to run the route for the day. On a typical excursion, they will start early, but not too early because enough shops have to be open to let them cover everybody on the route. Junk shop proprietors are most independent citizens and opening times are not consistent, a problem because you will feel compelled to visit at least 30 shops before they close. You will be absolutely positive that if you miss one shop, it will be the place with the big winner.

Once in a shop, you will have to stop in front of every picture to try to decide whether you are looking at a painting or a print. Both have value, but generally speaking the painting has the higher value. Telling a painting on paper from a print when both are framed under glass is a story in itself, particularly when the examination has to be made in the field under conditions that may be trying. The difference is one few experts have mastered for every example.

Oil paintings aren't too hard to distinguish from prints, although the less you know, the easier it is. Even where you see paint on a picture, what you have can be a watercolor that has been painted over a photographic portrait, for example, or a German genre scene painted over a print glued to a wood panel or to canvas. Pictures rejected by experts as painted-over prints have nevertheless been sold at auction, guaranteed to be oil paintings.

Conversely, some of the American Indian artists painted in gouache on paper in a manner that looks like a print, while also making silkscreen prints that look like gouaches. As an addition to the confusion, artists like Albert Bierstadt (1830–1902) commonly painted field sketches in oil on paper that was later glued to canvas.

There are even reproductions printed on canvas in oil paints in full color and then varnished thickly with a brush to simulate the strokes of impasto, and today there are museum shops stocking such misleading facsimiles. Detecting a print on canvas or a painted over photograph is tough for the beginner, although experience will tell you to look at the unpainted eyes to spot the photograph or to look for other unpainted areas that can be viewed under magnification. Sometimes the final answer can come only from the conservator in his laboratory.

Originals framed under glass, the watercolors and gouaches and drawings and once in a while the oils, can thus be difficult to distinguish from prints accented by hand. What you should remember is that the print you are trying to distinguish was commonly reproduced in a screen process. Under magnification, you may be able to find lines or dots in a pattern.

To use an oversimplification that will give you the idea, if you have a window screen in place in your home, look through it at the view beyond, and then directly at the same view, not through the window screen. This is what a coarse print is like, in comparison with a painting or a photograph. Keep in mind that quality prints may have very fine screens, hard to discern outside of laboratory conditions, and even then experts occasionally judge by what they sense and not what they actually see.

Of course, some prints are easy to distinguish from original drawings or paintings. Below the picture area, there may be a white border and on that border may be the name of the publisher with a copyright logo, the c in the circle. Or, the name of the artist may be signed with the number designating the particular print, as "10/20," the tenth print in a limited edition of 20.

In addition, you may find the press mark of the printing plate around the edges of the picture area. Some of this may be hidden by the framer's mat. Where you are unsure, the picture will have to be removed from the frame in order to ascertain whether it is a print.

This discussion is not to denigrate the importance of prints. They are just wholly different from paintings, making up a subject not usually within a painting dealer's expertise. Although prints are generally cheaper to acquire and easier to learn about, buying prints is not recommended as a way to begin buying paintings for investment.

Prints are a field unto themselves and knowledge about prints is not entirely applicable to paintings. For example, once you have determined that a work of art on paper is a print and not a painting, you must then go on to decide whether the print was mass produced or an "original," if you are to develop expertise on prints.

As a matter of good routine in the junk shops, you have to request information from the shop owners, but the data may be unreliable and the response at times even flippant. To a question about any old landscape of a mountain in oil on canvas, for example, the shopkeeper will invariably reply, "What are you looking for, a Bierstadt?" He means that, first, there never could be such a fine thing as a Bierstadt in his shop, and second, if there ever was one, you would want to buy it for a small fraction of its huge value and thus be a "stealer." He could be wrong on the first count.

You have to request the provenance of every possible purchase, too, but from the beginning, most of the shop owners know less than you would expect about what a painting is, and they care less. They cannot determine whether a painting was done professionally and they do not try to read difficult signatures. This is all a matter of the pride of the trade, to justify the keystone pricing with its uniform mark-up based on cost and not value.

Searching for the Signature

The shopkeeper will look with disdain at your next step, finding the signature and copying it onto a pad, along with any other information such as date or place. If the painting has no signature, however, you cannot buy it, regardless of how good the painting looks to you.

On the other hand, almost all the paintings you will find were signed some place, and searching for the signature provides worlds of data that is helpful in identification and evaluation. Paintings not signed lower left or lower right, where the signature can be expected, might be signed at the top or worked into a design in the body of the picture. Most of the time, if the signature is not in the obvious place, it was added at the spot where the balance of the composition demanded it. Looking at the balance will tell you where to find the name.

In rare instances, the signature may be below the lip of the frame, so that the picture will have to be removed from the frame to uncover the artist's name. When a picture is not signed at all, and the painter is unknown, the last legal if shabby recourse of some owners is to add a nameplate to cement an attribution to a particular painter. Although it may fool the uninitiated, a nameplate is not a signature in any sense.

Pictures not signed on the front require looking at the back. If the back is protected by cardboard screwed to the frame or by paper glued to the frame, consent of the shop owner is needed to remove the barrier because the original package is being diminished.

Many times there is writing on the back of the picture, or on the stretcher, or on the frame, if the frame was placed on the picture by the artist. You will be surprised by the frequency and the volume of writing on the back.

There are artists who title the work on the back and locate the scene and even give directions for cleaning the painting, in addition to signing and dating and perhaps specifying the oeuvre number. In a portrait, the sitter might be named. In a painting done as an illustration, the back of the picture or the stretcher might contain the title of the story, the publication, the date, and the size that the reproduction was reduced to.

Frequently, finding the signature wherever it is precipitates a new crisis. For whatever self-defeating impulse, many painters sign their names illegibly, although for collectors and investors the name determines the value. Reading signatures is thus part of the buyer's knack, an aptitude that is especially important during the learning time before well-known signatures become as familiar as your own.

To help yourself interpret signatures, you should go to gallery and museum exhibitions, buy the catalogs, and check the paintings on the wall for legibility of signature as if you were the artist's penmanship teacher in grade school. For the names you cannot read, and there may be a lot of them, copy the artist's scrawl right into the catalog. You will then have a permanent record of what the signature looks like, alongside the painter's printed name and the illustration of his work that may include the scrawl.

The trick in reading a signature is to remember that artists are people, hard as this may be to accept when their work is hung with such deference. Artists who are people have names like people, names like the ones in a phone book. It is necessary to relax to the reading and ask, what does the name look like that is familiar? When you see "Willlbms," that is not likely to be correct, and a little imagination might recreate the embellished symbols as "Williams."

If this does not work, find a place in the name where the letters seem clearest, and start there, filling the name in, forward and backward, as far as you can go. Some people are never able to read an artist's scrawled name, mostly because they move letter by letter from left to right, without any sense of the whole. Take it easy. Being able to read a signature is a critical part of buying whether in a junk shop or in a gallery that labels the work "signed illegibly," so the effort is worth making.

When a name does stump you, copy it as you see it, several times, and work on the deciphering whenever you have the chance. The name will probably become legible to you in an hour or a day, or you can get help. The amazing thing is that once you have read the signature, the name will seem so easy to read that you will not believe you ever had trouble.

Even after years of looking closely at thousands of signatures, though, there will still be some that veteran dealers simply cannot figure out, and may never decipher. When a dealer is really stuck, he shows the signature to everyone who passes through his shop. A dealer in Santa Fe had a watercolor signed "Paul" with an inscription. He took Paul to be the last name of the artist, and it did not occur to him that the signature was the author-illustrator Paul Horgan's (born 1903) given name.

Fine paintings with illegible signatures end up as the permanent possessions of those art dealers who are unable to price with confidence until they know the identity of the artist. Other dealers take care of the problem by making an attribution to the most important artist who could have done the work and then setting the highest price that could conceivably apply. If they get this price, they feel they have lost nothing, no matter who the artist was.

Ten years ago, a New York art dealer acquired a group of pictures that included a wash drawing of a Civil War camp scene signed J.B. Geyser and dated 1863. The quality was comparable to the best of the Civil War

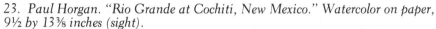

23. *Paul Horgan. "Rio Grande at Cochiti, New Mexico." Watercolor on paper, 9½ by 13⅜ inches (sight).*

illustrators, but Geyser was not listed in any reference or source book. Consequently, the dealer was unable to price the picture for resale because he could not determine the value. One day while casually reading a newspaper, he found an article on the making of a television mini-series based on real people affected by the Civil War, and the protagonist was Geyser, a Virginia artist who had reported on the war for *Harper's*. The handle to the drawing's value had been found.

The Books in Operation

After treasure hunters find legible signatures and before they look up the artists' names in the reference materials, they always make sure to ask the shop owners what the prices are on the art they believe to have been done by professionals. They are certain that after they have identified the artists, prices will go up. They also ask the dealer what he knows about the

24. J.B. Geyser. "Company D," 1863. Wash drawing on paper, 12 by 18 inches (sight).

art ("Nothing," he says. "It came with the furniture."). Then the treasure hunters take the pads with the signatures and retire to their lists, the "buyers with the books" in operation.

In the beginning when you try to find the signatures on the lists you have, it will be "no luck" most of the time. What looked on the wall as though it should be professional will not usually match the artists' names you are seeking. Either you read the signatures wrong, and misreading the first or second letters in the name can throw you off, or you could not yet tell a professional painting from a daub, or you have the wrong or incomplete books.

These first days, the answer can be a combination of all three. Reading signatures is intimidating when you are new at it. Also, there are countless artists whose work looks professional to the untrained eye but is not, generally because they copy professional artists. And, the trouble with the books is that at the start you may have only part of the books you need, the history books, say, and not the more detailed reference books. So, you go back to the shop, thank the owner but buy nothing, and ask him to call if anything special comes in. You leave your card and trudge on to the next shop.

On a typical early day, you may find one piece. In a month, after expanding your traveling library, you will find four or five. One treasure hunter once found four hundred paintings, the result of asking a country dealer whether he knew of anyone else in the neighborhood who might have art for sale. The dealer referred the treasure hunter to a specialist in autographs who liked art enough to have bought the estates of two local painters before learning he had no market for art.

Leaving your card is a mixed blessing. The junk dealers will seldom call. They don't themselves know whether what they find is worthwhile, and if they held themselves out as knowledgeable, they'd have to charge higher prices on selected things. If they do call, the likelihood is that when you get there, the piece will be nothing you can use. You can't buy it and the offended dealer never calls again. When you do leave a card, however, the dealer may at least remember you when you return, particularly if you have adopted a striking logo.

Once in awhile, a dealer phones and mentions a professional artist's name, so you ask him to hold the piece for you. As soon as you can, you go tearing over. Even then, the dealer may use the interim to figure out that if you would come to him in response to a call, he is giving the piece away at the price he quoted and he doubles the price before you can get there. If you can keep your temper under control, the piece may still be cheap.

The rare lucky instance makes it all worthwhile. A treasure hunter heard about a good ship painting while he was still earning his way, and he headed 50 miles east to see it. When he got to the shop, the picture was an obvious print, and torn at that. In nosing through a box of frames, however, there was one frame holding a painted landscape, a picture in wild colors that looked like what he had seen in the Larkin book, and the signature was a scrawl which seemed to be A.H. Maurer, a name on all the lists. The dealer's price was the frame price, $3, and the treasure hunter made the purchase.

Going back, he looked in Larkin and convinced himself that the picture really was a Maurer. At home, he took off the paper backing and found Maurer had titled the landscape on the reverse and had listed the European exhibitions the painting had been shown in.

He hung the Maurer on the wall, the first discovery good enough to have been by a painter in the art history books. The next Madison Avenue art dealer who came to visit him on another picture saw the Maurer immediately and asked the price. The treasure hunter specified a full price and settled for something less.

The purchase was good for the art dealer. For the hunter the sale provided a ticket of entry into investment in art, the realization that he could pick a winner in a junk shop and from it generate funds to buy a lot more works of art, never another Maurer of that type but many other paintings, some much more valuable. He had proved he could do it. He was an instant investor, able to buy from art dealers or at auctions, from funds he had generated on his own.

Other treasure hunters have had comparable experiences. One of them has mentioned his warm memories of going into a used furniture shop with the usual narrow aisles between high piles of every imaginable abandoned object. Eight feet beyond reach, against the back wall, was a huge scooped walnut frame containing a totally obscured painting. Like always, he started through the furniture, at first crawling over couches and chests and then, nearer the wall, sliding under bedsteads and tables on his belly until his nose touched the bottom of the canvas and he could just make out the hooves of a newborn foal, the name of the owners who were an 1890s racing family, and the artist's signature. His sense of "touch" was tingling as he slid back out, paid the $20 asked price, and never even regretted the slash in the canvas from the life-sized foal's withers to his haunch. The hunter had the painting restored, hung it for years, and ultimately sold it for $1,500.

This is how treasure hunters who want to become insiders operate. They are temporary pickers, until they amass the stake they need. They buy art offered at less than half the retail value and try to resell to dealers at half retail or more.

Locating appropriate dealers to sell to is not too hard if you are enterprising. The names come from advertisements, phone books, and conversations. You pick the ones who seem to handle the kind of picture you have, and you call or write, using a photograph as the description, adding the size, place of signature, medium, date, and condition. A Polaroid will do. If you have the signature the dealer wants, he'll get back to you.

A Prerequisite for Investment

Thus, experience in treasure hunting should be a prerequisite for serious collecting or investing in art, an experience derived from physically handling the works, in an environment where nothing is preselected for you. Your average used furniture store is just such an environment, a jungle compared to elite galleries and glossy auction houses where only art meeting certain spiffy standards is permitted entrance.

Junk shops really do have treasures, if you are willing to expend the legwork and face the disappointment of early trips that may produce nothing. It is no disgrace to have hanging on your wall a $1,500 painting that cost $20.

In galleries handling art done before 1950, the work is sanitized before you get to see it, simonized and spruced up like a new car in a Ford dealership. If you start with art chosen for you, you may short-cut the time devoted to the learning experience but you will miss the fundamentals of your education.

Those who treasure hunt, however, will in the end know as much about their kind of art as some of the employees who greet them in the slick galleries. They will know more than many of the 30-minute experts who superciliously counsel them in behalf of the plush auction houses. More to the point, they will have the "touch."

Besides, some of the art in the fancy galleries has come from the same kind of junk shop you will frequent. The most prestigious dealers cannot resist an occasional tour of the lesser antique shops, treasure hunting just as you do and leaving their cards so they can be called if "something special" comes in. When the dealers don't have time, their scouts are in the junk shops, competing with you.

Consequently, telling you to start learning about art by looking in used furniture shops is not exactly giving away a trade secret.

Some readers will raise the question of the morality of buying a valuable art work from a dealer for a nominal price. The appropriate response is that if you are not an expert, you are entitled to all the breaks you can find in buying through the exercise of your knowledge.

If you are an expert in the field, however, you should respond truthfully to a person who asks you about the value of what he is offering you, unless that person is a dealer. Dealers buy and sell for a living and are expected to protect themselves in setting prices on their merchandise.

Thus, there is nothing immoral in an insider buying a valuable art work at a nominal price, if the seller is a dealer.

CHAPTER 22

Whether, When, What, and How to Sell

By any standard, buying art is a lot simpler than selling. You have the money ready to buy, at least enough for the down payment. You scan the offerings within your specialization until your best piece comes along, and when it does, you buy the piece, if you can afford it.

That's all there is to the high spots of buying.

Selling as a Business Decision

As soon as you have acquired a work of art, however, more complex judgments are required. The first decision you have to make is whether or not to keep the piece.

When some casual buyers start out, they experience great difficulty choosing their purchases, and the act of acquisition immobilizes them for a time. They could not sell right away, regardless of the motivaton.

Such selling blocks are not unusual, and may take other forms. There are experienced antique dealers who readily buy and sell seemingly esoteric objects like diamonds or Navajo rugs with no knowledge at all of gems or weavings, but who find art baffling. When they acquire a pleasing work of art, they take it home, rather than setting a price for resale.

Keystone formulas are adequate for pricing their rings and rugs, but the folklore in the middle-level antique trade is that however unlikely any given work of art looks to be, it could be a masterpiece. Don't sell your paintings quickly, they say. You could be losing a million dollars.

Thus, some new collectors and even antique dealers can buy works of art and hold them without further emotional involvement, but they cannot sell easily. They are not objective about art. They cannot face up to selling art as a business decision, to be arrived at consciously at a time when there is no economic pressure to sell.

Instead, they wait until they are forced to sell because they need money or space, and then, having had no selling experience, they make the rashest decisions you can imagine. An antique dealer who buys a Raymond Jonson (1892–1982) drawing for $300 may ask $1,200 for it when he is flush and sell it for $350 or less when he needs money.

You Can Only Offer

For every collector, even the ones who step right out to buy, selling art brings a day of reckoning. The process of selling is not just the reverse of buying.

The legend you start with is, "When you have bought hard, you can sell easy." This means that when you have purchased art with all the safeguards and with resale in mind, reselling should be accomplished without difficulty. Despite the legend, though, reselling may not actually prove to be so easy. Reselling is simplified by following automatic investment plans like those we will be looking at, but even then, the process may still not prove to be quite as simple as it sounds.

If you purchased a representative work by one of the buzz names in American art, for example, and you paid a fair price, there should be a ready market for a profitable resale. Buying "according to the book" should have put you in a position to do well. You will still have to exercise good judgment in the process of reselling, however, because most of the errors made in art investment are made in selling, not in buying. If you are not prudent in selling, you can quickly undermine what was your "best" purchase.

The fact is, once you have decided to part with a piece you own, you cannot just sell in the same direct manner that you bought. You can only offer to sell. You can set the price and pick the time and the outlet and then put your art work up for sale, but you have no assurance you can effect the sale on a given day or that you will get your price. The decision is up to somebody else, the buyer, and the art market is relatively slow-paced.

The Illiquidity of Art

At the outset, we would have to admit that art is comparatively illiquid, although to a great extent the marketability is improving steadily.

The total dollar value of American paintings sold at auction increased from $4,400,000 in the 1975–76 season to $5,550,000 in 1976–77,

$12,400,000 in 1977–78, $14,600,000 in 1978–79, and $26,000,000 in 1979–80. The following year showed another substantial improvement, and in 1982 when one auction house admitted to a decrease in its American painting sales, the other houses all still claimed gains.

In the same five-year period, dollar sales of American watercolors and drawings increased more than eight times. And, in addition to these quantitative improvements, auction sales became much more frequent.

Nevertheless, the selling process is still chancy and slow for art compared to selling listed common stocks, the usual standard for liquidity in investment. Common stocks are marketed more easily than art works because they are clones. Single issues of stock provide a cluster of identical bits of ownership rights and are like peas in a pod.

Moreover, stocks are in sufficient multiplicity to lend themselves to daily averages, and averages sprout theories that aid investors by providing what appears to be a thread of reason in a tangle of names and numbers. The Dow theory, for instance, postulates that stock prices cannot be forecast with precision, but trends can be discerned through a reading of the stock averages over a period; once started, a trend will continue until its cancellation is manifested by having the same averages show its finish.

These stock averages are charted, and the charts foster countless analyses of short-term actions and long-term trends in the stock market. The numerical data, graphically presented, is read as formations, resistance levels, reversal patterns, channels, and so on. Next, these formations are seen typically as head and shoulder tops or bottoms, double or triple tops, rising or falling wedges, and runaway gaps, to the point that, as the old song went, every little stock movement has a meaning all its own.

The purpose of using charts to reflect stock averages is to show where the market has been. Chartists claim that history repeats itself, and the past tells the future.

Paintings Are Not Peas

In contrast to "peas in a pod" stocks, though, every painting is separate and unique. Paintings must be created, not just printed as a paper certificate, so the number of paintings is relatively limited.

Besides, two paintings of the same subject in the same size by the same artist done on the same day will have different values. Two watercolors of the same sidewheeler by James Bard and his brother, one viewed from the port side and one from the starboard, were recently given different pre-sale estimates at an auction, and at the sale the one with the lower estimate brought a higher price.

For these reasons, painting prices do not lend themselves to analysis through averages, as stocks do. Even without considering the refinements in value that are brought by variations in art due to medium, subject, and size, there are simply not enough pictures of any kind sold in the course of an entire year to produce a meaningful average price for any one artist, let alone to compare with the daily averages for one listed stock.

In a ten-year period, for example, there were only 61 Childe Hassam paintings sold at auction, and in two of those years, just two of his paintings sold. The averages are meaningless.

In the same period, 83 Hayley Lever paintings were sold at auction. Fifty of the 83 were sold in the two more recent years, after the Lever boomlet started, but even that volume would support very limited charting when you consider the differences among the paintings.

To provide enough data to be significant, a substantially greater number of artists would be required as by averaging the sales prices of all American paintings sold in a year. The annual statistics for the sales of American paintings have begun to be collected and may eventually prove to be of some value in the long view, but not for present day-to-day needs and not for any one artist.

In contrast to art, stock market analysts are full of theories founded on the available averages, and these theories generate automatic buy/hold/sell investment plans to guide diffident securities investors. The arts, however, are averageless, and similar investment plans cannot easily be formulated.

Fortunately, there are a few investment plans that are based on individual prices rather than on averages, and some of these can be modified to apply to art investment. Plans for art investment are worth looking at. They can help many art collectors, whether beginners or advanced, in buying and selling.

One advantage of these plans is the automatic feature, the sounding of signals for the benefit of the investors who need a push in making decisions. Another is the requirement of periodic review that enforces vigilance in art investment. Also, the more complex art plans call for a beneficial alliance with progressive dealers.

Some general texts on investment consider the purchase of art to be so long term that they discuss how to buy but they don't mention selling at all. Investment is obviously not just buying, however, and you will never really know how well you are doing in art until you try to sell something.

The Beginner's Fixed Fund

The issue of selling art can be reduced to four questions—whether to sell, when to sell, what to sell, and how to sell. Most attention has been paid to the fourth question, how to sell, although it is the unexplored first three questions which are the province of the automatic plans for art investment.

The question of whether to sell can be looked at in various ways. One way to decide to sell is involuntary and hurried, the result of a personal impetus, as when a strapped investor needs money right away. A second is voluntary, as when a prudent investor elects to make an unhurried sale for anticipated general economic or personal reasons, and a third is automatic, when conditions arise that were preset under a formal investment plan.

The simplest example of an art investment plan calling for an automatic response is the Beginner's Fixed Fund. Intended to be initiated when you are starting out, this plan involves your committing to art a fixed sum you can afford, while you are treasure hunting or otherwise learning how to buy.

The fund should be a maximum of about $1,000, and should amount to no more than two percent of your net worth. Within that top, buy your best pictures, with the intent of doubling your money in the near term, and you will have chosen a very rigorous but edifying method of learning the practicalities of the art market.

The Preset Signal Sounds

When you have spent the entire amount in your Fixed Fund, the preset signal sounds. From then on, you must sell part of what you hold in order to generate the cash required for your next purchase or you cannot buy. The point is that after you have exhausted your money in buying, you must sell before you can buy again. Regardless of the temptation, no further investment is permitted until you do sell.

That's a severe restriction, but if you start this Fixed Fund while you are a beginner, you will learn sales principles at the same time you learn to buy. In fact, the act of selling part of what you have bought will strongly augment your awareness of how to buy.

When all of your investment eggs are within the confines of a very little basket, you will watch those eggs much more closely. Taking one treasure hunter's log as an example, his $1,000 Fixed Fund covered the purchase of ten paintings, a lot more than you might have thought, before he received the signal to sell. All of these paintings were eventually sold, for a total of $3,075, enough to fund an expanded investment program.

One variation in this plan for the more adventurous is anticipatory selling. Because it took two months to locate and acquire the ten investment grade paintings in used furniture shops, a confident collector might begin selling without waiting for the automatic signal. When selling is done properly, it works to a collector's advantage any time it takes place.

Another Fixed Fund Example

For those beginners who seek art purchased in more conventional outlets, there are always underpriced art works in your specialization that can be plucked from dealers or auctions. All dealers have idiosyncrasies in pricing that can benefit you, and even the prestige auction houses sometimes provide opportunities for a prudent buy.

For example, the June 19, 1981 auction at Sotheby's in New York City listed 14 Hayley Lever paintings in the one sale, a sure way to depress prices and an instance of how consignors did not protect themselves by asking in advance what the content of the sale would be.

The most heavily backed Lever painting in this sale was the fourteenth lot, although even it sold for less than the midpoint of the pre-sale estimate. As you might have anticipated, eleven sold for less than the minimum of the pre-sale estimates and the other two did not meet their reserves at all, a sadness for the consignors.

Thus, if a Hayley Lever painting fit your specialization in American Impressionism or in twentieth century marines, you might well have been lying in wait for such good buys as lot number 243, a standard Lever subject estimated at $1,500 to $2,000 and sold for $950, more than 20 percent below the reserve you should have expected.

If you bought that Lever, the signal under the terms of your Fixed Fund would have sounded as you neared the $1,000 limit. You would have to sell the $950 painting before buying again, and to aid you, you would have in hand Sotheby's appraisal of about $1,750 plus the ten percent buying fee, or about $1,900 as the estimate of your asking price at retail.

Frequently, a canny bidder will then enter a work such as the Lever painting in a later sale at the same or an equivalent auction house like Christie's. He would obtain the same or a higher pre-sale estimate, making sure that the mix of lots was favorable this time, and would expect the winning bid at the second sale to be within the pre-sale estimate, thus reflecting true value.

CHAPTER 23

More Investment Plans

The Beginner's Fixed Fund is a good scheme for helping the collector get started in regularizing the buying and selling of his art. It frees him to buy, and then pulls him up short if he doesn't sell.

Other collectors, however, may be looking for either a more functional plan to serve a single long-range purpose or a more complex technique to guide their art investments on an automatic basis. This is where we get into Dollar Cost Averaging for the long-range purpose and into the Constant Dollar Series for sophistication.

Dollar Cost Averaging

Dollar Cost Averaging is a program to build a personal investment fund to meet a specific goal on a fixed date, as in a retirement plan or an installment purchase.

The program resembles buying a pension from an insurance company, where you pay in regular monthly amounts that accumulate to your account. When you retire in a given year, you will have laid away a nest egg from which you will be paid regular benefits. The amount you will receive as your pension will be commensurate with the dollars you paid in monthly, the duration of your payments, and the interest earned.

Similarly, you could enter into a Dollar Cost Averaging plan with a stock broker where you select a stock you wish to buy. The broker holds this stock for your account while you pay in regular monthly amounts for the required period. This stock plan is called Dollar Cost Averaging because what you eventually get in stock is the quantity actually purchased at the time of each payment you made, based on the market price of the stock that day. At the end of the period of your payments, the stock you will have acquired will be at a dollar cost that is the average of the prices you paid over the period of the purchase.

In art investment under Dollar Cost Averaging, you start by finding a gallery which will let you buy the portfolio of art works you choose with payment to be made at regular monthly intervals. As each piece in the portfolio is paid for, you take possession of it.

In this plan, the art you select is reserved for you. You pay in installments over a preset period with a definite termination date, regardless of the fluctuations in the value of the art during the period. You pay from your current income in an unchangeable amount at established times, as long as your plan is in effect. You do not sell.

The duration of the plan is by arrangement with the gallery. If the term is short, interest might not be assessed, as it might not be charged under a conventional installment contract to buy art. Longer terms mean larger portfolios that benefit the dealer. It could be stipulated that extensions or new agreements be entered into on renewal dates, thus providing a truer averaging.

By the time your Dollar Cost Averaging plan terminates, you will have received delivery of your entire portfolio. The plan assumes that the art you bought will be worth more than its cost, so you will have had an enhancement in value. A skillful art buyer will have selected a portfolio that gained substantially in worth, as opposed to the limitations faced by the investor in a conventional pension fund where the payout is in fixed dollars.

The Fulfillment of Your Purpose

Your Dollar Cost Averaging plan comes to its end at the preset time for the fulfillment of your purpose in initiating the plan. If your purpose was retirement, the preset time is the attainment of the retirement age you selected.

Next, you automatically start selling the art under a program you have formulated for disposition of your holdings, without buying. The disposition can be as a lot or piecemeal, depending on your needs. The proceeds of the sale are then available to satisfy your original purpose, presumably one for the long term, because the normal course of Dollar Cost Averaging is to meet a goal extending over ten or more years.

For example, a well-to-do investor aged 50 decides on a ten-year Dollar Cost Averaging plan of $200 per month to finance his retirement in part. He specializes in original illustrations so he decides on eight large paintings by F.C. Yohn (1875–1933) priced at $12,000 in total and one large Herbert Morton Stoops (1887–1948) Western illustration. At the end of the first year, he takes home two of the lesser Yohn paintings in the group.

25. Frederick C. Yohn. "Custer's Last Stand," 1929. Oil on canvas, 26 by 32 inches.

When the ten years are up, the investor has an extensive art collection in his retirement fund, and he can begin selling to produce income, in accordance with the marketing decision that had been made in advance. Exactly when to sell, and what and how, are questions for later.

This investor also applied the theory of doubling by choosing the Yohn illustrations because the artist was a first-tier illustrator in his day, but one who has not yet been rediscovered. Also, major Stoops illustrations that brought only a couple of thousand dollars five years ago sold at auction for as much as $25,000 in 1981.

The investor will have paid $24,000 into his Dollar Cost Averaging plan over ten years and reasonably expects these paintings to be worth at

*26. Herbert Morton Stoops.
"Monica Found Herself
Alone," 1926. Oil on canvas,
44 by 32 inches.*

least $60,000 in 1982 dollars at the time of his retirement, apart from changes in the worth of the dollar during the period.

Such value enhancement is a primary advantage of the plan.

Interim Selling

The disadvantages of Dollar Cost Averaging are, first, that the investor must be knowledgeable enough to have gained by committing his income for the period. That's easy. Anyone who buys art like an insider will profit from his purchases.

Second, the plan presumes that the investor will have sufficient income throughout the term and will not divert his dollars into other channels that may momentarily seem more appropriate. This is a fixed plan.

Third, if the investor decides on a series of short-term plans and prices are high when it is time to renew a plan, he must resist the temptation to wait for what might seem to be more favorable buying conditions. He must buy on a regular basis to achieve Dollar Cost Averaging.

Fourth, there is no provision for selling during the course of the acquisitions.

The lack of interim selling is the real rub in the plan. The proof of the art pudding is in the disposition of the art work you purchase. Errors in buying must be corrected as they occur, before the ultimate selling at the end of the program.

This is a reason for modifying Dollar Cost Averaging into a more flexible plan by adding a provision requiring you to analyze what you hold at the end of every two years. Then, you automatically sell at least ten percent of your art portfolio, just for the sake of selling, regardless of gain or loss and for no other purpose, and you reinvest the proceeds in a new acquisition for your portfolio.

Thus, under Modified Dollar Cost Averaging the investor who bought the eight Yohn illustrations could sell the weakest at the end of two years.

Selling refreshes one's mind.

Constant Dollar Series

The next automatic plan is the Constant Dollar Series for more experienced investors. In following this plan, you must decide on an aggregate amount of money to put into art. Approximately ten percent of your net worth is suggested.

The most opportune time to begin the plan is when prices are normal, but since no one can ever tell in advance when prices are normal, today will do. All of the money in the plan is invested in art, purchasing one "best" piece at a time, with no piece to cost more than 25 percent of your total budget.

In this Constant Dollar Series, you review your holdings monthly. If you find that any picture has failed to rise ten percent in value in a year, sell it and add any additional sum that might be required to keep the total dollars in the plan constant. Take your losses.

On the other hand, if any picture has increased in value by more than 100 percent since you acquired it, sell it. Take your profits and reinvest.

Hold on to the works that do not meet either selling signal. Let those middling profits ride.

Under this Constant Dollar plan, you keep a steady quantity of "dollars" in the plan, in the form of cash plus art. The experienced investor will expect to show substantial returns above the Constant Dollar level. With the excess of funds, start a second Constant Dollar plan, and continue these plans for as many years as they serve your purpose. In a rising market, you will have a series of Constant Dollar plans. If prices decrease, reduce the number of plans you have.

For example, suppose that for $1,000 you bought a small Dennis Malone Carter (1818–1881) genre painting of a child sewing doll clothes. If at the end of a year the value is still only $1,000, sell it. If its value is $1,250, hold it, but if its worth has risen to $2,000 or more, take the profit.

These are real values we are talking about. When we refer to a ten percent gain, we mean ten percent above the inflationary increment for the period. Some people count in nominal dollars and don't recognize the effects of inflation, although adjustments should be made yearly in your record keeping for significant rises in the cost of living.

Variable Ratio Plan

The final plan is the Variable Ratio concept for experienced investors.

You must accept that at some point, there will be a slowing of the art market. Major trends in art prices are long running, averaging 20 years or more rather than four years as in common stocks, but downturns will occur. Whether your portfolio was acquired under Dollar Cost Averaging or Constant Dollar plans or by a free-form program of your own, you must be prepared for that eventuality.

Under this new Variable Ratio Plan, veteran investors learn to recognize the difference between defensive and aggressive art works. Defensive works are by artists who are the cream of the first-tier. Thomas Hart Benton, Georgia O'Keeffe, Jasper Cropsey (1823–1900), Edward Hopper (1882–1967), Gilbert Stuart (1755–1828), and Frederic Remington, for example, would be defensive artists, along with Winslow Homer and Thomas Eakins (1844–1916).

At this point, Dennis Malone Carter, Hayley Lever, Henry Golden Dearth, Frederick Waugh (1861–1940), Julius Rolshoven (1858–1930), and George Herbert Macrum would be aggressive artists, from the second or third tier.

27. *Dennis Malone Carter. "Child Sewing Doll Clothes." Oil on board, 6½ by 4½ inches.*

Booming and Falling Markets

The theory behind the Variable Ratio Plan is that in a booming market, works by the aggressive artists are likely to sell disproportionately higher, while in a falling market, prices of the defensive artists are more protected against decline.

When the market bottoms, emphasis is on defensive art. The rally starts there, and as it settles into the upward trend, investors begin buying aggressive art works with vigor. Then, when the values of the aggressive pieces exceed the defensive, relatively, this is the signal of the weakening of the rally.

Consequently, when you start your Variable Ratio Plan at a time presumed to be normal, you should optimally have an equal balance between defensive and aggressive art works. As time passes, this ratio should change to conform to your opinion of whether the market is stable, rising, or falling.

While prices are going up, sell the aggressive artists and reinvest the profits in defensive artists who will be relatively cheaper and will guard against loss in any decline. When an aggressive painter like Charles Sprague Pearce brings $225,000 less ten percent for a small oil in a booming market, an investor tends to lose sight of what a fine Thomas Hart Benton painting could be bought for $202,500.

While prices are declining, sell the defensive artists at their protected prices and buy aggressive artists cheaply to prepare for the rise. As an example, sell Benton and buy a number of pieces on Pearce's level.

If prices rise steadily, as they may over a long period, and they never do decline during the course of your plan, you will still be well off. You will have a portfolio full of the prime defensive artists.

How bad can that be?

Plans Depersonalize Art

So much for automatic investment plans. Not every expert will agree with all parts of every plan, but the plans will at least make you think about selling.

The plans also raise questions about values. Do you know enough about appraisal to be sure of values for each work of art you are considering? If not, buy and sell only the pieces with values you are sure of, when you are following a plan.

These plans do compel collectors to become investors, as we have seen. Plans force sales. If you don't sell, you are just a collector. Plans also take the "I buy what I like" purchasers and prevent them from compounding their errors into "I sell when I like." Plans determine the buying and selling, individuals do not. The processes are regularized.

What the plans also do, though, is depersonalize art. Unlike investors in common stocks, collectors fall in love with particular pieces of art. They get involved, and won't sell.

There are people who put "halos" around art they own. A man who works in the outdoors adores a James Thurber (1894–1961) dog drawing. A woman who is a feminist finds it hard to part with a Georgia O'Keeffe watercolor, although in truth, works of art don't know who owns them and don't reciprocate warm feelings.

Plans do emphasize reality. Using plans eases the indecision in both buying and selling, automatically taking care of the question of whether to sell as well as when and what to sell.

Thus, art investors who follow plans may get more action than do informal investors. The planners are buying and selling regularly, and between times they are analyzing whether to buy or sell. In addition, investors in art plans are more certain of profits, but the amounts may be smaller.

Finally, investors in plans are controlled by more mechanical procedures, requiring fewer personal decisions, and timing is their key to selling. Speed of action is called for, though they may sometimes be frustrated by the relative illiquidity of art.

Principles to Watch_____

For the "free form" collectors who are following their individual investment programs rather than specific plans, there is nothing automatic to fall back on. There are only general principles to be applied.

The basic principle is that the investor know himself. In addition to a yearly assessment of his personal economic state, he must continually consider his own lifestyle changes that come with age and experience. A person's likes may move from simpler things to cerebral and sometimes back again in art. The reverse is equally possible, and his art portfolio should reflect his status.

Although most collectors do not use a formal plan, when to sell may still be easy for them, in theory. Generally, you sell when your reading of sales prices indicates that the trend of your specialization has neared its peak or is starting into a decline.

The analysis is mathematical, keyed to money which is the way our society keeps score, but the reading should also be by the emotions. You should be listening constantly to the emanations from the veteran dealers and the other experienced resellers. Are they losing confidence in the stability of art prices in your specialization? If so, you may want to consider selling now.

There is a touch of crowd psychology in market trends, in addition to the cut and dried direction of the numbers. You should recognize that the market rises and falls partly because of influences other than facts. If you go strictly by prices in deciding what will be, you may be missing the nuances that would tip you to what is.

When the stock market fell apart in October 1929, it was because mass psychology played an important role, not just statistics. Like the stock market, the art market may decline when people think it will decline, and that's the key you should be listening for.

When to sell is equally as important as whether to sell, and your analysis of this question should be from two factual sides, the external conditions outside of art as well as the technical inside factors we have been exploring.

The external conditions are general economic indicators like the Dow-Jones stock averages, interest rates, commodity prices, the cost of living index, gross national product, construction index, and so on. There are also political factors such as threats of war and presidential acts. When the public ceases to believe that the party in power is behaving rationally, prices may suffer.

The Theory of Art Lag

The reason for watching the externals is of course that business cycles do act upon the art market as well as on the stock market. Stock prices react more violently than art does, having suffered a major decline on the average of once every four years for more than a century.

The art market has these longer cycles we have seen, and in addition, the levelling off in art prices that may come will generally lag four to six months or longer behind stocks. This is the theory of art lag which is a compensation for the lack of the liquidity you find in stocks.

In art, when the signs appear, you cannot expect to sell in a day, but you don't need to. There is time. In stocks, you can sell in a day, but when the signs appear it may be too late. The experts may already have discounted what is about to happen.

In times of stagflation, the experts anticipate that stocks may react negatively to the stagnation, while art responds positively to the inflation. Art offers the double blessing of high appreciation in inflation plus some protection in deflation.

Art Is a Gentle Game

What it gets down to is that buying stocks is for gamblers. The stock market makes for anxiety, high blood pressure, and addiction. The stock game is generally played for the sake of the game itself, and players seldom quit. The most experienced stock investors lose as well as win.

Investment in art, however, is relatively serene. The risk of loss associated with high rate of return investments like some collectibles is not substantial at all for the knowledgeable art investor. There may not be equal liquidity or posted daily prices in art, but there is time to read the omens and think before you act.

Art is a gentle game, in the old-fashioned sense.

CHAPTER 24

The Theory and Practice of Selling Art

In addition to the generalized principles we have been examining for selling art, there are technical signs of change you can see inside the art market that take fairly specific forms. Some of these forms are open and factual series of events, usually expressed in numbers, and you can easily scrutinize their movements, if you know what to look for. The mathematical variations in the forms could even be charted.

The Breadth of the Market

One sign of change that investors without automatic plans can weigh for guidance in buying and selling is the breadth of the art market. This is indicated by the number of different artists being offered for sale at any given moment, as well as which artists they are.

This breadth factor is disclosed in the indices to auction catalogs, for example, and in magazine advertisements by galleries. Second- and third-tier artists may be appearing more frequently, including some whose names you have never seen before and will have to investigate in reference books.

When you start seeing these new names, you are in an aggressive market, and when there are a lot of new names, the market is peaking.

Second is the theory of outright discoveries. No matter how many second- and third-tier artists have unexpectedly sold for high prices in an aggressive market, there are others still out there to be bought cheaply compared to what they will be sold for after they are discovered by dealers. The greater the number of discoveries, the stronger the market.

A third indication is the number of new highs in sales prices for individual artists. These are announced in auction house publicity releases mailed to known investors. Ask to be put on the house mailing list.

By publishing these announcements of record art prices, auction houses have begun a conditioning of investors that they must maintain lest they inadvertently weaken the market. If at some point the auction houses start claiming fewer new highs, the market will be seen as weakening, and art investors will take that as a sign to sell.

Fourth, look at the bellwether artists. In a rising market, when a leading painter like Winslow Homer hits repeated new highs in price, this signals continued strength in the market. Collectors of lesser artists become confident and buy in their own specializations.

A variation of this is to pay attention to the bellwether buyers, the insiders who set the trends relative to high priced art and who purchase in amounts over $100,000. When they who are presumed to be experts buy, you may think you should buy. Other bellwether buyers include the art funds, if you are able to obtain timely details on what the funds are buying and selling.

Don't concentrate on the consignment dealers, though. They always function as sellers, under any condition, in any market.

The Theory of Contrary Opinion

Fifth is the theory of contrary opinion. Holding to the view that the buying public is always wrong, the theory goes, you should sell when mass optimism is at its highest.

This is the cynic's view, "sell when the good news is out." The little people are always mistaken, these theorists say, so do the opposite.

On the other hand, there is the populist theory of the behavior of smaller investors. Concentrate on the movement of art works sold for less than $1,000, it is said, because the smaller investor is the first one hit by economic downturns. He then reacts through his visceral feelings rather than listening to the experts who are right, on the average, only about 50 percent of the time.

Most price changes result from popular interpretations of the facts, not necessarily the facts themselves, so pay attention to what people say they do, not always what they really do.

Sixth, there are the seasonal factors we have looked at before. The art market is historically strongest in the spring and the late fall. When the market is not strong in the right seasons, the signal is one of overall weakness.

Seventh is the theory of Collateral Markets. How are art sales in England? In Canada? How are sales in specializations other than yours?

Finally, there is the utter opposite to all of the usual approaches, the random walk theory which holds that yesterday has nothing to do with tomorrow. Therefore, prices have no memory. You should ignore what paintings and sculpture have been bringing at auction, the random walkers say, and look only to the intrinsic value of the one piece you are selling.

Forget the statistics. Think of selling as a knack, not a science, they advise, and look to your own intuition. It works as well as anything else does when you consider how inexact and contradictory the other theories are.

The Maxims of the Trade

After examining the automatic plans and informal theories covering whether, when, and what to sell, we are left with the maxims of the trade. These are the pithy sayings that epitomize selling practices in the art business and provide the essence of the accumulated wisdom of the market, although sometimes the physical enjoyment of stringing the words together seems to take precedence over the meaning of what is being said.

On whether to sell, for example, the old saw is, "If today you would not buy a work of art you already own, sell it." Do it as soon as the original reason for buying no longer holds. Sell any art work you bought believing it had good prospects because of a proposed retrospective exhibition or a biography that never materialized.

Also, "Never quarrel with the implications of sales prices, but do what they indicate." Never try to outguess the art market, but obey the manifested trends.

In addition, "There are no keepers in art." You can't take art works with you when you go. Make timely sales because the pieces will be sold sometime, anyhow.

These are sayings emphasizing objectivity. When the signals say sell, sell, and vice versa.

If you hold a loser, "Learn to take a loss quickly." Also, "Cut your losses and let your profits run." The most critical requirement in any investment program is training yourself to accept losses and deal with them.

If you were to sell only the profitable pieces and keep the losers, you would eventually have only losers. So, when prices start to move downward in a confirmed trend, don't hesitate. Sell the losers. When a school of art or a subject is becoming unpopular, like paintings of people smoking or violence or ancestral portraits, sell.

And, "If you ever have three straight losses, sell everything and start over."

Psychiatrists and Accountants _____

If you hold a winner, "No one ever went broke taking profits," but, "Don't try to get the last dollar." No one can predict the absolute bottom or top price, and many opportunities are lost through hanging on too long rather than concentrating on protecting your "best" picture and moving in your optimum time.

"It is better to sell art too soon than to risk overstaying the market."

In addition, "Take your profits when better gains are likely in another work."

Also, after selling at a profit, "Pause before reinvesting." Don't be rash just because you have money to spend.

In general, "When you have been fully invested for a year, start selling."

Also, "There is no need to be in the art market under all circumstances." When you pull dollars out of art, invest defensively.

Nevertheless, you must "avoid switching too frequently." For one thing, the commissions for buying and selling art at auction or through dealers are too costly.

In addition, "Psychiatrists are the best investors in art. Accountants are the worst."

And finally, "The art market has no past." That's for the random walkers.

Obviously, the plans, theories, and maxims overlap and even contradict themselves. Nevertheless, the essence of what is right for you will come through to you, and this is what you should follow. Random walk if you must, but the rest of us will be learning from and applying the plans and theories of the past, as condensed into the maxims that fit us.

How to Sell _____

The last part of collecting art is how to sell.

The underlying maxim here is, "When you have a buyer in hand, don't let him get away." Don't be overly rigid in what you are asking. You may be a long time between buyers.

In selling, one way is directly to another collector or investor, at the retail price or as close to it as you can get. Lower priced works are the easiest to sell privately.

Your specialization will help—you may even know private buyers to contact. If you do not, you can run a classified advertisement in an art magazine or in your daily newspaper. Selling by mail works, although you have to exercise some caution to avoid thieves and nuisances.

Another way is to try to sell to a dealer. It is sometimes easier and cleaner to sell to a dealer than it is to a friend.

In selling to a dealer, the relationship is finished when the transaction is done, unless you were fraudulent. While the dealer buys art at his own risk in terms of defects, you may end as guarantor to a friend who might develop a frivolous objection to the work of art months after the purchase.

The dealer may even pay you more than you would feel warranted in asking from a friend. You should expect to receive at least 50 percent of the retail price when you sell to a dealer, but you can do better if you approach a dealer with the same specialization you have or if you contact a new dealer who needs inventory. Some dealers may even be willing to pay 100 percent of what you consider retail to be. They may have a special customer for the piece.

When you are offering your art to a dealer, the recommended practice is to dress well and to praise the virtues of what you have to sell.

If you have a desirable piece, the dealer may tell you that he can pay more than auction prices because he is buying privately from you. What he pays you will not be published, he says, and he can therefore charge the ultimate buyer more. You do not need to believe this explanation.

Getting the Dealer to Offer

Your objective as the seller is to get the dealer to make an offer. You should have researched the price of your art before calling on a gallery, but even so, private sellers are never entirely sure of how much they really know vis´a vis one they conceive of as an expert like a dealer. They are afraid that the number they pick as an asking price will only be a fraction of true value. They think they might put a hundred dollar price tag on a five thousand dollar gem.

In contrast, the dealer will use his experience to try to lead the seller into setting the price or at least he will attempt to get a feeling of the range of prices that would be acceptable to the seller. If the seller says he has no idea of price and he refuses to state an amount, and it does not appear that a purchase can be effected, a dealer who is independent may even tell the seller to come back after he has done his homework in establishing a price.

In negotiating on a California landscape by Julian Rix (1850–1903) worth about $1,500 at retail, one seller who had been sent away because he had no asking price actually did return. He said he had obtained an appraisal at the Fine Arts Department of the local university and he wanted "four" as his price.

The dealer did not know whether the seller was talking about $4,000 or $400. Either sum could have been recommended by the professor who was an unpredictable amateur appraiser, and the dealer was relieved to learn it was the latter. He then offered $350.

However low you set your asking price, dealers will always bargain on it because they expect there will be air in what you ask. Moreover, dealers say they believe that if they don't bargain, you will think you asked too little, and they want to maintain a satisfied atmosphere.

The Dealer's Fault-Finding

The refusal to make an offer to a private seller who has no idea of what an art work is worth is one of the most aggravating devices of any dealer. Actually, it is the dealer's ethical obligation to set the price in a transaction with a seller who is not an expert and who relies on the dealer's professionalism.

Another irritation is for the dealer to find every possible fault with the piece while examining it for purchase, even to naming defects that don't exist. The signature doesn't look authentic. The painting has been cut down in size. The paint has been skinned in an old cleaning. The subject is one that won't sell. When the work is a bronze, it is a poor casting, badly chased and patinated. Then, after reciting a litany of flaws that prove the piece to be absolutely worthless, the dealer makes an offer anyhow, a low one.

A ploy when you have a large picture, too big to go under your arm, or a heavy bronze, is for the dealer to get you to bring the behemoth into his gallery rather than looking at it in your place. The change in location provides the dealer with a tactical advantage because you will probably reject the thought of lugging the work back home, even if you have to accept less than you had anticipated.

A dealer's primary objective is of course to buy at as low a price as he ethically can. He has at hand the latest inside information about trends, auction results, what other dealers are doing, museum purchases, promotional campaigns, books to be published, exhibitions coming up, and so on. He knows what will be featured in magazines because he is solicited for ads.

All of the bargaining advantages are with the dealer. When you walk into a gallery with a small Joseph Sharp painting under your arm, the dealer will use his experience to probe to discover the price he knows you must have in your mind, consciously or unconsciously.

As a last resort, he may even ask what the highest price is you can conceive of for your piece. One cagy dealer who did just that was surprised to hear "$2,500" instead of the $25,000 he could have expected. He has told the story to other dealers a hundred times.

A more subtle dealer approach is to suggest that you leave your art work with him so he can look into its authenticity, and then ask you what he should insure it for while he holds it. He would consider your insurance evaluation to be the same as your asking price.

You Can Shop Around

If you are not satisfied with the dealer's response, you are at liberty to try another dealer. You can shop around, although dealers hate this.

When dealers suspect you are shopping, they may respond by acting in concert, phoning ahead of you to set up the same kind of "ring" that controls auction prices. Then you will never get an offer from any local dealer higher than the first one you received.

In defense of dealers, they have to anticipate evasions and outright lies. There are sellers who will call or write an expert for a free informal appraisal and then claim to have had a formal appraisal from the expert at four times the round figure he gave orally.

A man from Maine came into a collection of original illustrations that had been given away years earlier by a publisher. The new owner contacted every expert he could reach, to find out what he had and what it was worth. Most experts are suckers for letter writers who seem to be ignorant and sincere, but they tend to put big prices on items they do not think they can buy. Before the owner wore out his welcome, he had learned just enough to price his paintings prohibitively high. He still has them.

When dealers learn that a seller is under pressure and has no other outlet, they can be cruel. There was a Thomas Moran landscape of Long Island discovered in an attic during an estate appraisal in Alabama. The painting was in poor visual condition. The surface paint had cracked to the point that the picture was not suitable for auction, but the defect was entirely restorable.

The heirs did not know what to do. They delayed bringing the painting to the attention of New York City dealers, and when they did, they could not get an offer above $20,000. It appeared that the "ring" had been alerted. The New York dealers also discouraged possible private buyers who asked for their opinion. The claim was that the painting's condition was fatally flawed.

When the heirs ran out of time because the estate had to be settled, they were lucky to find a small Southern dealer who paid them $40,000. The painting was restored, but the Southern dealer still could not find a customer because the early knocks on the picture had survived. He was forced to take the picture back to one of the same New York dealers who had bad-mouthed the condition in the beginning. The larger dealer accepted the picture on consignment at $150,000, gave it his imprimatur, and sold it.

As another example, some collectors try to sell privately and cannot. They may then think it is obligatory for the dealer to buy back art he sold them, at the price paid. There are dealers who will do this, if the current value is not less than it was originally. Other dealers will accept a return only if there is an extra profit in it, while a third group will as a matter of policy never take back art they sold. This is a condition to be covered in the original bill of sale, rather than to have it arise in an emergency.

The moral to these stories is that people who are not experienced in handling transactions in art may trip in selling, unless they become knowledgeable or find a knowledgeable agent. Dealers are not good samaritans. They are in business to make a profit.

Consignment with a Dealer

When you can't sell privately and you can't sell outright to a dealer, the next choice is to put the piece on consignment with a dealer.

This is often an easier ford to cross than selling directly. The dealer doesn't have to put up any money. When a dealer buys, he must watch what he pays because he must at least make a greater profit than he would earn by investing the purchase money elsewhere. If he takes art on consignment, however, he has no out-of-pocket payment of any kind to make.

There are two ways for you to effect a consignment. The one the dealer prefers is to have you agree on a net cost to him, as if you were selling to him—except that you don't yet get paid. Then, the dealer will add on whatever he feels appropriate to come up with a selling price. Some dealers will insist on this arrangement, if you permit it. After all, they say, you must know what you want for the piece.

A fixed net like this is a multiple benefit for the dealer. He is buying without paying and he still has the right of return. When the art is worth more than the consignor suspects or when it increases in value, the owner's share remains constant but the dealer's share rises smartly. If the owner asked for a thousand dollars for his end and the dealer originally priced the art at $1,500 so he would take a third as his commission, a rise to $2,000 in value would have the owner and dealer sharing equally.

The more usual consignment is for you to agree with the dealer on the selling price and on the dealer's commission which is negotiable. However much the price might rise, the dealer's commission is fixed at, say, 30 percent. This is the fairer basis for the seller.

When you leave the piece with a dealer, though, be sure to get a receipt that fully describes what you left, including the exact physical condition of the work and its frame or base. The receipt should also state both the selling price and the rate of commission and should list the terms of the agency.

Keep in mind that if the dealer has trouble selling your art, he may elect to ship it out to sub-dealers any place, without telling you. If the dealer does not want to hang your picture for exhibition, he does not have to. The dealer may not advertise your work, or insure it. He may not tell you when the piece is sold, and he may not pay you unless you demand payment.

All of these contingencies should be covered in the receipt. And remember, the bigger the dealer, the more exposure your piece gets, but the less leverage you have in your relationship.

A fourth method of selling is at auction, a process we have already covered at length.

The Selling Sequence

The way you actually sell depends on how much time you have and how much trouble you are willing to take.

When you can, sell privately because this is the best way to try to dispose of your art work. You should make the most money.

If you cannot sell privately, attempt to sell to a dealer. That's the quickest disposition.

If this does not work out either, put your art on consignment with a dealer, at an agreed price and commission.

If your piece does not sell through the dealer in a specified period, go to auction.

You will not lose anything but time by trying the other methods first. Don't rush. You will learn by going through all of the steps called for in effecting your own sale.

Alternately, it is possible to dispose of art by giving it to a charity. There are tax advantages too complex and too changeable to describe here. You can also bequeath art in your will, to provide ever-increasing benefits for the estate.

When you do sell art regularly, you demonstrate to the Internal Revenue Service that you are an investor rather than a collector, for the tax advantages that may occur.

If you sell more than a few pieces, however, you may slide over into becoming a dealer, with different tax consequences requiring professional analysis. Investors who have been acquiring art over a period of years frequently do begin acting like dealers and selling on their own. They have the inventory and the background for selling so they use their homes as bases and off they go.

Even if the investors are only part-time dealers, they can exaggerate a little to the auction houses when they sell at auction and ask for a dealer's discount on the commission.

There is good in almost everything, when you look for it.

CHAPTER 25

The Mop-Up

Now that you are acquiring art, finding out how to buy gives way to learning how to do the housekeeping on the works of art in your portfolio.

This is the mop-up. You will have to assume the responsibility for such tasks as framing and hanging pictures, physical handling and storage, crating and shipping, insurance, taxes, art management, record keeping, and the like.

Seeing Beneath the Surface

As an investor, you must deal in futures, not only in what the price of a painting may rise to over a period of time but also what added value a defective painting will take on as soon as it has been made visually perfect. At this stage in the development of your touch, you should be able to look at any painting, no matter what shape it is in when you first see it, and visualize the fully cosmeticized picture.

To most casual buyers, collectors, and even dealers, paintings look to be absolutely unsuited for purchase when they are damaged, dirty, unvarnished, or unframed.

A painting in otherwise fine condition may be regarded with suspicion by the half-knowing even if the sole defect is that the surface is unvarnished. Some buyers will reject an unvarnished painting simply because it does not possess the sparkle that varnishing would add. This complaint is also voiced when the varnish was improperly applied and the gloss has faded irregularly, leaving matte spots.

You should by now be seeing past surface defects like dirt, to appreciate the real work of art a conservator will unearth.

The Role of Framing

In addition, it is difficult even for experts to believe how critical the role of framing is in enhancing as well as protecting a painting.

There are, for example, paintings seen in a color photograph without the frame that are stunning, but in a gallery you could pass by the same painting without a second look when the frame detracts. A painting on the somber side with dark blue detailing will be severely diminished by a darker frame in an off shade of green.

When a painting is badly framed, few buyers will see it as their "best."

Some of the same conservators who restore paintings also deal in frames to complete the package, but most do not. Generally, the choice of framing will be up to you. Ideas for styles and finishes can come from the conservator, museums, auction houses, and galleries, as well as from your frame shop.

The goal in framing is to achieve a balance, making the frame secondary to the picture and yet functional in protecting the picture, defining its area, and connecting it both to the wall it hangs on and to your other pictures. The frame must be neutral and subordinate to the picture while independently handsome and compatible. The frame that is right for you is the one that looks right on your picture, on the wall.

Simple Picture, Simple Frame

The general rule of the trade is that a simple picture calls for a simple frame and a complex picture a complex frame, although some authorities suggest the reverse. When in doubt, select a simple frame.

If protecting an unframed picture is in question, you should act promptly because a painting that is unframed when you get it may warp or become edge worn unless you secure it in a frame. On the other hand, a painting framed by forcing it into a space that is too tight is a greater danger, compressing the stretcher bars and ballooning the canvas. The solution requires chiselling away the rabbet of the frame until the fit is eased.

As you might expect, a great many paintings are on stock stretchers in sizes such as 16 by 20, 20 by 24, or 24 by 30 inches. This means you can purchase stock frames to fit the stock stretchers, but look at your painting inside several stock frames before you select one. Be sure of suitability. Treat buying a frame as carefully as you did buying the picture.

Ask your frame source to mount the picture in the stock frame for you. If you do the job yourself, do not nail the painting into the frame you buy. Instead, use two-inch mending plates with screw holes in both ends. Bend each plate with pliers so an end can be screwed to one of the sides of the frame, the other end extending over the stretcher to hold the picture tightly in place.

One Knowledgeable Framer

When you need a custom frame, you will find there is at least one knowledgeable framer in almost every area. This is the expert who does the work for the professional artists, museums, and veteran dealers.

Seek him out because there are other framers who will do anything irresponsible you can visualize in derogation of the integrity of the art. A framer can casually destroy the value of a work of art by cutting down its size, by throwing away old mats and backings with titles and dates on them, by using new mats or backings that can stain, or by irrevocably glueing a drawing to a board.

The usual approach of a framer to his task is that bigger is better. The more elaborate a frame is, the richer he will claim it looks, and the wider a mat is, the more flattering he will say it is. You will have to curb his salesmanship. In general, simpler is safer.

The choice of a new frame is a matter of aesthetics. You should select the design of the frame to fit the period of the picture. It is inappropriate to choose a frame style of a significantly later period than the picture, and it may be misleading to choose a style that is much earlier.

For the surface of the frame, gold leaf is almost always suitable.

An Extension of the Painting

A liner or insert may be used inside the frame as an extender, and the modern practice is to cover this liner with a neutral gray fabric instead of a matching gold leaf. This kind of contrasted framing has become a contemporary uniform for paintings of any period, but it is also possible to think of the frame as an extension of the painting instead of as a visual stop. For medium and small paintings, a frame will make the painting look larger if it continues the same colors that are dominant in the painting.

Even when the painting comes to you framed, as it generally does, you will have to decide whether reframing would be an improvement. Most dealers will have made the change whenever reframing would better the appearance of a painting. Dealers are suspicious of old frames anyhow. An old surface may flake or break loose when the picture is in transit, on exhibition, or even while just hanging on a collector's wall.

When the frame is original and reframing is being considered only because of surface damage or staining, however, a conservator or a cabinetmaker can be engaged to repair the frame to preserve the artist's own package.

Old frames should be retained even if they must be removed from the paintings. Museums and major collectors know how to ask for them because the artists may have designed or constructed the original frames, have selected them as part of a planned decorative combination, or have made markings on them contributing to provenance.

Crating and Shipping

The physical handling of art includes crating and shipping. These services are expensive.

A recent shipment from New York City to Albuquerque of a $2,000 35 by 30 inch painting in a five inch frame cost $261.19. The crating portion was $128.50 and the basic air freight was $75.99, expenses that make the shipment of lower priced paintings prohibitive by conventional means. The total of incidental costs for an average painting bought at auction in a distant city, with bidding agent's fees and buyer's premiums included, can add one-third or more to the cost.

Alternatives to conventional crating and shipping would be the use of double corrugated mirror cartons as containers and bus lines like Greyhound as carriers. The shipment should be insured in transit. Bus lines may be cheaper on insurance, too, but you need to inquire about the carrier's insurance limits. Some carriers offer only nominal maximums and others cut off at $1,000, a paradox when the carriers' own crate and freight charges may exceed 25 percent of the insurance limit.

More paintings are being shipped to exhibitions and sales than ever before, so if you are the shipper, you may wish to make your own wooden crates.

There are two basic principles. First, you need four inches or so of interior clearance in all directions from the point where the painting is to be positioned. This clearance is to avoid an object piercing the front or back of the crate and penetrating the picture, but a practical compromise on dimensions may be adopted to avoid excessively thick crates.

Second, the top of the crate must be screwed on rather than nailed. The ends, sides, and bottom of the crate can be nailed together, but the top is screwed on to avoid vibration from hammering after the picture has been placed in the crate.

To construct the crate, use ¾ inch lumber for the ends and sides. Figure the interior size you need by adding about eight inches to the picture's height, width, and thickness. This produces a crate thicker than usual, but safer. Conventional commercial crates are thinner, adding only two inches to the thickness of the picture and then adjusting that measurement to the next wider size of standard ¾ inch lumber.

Cut the ends for the crate to the same dimension as the width of the interior size you want. For the sides, add one and a half inches to compensate for the thickness of the ends. For the facing panels of quarter-inch plywood or masonite, add one and a half inches to both the width and the length.

Thus, if your framed picture is 28 by 38 inches, you need an interior space of about 36 by 46 inches. The ends are 36 inches, the sides 47½ inches, and the panels are 37½ by 47½ inches. The wood and the masonite can be custom cut for you in a lumber yard. The sides are nailed to the ends to form the framework, then the bottom is nailed on. Use special nails that bond like screw nails.

The picture must be wrapped in a sealed polybag, taped into a protective overwrap like bubbled polyethylene film, and packed quite firmly, equidistant from all parts of the crate. The picture must be cushioned, there must be no chance of any internal contact of the walls of the crate with the canvas, and there must be no room for movement in transit after the top of the crate is screwed on.

Crating sculpture is more complicated and optimally involves belting to be fastened outside the crate. This should be done by an advanced fine arts packer, and you must beware the moving man technique that relies on wrapping and stuffing rather than belting or interior bracing.

If you are shipping the art for sale by an auction house or dealer, you pay the cost of transportation. When an auction house is shipping to you, you also pay the cost. When you are buying a moderately expensive work from a dealer, he will probably absorb the crating and shipping cost, but you should make that a part of your purchase agreement where it is appropriate. If you are buying an expensive piece from a dealer on approval, he will usually pay for the outgoing crating and shipping if you are a known customer, but if there is any return, he will expect you to pay.

Eyes and Wire

Before paintings are crated for shipment, the hanging wire is removed to prevent damage to the painting. The screw eyes for the wire are also taken off so the back of the framed picture will lie flat. The eyes and wire should be placed in a box and shipped with the picture, but this is seldom done.

If the shipment is to you, the task of rewiring will be yours. There are new ways to hang pictures, but the old ones still work.

Obtain two screw eyes of a gauge and length suited to your picture and a quantity of picture wire in a thickness appropriate to the weight of the picture. The length of wire required is approximately the width of the frame plus 15 percent for slack plus a total of 12 inches for winding at the ends. A frame 20 inches wide calls for 20 plus 3 plus 12 equals 35 inches of wire.

The spot for the screw eyes should be about 25 percent below the top of the frame, in the center of the vertical sections of the frame. Be sure the spot selected is not so thin that the screw end will penetrate through the front of the frame. When the wire is fastened to the eyes, the first coil of the wire is always a knot.

The hanging point should be about ten percent below the top of the frame. The type of hanger you use depends on the weight of the picture and the composition of the wall.

Where You Hang

Where you hang the picture is a compromise between your best spot and the spot with suitable lighting, temperature, humidity, freedom from pollutants, and physical protection. Regardless of where you would most like to see the picture, you must avoid direct sunlight and you should stay away from fluorescents that are not corrected for usage with art.

Track lights are better than close-up picture lights mounted on the wall or on the frame itself. Exposure to any natural or electric light that is bright may discolor or embrittle, and you must remember that there are seasonal changes in the direction and intensity of sunlight.

Rotating your pictures semiannually may help in protecting them, although you will find when you place the pictures in different settings that some pictures look right only in one spot. This is a phenomenon of colors and light.

The ideal temperature for art is about 72 degrees and ideal humidity is about 50 percent. Avoid extremes of heat or cold. Add moisture to the air when the humidity is much below 50 percent. Otherwise, low humidity may cause flaking and cracking. High humidity may cause mold. If you move a painting on millboard from an island to a desert without a conservator's advice, you may see the board crack open, but the mold will be discouraged.

Avoid hanging paintings in bathrooms, in kitchens, near pools, over radiators, over fireplaces without mantels, and in sprinklered areas.

The Burglar's Guide

In homes, you will generally find the best pictures hung in the master bedroom, the second best in the living room, and the poorest in the kitchen. This is the uncultured burglar's guide to value.

A more appropriate functional distribution is to group paintings for hanging in accordance with compatibility to your eye. One approach is to have different aspects of your specialization on different walls or in different rooms.

As we have seen, the picture frames should have been chosen with the first duty to the picture and not to the room, but when the pictures have similarities, proper frames will have similarities too. Also, if the pictures fit the room, frames subordinated to the pictures will fit the room equally well.

Do not hang pictures in spots where there can be accidental contact. Place tables below pictures hung in entrance halls. The tables should keep people from fingering the paintings, an infantile compulsion. Be sure no table lamp makes contact with the picture or causes overheating. Do not hang pictures where doors can swing into them.

Be safety minded.

Art Requires Little

Despite all these warnings, though, art requires little maintenance. Common sense rules apply. There is no program needed for daily care, and in fact, art works are better off without overzealous attention. Don't get carried away.

The curator of a major museum brought a friend to a dealer's gallery to recommend the purchase of an 1880s watercolor. At the same time, the curator cautioned against defects in the original framing he said would demand immediate correction.

The dealer remained mute, but the original frame had been in place for a century without causing any damage and might well have lasted another hundred years in the absence of the knowledgeable but impractical curator.

The maxim is the old "Don't fix what isn't broken."

Even the compulsive housekeeper who cannot leave art works alone must never wipe pictures that are not behind glass. Cloths or feather dusters might catch in the surface and pull or smear. The only acceptable dusting agent is a soft three inch camel's hair brush or its equivalent. Brush gently. Apply no wax or solvent or water.

It seems unnecessary at this point to warn against spitting on fingers to wipe paintings, but that is the most common gaffe. Don't do it.

The frame and back of a picture can be cleaned gently with the soft brush attachment to a hand vacuum on the setting providing the lowest power. When in doubt, stay with the camel's hair brush, if you can afford one. Never apply pressure to the face or back of a picture.

Every six months, you should shine a bright flashlight on the paintings that are hung, aiming the light both perpendicularly and on raking angles, to see if there is any indication of flaking or cupping. You should also check for new dangers of accidents and for environmental changes in light, heat, and dampness.

Front to Front and Back to Back

Paintings that are not hung must be stored carefully. Most damage comes from stacking without being sure the contact is frame to frame. See that nothing leans on the corners of the canvases. Stack front to front and back to back. Keep an eye on those hanging wires.

If you have only a few paintings that are not hung, put protective boards front and back. If you have many, convert a closet to painting storage, as long as the temperature and humidity are suitable and the door is the full width of the closet.

Build as many slide-out floor to ceiling frameworks in wood as you need and suspend them on ceiling tracks inside the closet. Face each framework with pegboard so pictures can be hung on both sides, and allow spacing between slides for the thickness of the pictures. Fifty average size pictures will fit in one closet.

Any recessed area in a closet can be shelved for sculpture and for drawers to hold works on paper.

CHAPTER 26

Final Learning Tools

People in the art business know the least about the physical characteristics of works on paper, so they are properly hesitant about handling works on paper when housekeeping, framing, or conservation is required. Dealers know that damage to a work on paper can take place within a year with exposure to an innocent-looking hazard. The result may not be reversible through conservation, as, for example, an injury to an oil painting might be.

Damage to Works on Paper

Not all framers are professionals, even in dealing with a material as familiar to them as paper, so a collector must know enough about the theory of framing paper to protect himself. Watercolors, drawings, and prints should always be behind glass or destaticized plastic sheet, but non-glare glass is to be avoided because it visually deadens colors. The backs of frames must be sealed with paper.

A gouache may resemble an oil painting because of its impasto, but a gouache on paper may flake unless it is framed like a watercolor.

Pastels require the most delicate handling and framing because the pigment is bound to the paper only by the friction of the dry application. A force as weak as static attraction will pull pastel from the paper.

Damage to works on paper can come from many causes. One attack can be environmental, coming from excess moisture in the air, producing rippling of the paper and permitting mold at humidity readings of 70 percent or higher.

Also, ordinary wood pulp paper in mats and boards used for framing will darken in time and embrittle the works on paper it touches, as will excess heat from stoves or fireplaces. Sunlight and fluorescents that are not shielded can cause fading. The framing of every work on paper requires the mat, mounting board, and backing to be 100 percent ragboard that is acid free. In museum practice, mounting hinges are made from mulberry paper and are applied with flour paste.

Man is another hazard. Old paper is fragile and should be picked up with two hands to avoid tearing. Soiling from handling is common.

The point in dealing with works on paper is that the material is unforgiving and requires professional attention at every step.

Insurance Against Calamities

Good housekeeping for works of art is mainly protection against the gradual deterioration of physical condition, while protection against calamities like theft and accidental damage is commonly provided by insurance. The type of insurance you buy depends on the risks you want covered and on how much you are willing to spend. The cost may be less under a standard Home-owners policy, if the more limited coverage satisfies you.

Works of art are not prone to casualties. Art theft is not as prevalent as auto theft because thieves don't usually have the touch to pick the most valuable work of art in a room full of art. You will be surprised, for example, if you ask a friend who is not an expert in art to give you his idea of the relative values of the works you own. What is obvious to you at this point may not be apparent to him at all, and would probably be less obvious to a burglar who is choosing under pressure.

Moreover, the singularity of art makes it difficult to "fence." Even burglars have problems with the illiquidity of art compared to cash, coins, diamonds, guns, or television sets. Stolen art works cannot safely be put up for public auction because of the exposure. Consequently, the rate of recovery is high on stolen art works of importance.

And, works of art seldom collide like cars, although Whistler's Mother did pass the Mona Lisa on the New Jersey Turnpike in the 1960s.

There are some special risks that might concern you, however, such as hazards affecting art works in storage, in transit, on exhibition, for sale, or damaged accidentally by visitors to your home. You will need to determine whether these acts are covered in the less expensive insurance policies. You should also ascertain whether you will collect for loss of value due to damage, in addition to the cost of repair. Even after a torn painting is cosmetically restored, its value has been diminished, perhaps substantially.

An alternative to the Home-owners policy is a scheduled form of all-risk coverage, where your insurance agent will advise you concerning how much of your art you should individually list in the schedule, and in what amounts. He will also guide you in selecting the appropriate deductible.

Valuable art calls for all-risk insurance, especially when the art travels.

Keep Adequate Records

Taking out insurance coverage demands that you keep adequate records and store them off the premises. If you ever do experience a major loss, you will be negotiating with a hard-nosed claims agent rather than your friendly sales agent, and beyond the claims agent is arbitration or the courts.

When you take out an insurance policy to protect yourself against loss, you are wasting money unless you also prepare yourself to be able to establish the amount of any loss. With your insurance policy, you should preserve written documentation of your art, including the description, size, medium, title, artist, date, name of seller, and the original bill of sale.

Review the value of your holdings annually and get current appraisals, if needed. Use an appraiser who is acceptable to your insurance carrier.

Consider installing burglar and fire alarm systems that may earn you a lower insurance premium.

In addition to the written inventory of your art, take color photographs. Put a ruler and a color chart in the picture. Photographs taken professionally for insurance purposes should cost about $25 an hour plus expenses, although you might prefer a videotaped record at about $50 an hour. This pictorial record should be processed away from your home community, for security, and should be kept with the policy and written records.

Taxes Are Complex

Taxes relative to art cannot be treated here because they are complex and changing. From the standpoint of investment and tax planning, however, art is distinguishable from many other investments because it does not generate current income and because its gains accumulate until you elect to realize on them. No income tax is paid while the value of the art appreciates.

As a special situation, you should explore charitable donations of art because there may be substantial tax savings. Under some circumstances, the fair market value of art donations may be deducted instead of your lower cost, but this must be determined with your accountant.

One goal to be adopted right at the beginning of your program may be to try to establish yourself as an investor for tax purposes rather than as a collector, to gain advantages on deductions. Your accountant should get you started on the most advantageous path.

If you sell more than six pictures a year, though, the Internal Revenue Service may classify you as a dealer, putting you under totally different tax regulations.

Tax issues of significance are reviewed by an Internal Revenue Service advisory panel of art experts.

A Card for Every Work

The data you need for insurance and tax purposes should be kept separate from your investment planning records.

For your personal planning, make out an index card for each work of art you acquire. Enter a full description of the piece, including the price and any additional cost. Put down the reasons for your purchase. State why the piece is your "best" at the moment of purchase, what you believe the current value to be, why, what you expect to sell the piece for, when, and to whom.

Then, when you are reviewing your holdings periodically, you can work from the cards. You can determine whether you would still buy the piece if it came up anew. You can see whether your targets are being realized.

When you have attained your goal and you sell, close out the card with the conditions of the sale.

An Entry Meatier than Most

As an example of an entry card much meatier than most, here is the Young-Hunter painting mentioned previously:

YOUNG-HUNTER, JOHN. "Purple and Gold." Oil on canvas, 35 by 30 inches, signed lower right, not dated. Listed, not shown, in Sotheby's grab-bag sale April 4, 1981, as lot #186, provenance estate of artist, exhibited Royal Institute Galleries, London, Summer Exhibition, no date. Pre-sale estimate $700 to $1,000.

The *Illustrated Encyclopedia* describes Young-Hunter as a Taos, New Mexico painter born in England in 1874 and refers to a signature example in the artist's autobiography, p. 146, which is a full color reproduction of this same "Purple and Gold," a warm-toned female nude wearing gold jewelry, kneeling against a purple backdrop. Our pre-sale estimate of the current retail value in average condition with no additional provenance was $7,500, but because we could not see the painting itself before buying and had to rely on an agent's opinion, we set a maximum bid of $3,100. The cost to us proved to be $2,000 plus ten percent agent's fee plus ten percent buyer's premium plus 13 percent crating and shipping, or $2,660.

Our incoming inspection indicated the painting to be in pristine condition except for black toning on the nude body. The frame was original with six exhibition labels including a juried award at the Western State College of Colorado in 1945.

The black toning was removed by a conservator to uncover the golden body tones illustrated in the autobiography. The quality of the entire package made "Purple and Gold" a strong "best" for a number of potential buyers, including Taos and figure painting specialists. The current value was reappraised at $12,500, for realization within two years through private sale.   10/15/81.

A more typical example is:

NASH, WILLARD. Charcoal on paper, sight ten by eight inches, portrait of an Indian woman staring dreamily off to right. Initialed WN on left shoulder. Drawn on tan wallpaper with printed serial numbers. Tastefully framed with French mat. Cost $75 from private dealer.

This is a "best" drawing by a member of Los Cinco Pintores in Santa Fe in the 1920s. The Indian subject was a known model of Santa Fe artists. The printed serial numbers on the paper will be disfiguring for some buyers but attractive to others because it is typical of the place at an arty time.

Current dealer's value, $150. Goal, $600 as retail price, to be realized within three years, by private sale.   6/15/81.

Biographical Cards

A second set of index cards should contain biographical and pricing records of each artist whose work you own. For most artists, the data is readily available. Biographical material can be taken from recent books and catalogs, and prices from an annual of auction prices.

For some artists, however, the data will have to be assembled as a research program. George Herbert Macrum is an example of a painter who

28. *Willard Nash. "Indian Woman." Charcoal on wallpaper, 10 by 8 inches.*

was second-tier immediately after the turn of the century but whose life record has since been lost.

MACRUM, GEORGE HERBERT. Born about 1870, probably in Pittsburgh, died about 1945, probably in Europe. American Impressionist painter and teacher, studied at Art Students League 1902–03 in New York City with Frank Vincent DuMond. Traveled in Europe before 1910 and settled in Woodstock, New York, studying with Birge Harrison.

Listed in *Who's Who in America*, *Who's Who in American Art*, and referred to in *Mallett's*, Fielding, and Benezit. Exhibited in the

National Academy, Society of Independent Artists, Pennsylvania Academy of Fine Arts, Salon des Beaux-Arts, and elsewhere in Europe and in commercial galleries. Work in Pennsylvania Academy of Fine Arts, Art Gallery of Ontario. Awards, Appalachian Exposition 1911, Salmagundi Club 1914, Panama-Pacific Exposition 1915.

Preferred medium, oil on canvas. Preferred subjects, Catskill and European landscapes and New York City scenes. No significant auction record.   3/10/80.

This biographical record would be read in combination with painting cards such as:

MACRUM, GEORGE HERBERT. "Overlook," oil on canvas 24 by 30 inches, signed lower right G.H. Macrum/1907. In original gold leaf frame with title printed on frame at left. Canvas was wax lined onto board about 1960 without wholly correcting the cracked paint. Scene is landscape at Woodstock, New York, in Impressionist style typical of Woodstock School. Painting was exhibited at Pennsylvania Academy of Fine Arts in 1908.

Cost $450 at 6/6/78 local auction in New York City. Acquired to supplement collection of Macrum paintings rather than for immediate resale. Initial value set at $3,000.   7/1/78.

Raised to $5,000. This is a "best" landscape painting by Macrum, done relatively early in the development of American Impressionism.   1/1/82.

Back to the Start

The completion of these index cards is to provide you with one more learning tool, the last step in regularizing art for you in your role as the careful collector. You are now a specialist with your own personal touch to be exercised in this program that was tailored precisely for you.

You will find you are a different sort of art collector than you were in the beginning. You will be looking at art with the eyes of experience, and what you did early on may no longer satisfy you.

Your next task will be to go all the way back to the start of your buying, to upgrade your holdings in line with your current awareness. Sell whatever is no longer your best and reinvest the proceeds.

Learning about art is an escalating process. You will never know it all, no matter how tight your specialization, but you will know as much as most other people in the art business, and maybe more.

Graduation Exercises_____

The key to buying like an insider is confidence, the assurance that with your new approach you can walk into a place that has a large quantity of unsorted art for sale and expect to come away with a gain of $250 to $500 or more from that one venture.

The Albuquerque ARTSwap in the Old Airport Terminal seemed like a good example. The press release in the morning newspaper for May 6, 1983 promised a sale of pre-owned art consigned by those who were "tired of the same old paintings on your wall, that boring piece of sculpture you've had for years and years." Something like the ARTSwap would be an appropriate group to host your graduation exercises. You would be looking in a haystack, because the old paintings and sculpture from private sources would be few compared to the new daubs and prints that would be loaded into the Terminal by local artists and galleries.

When you got there, you would at first have been disappointed. Tables and walls were covered with modern prints by amateur and part-time artists. The bronzes were by unlisted sculptors. Pressing through, however, turned up a more promising Fritz Scholder (b. 1937) lithograph that was signed, but the price was $3,000, more than retail. Next came a Childe Hassam (1859–1935) lithograph, beautiful but overpriced at $1,200. On the table were two small Bruce Lubo (b. 1911) oils, the kind he painted in his shop window and not his "best" let alone yours.

On the wall beyond, though, was a 24 x 36" oil on masonite of three Indians by Marjorie Rodgers (b. 1927) priced at $250. If your specialty is the West, you would know Marjorie Rodgers because her work appears in full color in *Contemporary Western Artists*. The quality of the painting was good enough to be your "best," and the gallery price of a similar work would be about $1,000.

There was also a signed lithograph by Jean Jansem (b. 1920) at $75. You might not know Jansem because he worked in Paris, but a look at Benezit would tell you that his paintings and prints are commodities on the world art market. The *International Auction Records* show that this print brought $180 as long ago as 1979. If the print suited you, it could be your "best."

No doubt your personal specialization would have turned up other works of art at the Terminal that could have been particularly for you. There was, for example, a superbly printed George Grosz (1893–1959) art book of the 1920s with 16 frameable color plates and 67 plates of drawings priced with two other quality art books at $14, but why go on? The point is that even at as unlikely a spot as an ARTSwap in Albuquerque, you can buy fine things and, if you wish, make money.

Good hunting!

Selected Bibliography

Alburquerque Journal. "Western Art Worth Soars." June 1, 1980, p. D-3.
———. Steve Penrose, "Taping Your Treasures Pays Future Dividends." October 22, 1980, p. B-1.
———. A. M. Fenimore, "Lost and Found—City Accounting Firm Uncovers a Hidden Artistic Treasure." May 17, 1981, p. E-13.
Albuquerque Tribune. "Buying Gems a Tricky Business." Nov. 3, 1980, p. D-2.
———. "Masterpieces Shrink from $250,000 to $120." Aug. 14, 1981.
Americana. Jeffrey Hogrege, "American Bronzes." Aug. 1980, p. 26.
American Art Review. Los Angeles: Kellaway Publishing Company, beginning 1974.
American Society of Appraisers. "Information on the Appraisal Profession." Feb. 1981.
Appraisal Studies. Southhampton College, Long Island, N.Y. Home course.
Art & Antiques. Lorel McMillan, "Donating Art to Charity." March 1980, p. 44.
———. Gwendolyn Owens, "Caring for Your Watercolors." May 1981, p. 14.
———. Investment report, "American nineteenth century paintings near top of high risers." Apr. 6, 1981, p. 5.
———. "Investing in Collectibles—The Melina Formula." Apr. 20, 1981, p. 2.
———. "American Paintings: Extraordinary Prices for Certain Major Works—Particularly Westerns." May 18, 1981, p. 3.
Art Investment Corporation. Statement, Jan. 1, 1981. Santa Fe.
Artists of the Rockies. "G. Harvey auction at Burt's Place." Summer 1979, p. 58.
———. "Fourteenth Annual CAA Exhibition." Fall 1979, p. 2.
———. "Western Heritage Sale/Fine Art and Texas Cattle." Fall 1979, p. 80.
———. "Around the Easel." Summer 1980, p. 5.
ARTnews. Janet Wilson, "Celebrating the American West with Harry Jackson." Dec. 1978, p. 58.
———. Richard Blodgett, "The rip-roaring record-breaking western art market." Dec. 1979, p. 102.
Barker, Virgil. *American Painting.* New York: The Macmillan Company, 1950.
Benezit, E. *Dictionnaire des Peintres, Sculpteurs, Dessinateurs et Graveurs.* France: Librairie Grund, 1976.
Bermingham, Peter. *American Art in the Barbizon Mood.* Washington: Smithsonian Institution Press, 1975.
Bettens, Edward Detraz. *Picture Buying.* New York: privately printed.

Blodgett, Richard. *How to Make Money in the Art Market*. New York: Peter H. Wyden, 1975.

Brown, Milton W. *American Painting from the Armory Show to the Depression*. Princeton: Princeton U., 1955.

Domit, Moussa M. *American Impressionist Painting*. Washington: National Gallery of Art, 1973.

Dykes, Jeff. *Fifty Great Western Illustrators*. Flagstaff: Northland Press, 1975.

Eagle, Joanna. *Buying Art on a Budget*. New York: Hawthorne Books Inc., 1968.

Engel, Louis. *How to Buy Stocks*. New York: Bantam Books, 1972.

Fielding, Mantle. *Dictionary of American Painters, Sculptors and Engravers*. With addendum. New York: James F. Carr, 1965.

Fink, Lois Marie and Joshua C. Taylor. *Academy: The Academic Tradition in American Art*. Washington: Smithsonian Inst. Press, 1975.

Frankenstein, Alfred. *After the Hunt*. Berkeley: U. of Cal. Press, 1975.

Gardner, Helen. *Understanding the Arts*. New York: Harcourt, Brace and Co., 1932.

Gerdts, William H. and Russell Burke, *American Still-Life Painting*. New York: Praeger Publishers, 1971.

Gettens, Rutherford J. and George L. Stout. *Painting Materials*. New York: Dover Publications, 1966.

Groce, George C. and David H. Wallace. *The New York Historical Society's Dictionary of Artists in America 1564–1860*. New Haven: Yale U. Press, 1957.

Hardy, C. Colburn. *Dun & Bradstreet's Guide to $Your Investments$*. New York: Lippincott & Crowell, 1981.

Hind, C. Lewis. *The Consolations of a Critic*. London: Adam and Charles Black, 1911.

Hislop, Richard, ed. *Auction Prices of American Artists*. England: Art Sales Index, 1982.

Hoopes, Donelson F. and Nancy Wall Moure. *American Narrative Painting*. Los Angeles: L. A. County Museum of Art, 1974.

House & Garden. Mary Roche, "Art for Everybody." Oct. 1971, p. 31.

————. Nan R. Piene, "Buying art as an investment." n/d, p. 68.

Howat, John K. *The Hudson River and Its Painters*. New York: The Viking Press, 1972.

Isham, Samuel. *The History of American Painting*. New edition with Royal Cortissoz. New York: The Macmillan Company, 1927.

Jackman, Rilla Evelyn. *American Arts*. Chicago: Rand McNally & Company, 1928.

Johnson, Allen, Dumas Malone, and Harris E. Starr, eds. *Dictionary of American Biography*. 21 vols. New York: Charles Scribner's Sons, 1921–1944.

Keck, Caroline K. *A Handbook on the Care of Paintings*. Nashville: American Assoc. for State and Local History, 1965.

Larkin, Oliver W. *Art and Life in America*. New York: Rinehart & Company, 1949.

Leffler, George L., revised by Loring C. Farwell. *The Stock Market*. New York: The Ronald Press Co, 1963.

Levy, Florence N. *American Art Annual*. New York: The Macmillan Company, beginning 1899. Washington: The American Federation of Arts, 1913 to 1933.

Loeb, Gerald M. *The Battle for Investment Survival*. New York: Simon and Schuster, 1965.

Loria, Jeffrey H. *Collecting Original Art*. New York: Harper & Row, 1965.

MacDonald, Colin S. *A Dictionary of Canadian Artists*. Ottawa: Canadian Paperbacks, beginning 1967.

Maine Antique Digest. Lita Solis-Cohen, "A Limited Partnership for Antique Investment." Sept. 1980, p. 32-A.

———. Lita Solis-Cohen and Samuel Pennington, "IFAR—Doing Something About Art Crime." May 1981, p. 7-A.

———. "In Quest of Quality." July 1981 editorial, p. 2-A.

———. "Bard 'Highlanders' Sail at $16,000 and $20,000. Oct. 1981, p. 28-B.

———. George E. Jordan, "Morton's Louisiana Purchase." Dec. 1981, p. 1-C.

Mallett, Daniel Trowbridge. *Mallett's Index of Artists*. Two vols. New York: Peter Smith, 1948.

Marlor, Clark S. *A History of the Brooklyn Art Assn*. New York: James F. Carr, 1970.

Mayer, E. *International Auction Records*. France: E. Mayer, beginning 1966.

Mayer, Ralph. *The Artist's Handbook*. Revised. New York: The Viking Press, 1970.

McGlauflin, Alice Coe. *Who's Who in American Art*. Washington: The American Fed. of Arts, 1935, continuing as New York: Jaques Cattell Press.

Money. "Top-quality objects in art." Sept. 1979, p. 47.

———. Patricia A. Dreyfus, "Figuring Your Own Odds in a Slump." Sept. 1979, p. 48.

Monro, Isabel S. and Kate M. *Index to Reproductions of American Paintings*. First Supp. New York: The H.W. Wilson Co., 1964.

New York Graphic Society Ltd. *Fine Art Reproductions*. Greenwich: 1968.

The New York Times. Susan Heller Anderson, "The Lord of the Auction House." Nov. 23, 1980, p. F-9.

———. Ernest Dickinson, "Appraising the Appraiser." Jan. 4, 1981, p. F-13.

———. "News on the Gallery Tour: Arnold & Porter." Mar. 8, 1981, p. F-19.

———. Steve Lohr, "Theft and Fraud in Fine Art." Mar. 22, 1981, p. F-13.

———. Rita Reif, "Art Auctions: 'Half Theater, Half Casino.' " Sept. 27, 1981, p. D-1.

———. Carol Lawson, "A Group Shopping Spree Stocks a Museum with Art." June 20, 1982, p. H-28.

———. Grace Glueck, "When Money Talks, What Does It Say About Art?" June 12, 1983, p. H-1.

Pitz, Henry C. *200 Years of American Illustration*. New York: Random House, 1977.

Porter, Sylvia. *Albuquerque Journal*, "Follow Investment Basics for Stock Market Success." Dec. 18, 1980, p. G-12.

———. ———, "Tax Shelters a Critical Concern." Dec. 21, 1980, p. G-3.

———. ———, "Learn How to Insure Items." Jan. 2, 1981, p. B-4.

———. ———, "The New Buyers Profiled." May 13, 1981, p. C-6.

Portfolio. Avis Berman, "The Making of a Collection." Summer 1980, p. 62.

Physics Today. Stuart Fleming, "Detecting art forgeries." April 1980, p. 34.

Reed, Walt. *The Illustrator in America 1900–1960s*. New York: Reinhold Publishing Corp., 1966.

Reitlinger, Gerald. *The Economics of Taste*. New York: Holt, Rinehart and Winston, 1964.

Rocky Mountain News. Jerry Ruhl, "Art for art's, and money's sake." April 21, 1980, n/p.

Rose, Barbara. *American Art Since 1900.* New York: Frederick A. Praeger, 1967.

Rush, Richard H. *Art as an Investment.* Englewood Cliffs, N.J.: Prentice-Hall, Inc., 1961.

Rutledge, Anna Wells. *The Pennsylvania Academy of the Fine Arts, 1807–1870.* Phila.: The Amer. Philosophical Society, 1955.

Saarinen, Aline B. *The Proud Possessors.* New York: Random House, 1958.

Samuels, Peggy and Harold, edited by. *The Collected Writings of Frederic Remington.* Garden City, N.Y.: Doubleday & Co., 1979.

————. *Contemporary Western Artists.* Houston: Southwest Art Publishers, 1982.

————. *Frederic Remington, A Biography.* New York: Doubleday & Co., 1982.

————. *The Illustrated Biographical Encyclopedia of Artists of the American West.* Garden City, N.Y.: Doubleday & Co., 1976.

Seddon, Richard. *Art Collecting for Amateurs.* London: Frederick Muller Ltd., 1965.

Solomon, Irwin. *How to Start and Build an Art Collection.* Phila.: Chilton Company, 1961.

Snodgrass, Jeanne O. *American Indian Painters.* New York: Museum of the American Indian, 1968.

Southwest Art. Gary Russell Libby, "100 Years of Western Illustration." Oct. 1980.

Stauffer, David McNeely. *American Engravers upon Copper and Steel.* New York: Burt Frankling, 1964.

Stout, George L. *The Care of Pictures.* New York: Dover Pubs., 1975.

Suehsdorf, Adolph. *How to Invest Safely and for Profit.* Greenwich, Conn.: Fawcett Publications, 1960.

Tanner, Clara Lee. *Southwest Indian Painting.* Tucson: U. of Ariz. Press, 1957.

Taubes, Frederic. *Restoring and Preserving Antiques.* New York: Watson-Guptill Pubs. 1969.

Thieme and Becker, *Allgemeines Lexikon der Bildenden Kunstler, 1907–1948.* Germany.

Toffler, Alvin. *The Culture Consumers.* New York: St. Martin's Press, 1964.

Town & Country. Leon Harris, "Going Going Going Up!" Sept. 1980, p. 131.

Towne, Morgan. *Treasures in Truck and Trash.* Garden City, N.Y.: Doubleday & Co., 1950.

Towner, Wesley. *The Elegant Auctioneers.* New York: Hill & Wang, 1970.

U.S. News & World Report. "Investing in Art." Sept. 11, 1978, n/p.

————. "Investing in Art." Nov. 19, 1979, n/p.

Vollard, Ambroise. *Recollections of a Picture Dealer.* New York: Dover Pubs., 1978.

The Wall Street Journal. Beth Nissen, "Cowboy Art: Where the Deer and the Antelope Pay." n/d.

Western Art News. "Buy at Auction without Leaving Home." May 1980, p. 1.

Witt, Robert Clermont. *How to Look at Pictures.* London: George Bell and Sons, 1909.

Young-Hunter, John. *Reviewing the Years.* New York: Crown Pubs., 1963.

Zigrosser, Carl and Christa M. Gaehde. *A Guide to the Collecting and Care of Original Prints.* New York: Crown Pubs., 1965.

Index

Peggy and Harold Samuels have been private dealers in American art for 20 years. Peggy Samuels was an editor at *Woman's Day*. Harold Samuels was a corporate lawyer before, as he says, he "went straight." They have written many articles on art and their books include *The Illustrated Biographical Encyclopedia of Artists of the American West*; *The Collected Writings of Frederic Remington*; *Frederic Remington, A Biography*; and *Contemporary Western Artists*. The Remington biography was a *New York Times* "Notable Book of the Year."

Listed in *Who's Who in American Art* and *Who's Who in the West*, the Samuelses are also antiquarian bookmen and lecturers on investment in art. They live in Corrales, New Mexico, near Albuquerque.